The
Wardrobe
Project

The Wardrobe Project

A YEAR
OF BUYING
LESS AND
LIKING
YOURSELF
MORE

Emma Edwards

WILEY

First published 2026 by John Wiley & Sons Australia, Ltd

ISBN: 978-1-394-37681-0

 A catalogue record for this book is available from the National Library of Australia

Registered Office
John Wiley & Sons Australia, Ltd. Level 4, 600 Bourke Street, Melbourne, VIC 3000, Australia

For details of our global editorial offices, customer services, and more information about Wiley products visit us at www.wiley.com.

Wiley also publishes its books in a variety of electronic formats and by print-on-demand. Some content that appears in standard print versions of this book may not be available in other formats.

Trademarks: Wiley and the Wiley logo are trademarks or registered trademarks of John Wiley & Sons, Inc. and/or its affiliates in the United States and other countries and may not be used without written permission. All other trademarks are the property of their respective owners. John Wiley & Sons, Inc. is not associated with any product or vendor mentioned in this book.

Cover design and illustration by George Saad

Set in ITC Berkeley Oldstyle Std 11.5/14.5pt

Icons: Paper receipt: © Creatives/Adobe Stock; Unboxing: © blankstock/Adobe Stock
Post-it notes: © Pixel Embargo/Adobe Stock
Printed and bound by CPI Group (UK) Ltd, Croydon, CR0 4YY

C9781394376810_111125

The manufacturer's authorized representative according to the EU General Product Safety Regulation is Wiley-VCH GmbH, Boschstr. 12, 69469 Weinheim, Germany, e-mail: Product_Safety@wiley.com.

For Doreen

My fantastic gran, who was never ashamed of having a visible underwear line, and who proudly wore her signature homemade chambray trouser sets, sternly replying 'well, I'm comfortable' to anyone who questioned her sartorial choices. I miss you more than words.

Contents

'Your parcel will be delivered today'   xi

The chokehold of clothes   xvii

Creating the Project   xxvii

Preparation   1
  Wishlist items   2
  The rules   3

January: The beginning   11
  To embrace or withdraw?   13
  The urge to purge   15
  Cataloguing my clothes   16
  The stories hanging in our wardrobes   18
  Chapter summary   23

February: The mirror to myself   25
  Meeting my 'fantasy self'   27
  The outfit in my head vs on my body   29
  Signs your fantasy self is tapping your card   30
  The 'almost' trap   31
  Chapter summary   42

March: The steer into the skid | 43
The allure of looking 'polished' | 47
You're not going to look like the picture | 49
Whipped cream: An alternative to chasing polish | 53
Chapter summary | 58

April: The resistance | 59
The perils of a change of season | 59
The curious case of trends | 61
It's okay to just look... okay | 63
The clutter factor | 69
Chapter summary | 71

May: The classroom of my mistakes | 73
Buying mistakes I'd been stuck in | 75
The outcome? A wardrobe that doesn't work | 80
Excuses we make to buy things | 83
Lessons from items I've loved | 86
The capsule wardrobe fallacy | 87
Chapter summary | 94

June: The shift | 95
The unfamiliar territory of not wanting anything | 97
Urgency as an indicator of mindless buying | 99
The human behaviour element of fast and
slow fashion | 102
Slowness fosters creativity | 103
Chapter summary | 108

July: The breakthrough | 109
From beige iced latte to punchy espresso | 110
Having enough and being enough | 113
Finding confidence outside of buying | 116
The therapy of spending | 119
Chapter summary | 131

Contents

August: The holiday and the three-year-old bikini 133
Spending runways 134
There's so much more to life and money than clothes 136
Liking doesn't have to mean buying 137
Values-based spending 140
Adding more variety to your spending 142
The 'yes, and?' method 143
Understanding your buying decisions 144
Slowing down your purchase decisions 148
Chapter summary 153

September: The rebellion 155
The default option: Buy something new 157
Body acceptance, is that you?! 158
The 'flattering' lie 160
Ten ways to dress for resistance 163
The weight of weight 164
Weight-fluctuation-proofing your wardrobe 167
Chapter summary 172

October: The outfit repeater 173
You don't need a new outfit for every single event 174
Outfit repeating is cool 178
Embracing style formulas 180
Chapter summary 181

November: The clear out 183
My top five most worn items and what they taught me 188
Chapter summary 191

December: The end 193
My mindful buying toolkit 196
The Rule of Three 199
My beliefs about clothes pre- and post-Project 201
Chapter summary 210

The emergence 211

The key shifts I never expected 212

Not buying clothes freed me up to do so
much more 214

Buying again 216

...And then I hired a stylist 219

How to be your own personal shopper 221

Dressing differently 225

Style formulas 225

Wardrobe optimisation 228

Moving forward 229

I am forever changed 233

Epilogue: The integration 241

Advice for your own Wardrobe Project 244

Four mindset anchors to take into your Project 247

Let's keep in touch 249

Acknowledgements 251

'Your parcel will be delivered today'

… the text message says. I immediately begin counting down the hours, jumping out of my seat at every rumble up my driveway. Maybe that's the delivery bloke. Finally, a knock at the door. I skid on my socks to the front door and hold out my hands to receive the package from the postie.

Slamming the door shut after one too many choruses of 'thanks so much!', I pace to my bedroom and start tearing the plastic open like a lion devouring prey. The fucking tape won't tear. I get angry and stomp off to find the scissors.

I grab a kitchen knife instead. After hacking into the package, I lift out and unfurl a black dress. It's crinkled from being packaged up, and it doesn't look as nice as it did online. I slip the dress on, choosing to ignore the fact I'm wearing an ill-fitting bra and underwear that's cutting me up like a Christmas ham.

Staring into the mirror, I tilt my head to one side and sigh. The dress looks nothing like I hoped it would, but I can't work out if that's because my hair is messy and I'm not sure whether I brushed my teeth today, or if it's because one of my thighs alone probably weighs more than the model wearing it in the picture on the website. Or maybe the dress just isn't that nice.

I hear three chimes coming from the other room. It's my ten-minute calendar warning for my next meeting. I take the dress off, put it back in its packaging, contort myself back into my leggings and sit down at my desk. In my head is a weird mix of disappointment and justification that I can't quite reconcile. I join my meeting and get on with my day, but it won't be long before the next shiny thing catches my eye and promises me the world.

Hello reader, and welcome to my brain. You might relate to this story. You, too, might be one of those people who has at one point thought a new piece of clothing was the answer to all your problems—or to a bad day, a crisis of confidence or the societal pressures that magnify our manufactured flaws.

Clothes have had a power over me for as long as I can remember. They'd always be the thing I'd want to spend my money on, and a cute outfit would be the first thing to derail my budget, even once I'd got most of my financial ducks in a row—the one behaviour that always tripped me up was wanting to buy a new outfit.

Fashion is weird, right? On the one hand, we need to wear clothes for warmth, just like we need to eat food to survive, but our relationship with these things is far from utilitarian. I'm certain a good burger can begin to mend a broken heart, and an online clothes order has dragged me through all manner of life's stressors, but we don't consume these things out of necessity.

A couple of years ago, I started to realise I was on a hamster wheel when it came to my wardrobe. I was always searching for the next thing, never quite satisfied with what I had, or the way my clothes made me feel. I was searching for something, and I was searching for it on a rack.

Curious as to why I could go from living my life perfectly normally one minute to punching in my credit card information with desire surging through my body the next, I started to really look at the way I was buying clothes and the feelings I had when I was buying them—and I didn't like what I saw.

I've struggled with my confidence and self-image in varying capacities my entire life, and I'd started to realise I used clothes as a way to buffer those emotions. Hated what I saw in the mirror? I could buy something and feel better for a bit. Buying clothes felt like I was taking control, but really, I was fuelling the fire.

And this habit got expensive. I worked out I had spent thousands in one year on clothes—which might be fine if I felt good in what I was wearing, but I didn't. I still lusted after outfits I saw on social media and longed for the day I finally looked the way I wanted to.

So I decided to conduct an experiment—one whole year without buying clothes. It was my attempt to change my relationship with clothes, and myself, step off the wardrobe treadmill, and stop relying on new outfits to feel any semblance of confidence in the way I looked.

This book contains everything I learned from interrogating my clothing consumption habits for a whole year, and what happened afterwards. Spoiler alert: I made it to the end, and I learned a heck of a lot along the way.

I learned so much that I created The Wardrobe Project—a movement aimed at getting women to stop looking outside of themselves for their style and confidence, and to find freedom with who they already are and what they already have.

The Wardrobe Project is now a book, a social media platform and a six-week behaviour change community program (thebrokegeneration.com/the-wardrobe-project-challenge) where we work on our clothing spending habits together.

This book will become your companion for navigating your own consumption habits when it comes to your wardrobe. Consider it a wise and witty (if I do say so myself) friend that tells you what you need to hear, without berating you or judging you.

It's my hope that this book will help you identify patterns of unhelpful spending in your own life, step off the dopamine-powered hamster wheel of clothing consumption, and finally feel like you not only *have* enough, but that you *are* enough.

In this book you will find:

∞ month-by-month instalments of my own personal year without buying any clothes, including the realisations, the resistance, the breakthroughs and everything in between

∞ teachings about how to extract deep learnings about yourself from your own wardrobe, regardless of whether you're crackers enough to do the full year challenge yourself

∞ stories from real people who have gone through The Wardrobe Project group program and learned about themselves and their buying behaviour

∞ insights from a survey of 1500 women about their clothes-buying behaviour

∞ item reports, breaking down what specific items in my wardrobe taught me about my buying habits

∞ intention unboxings: deep dives into some of the granular reasons we find ourselves wanting to buy clothes, exploring what they mean for our relationship with our wardrobe and ourselves.

While this is a book about not buying, it is not a book about *never* buying. Make no mistake, you will not find me telling you to quit buying clothes altogether. I love a slappin' outfit as much as the next girl. But I want this book to scrub your mind of all the ways you've been *conditioned* to consume clothing—from emotional soothing and trying to be who you've been told to be, to retailer tactics, algorithmic advertising and our worsening addiction to dopamine. I want to create space for you to understand your buying patterns and rediscover the joy in your wardrobe and getting dressed. It's more than okay to enjoy clothes, but to fully do so, we have to learn to separate style from spending. When we do, it benefits our finances, our confidence and the planet.

This quote from Avery Trufelman from the podcast *Articles of Interest* comes to mind:

> *There is this myth that it's frivolous or unproductive to care about how you look. Clothing and fashion get trivialised a lot. But think about who, culturally, gets associated with clothing and fashion: young people, women, queers, and people of color. Groups of people who, historically, haven't been listened to, have expressed themselves on their bodies, through their style, their hair, their tattoos, their piercings and what they wear.*

It's not wrong to want to look good or to find joy in clothing—it just needs to be on your terms, not via a standard that's been dictated to you by patriarchal capitalism that's profiting off your insecurities.

Oh and one final thing. This is not a fashion book. I am as far removed from the fashion industry as billionaires are from reality. You won't find me talking about runways and collections and designers and trends. This is a book about regular, schmegular style as a regular, schmegular person that will help you break free from the expensive 'wardrobe treadmill'. This is also not a sustainability book, though the outcome of the shifts you'll experience after reading will certainly benefit the planet. More than anything, this is a book about taking back your power, changing the way you see yourself and breaking the cycle of outsourcing your identity to consumption.

Let's get started.

If you enjoy this book, head to www.thewardrobeprojectbook .com or resources on helping you start your own Wardrobe Project.

The chokehold of clothes

For as long as I can remember, clothes have been my 'thing'. You might read that and think 'okay, she's into fashion', but I wouldn't really describe myself that way. I wasn't ever particularly fashionable, nor would anyone describe me as a *fashion girl* in the way some people are. I was more so a product of the 90s and 00s 'shopping' culture. Shopping was a legitimate hobby for me back then, even if it was less high-end retail therapy and more rocking around my hometown with a fiver to spend on a studded black T-shirt from the sale rack.

I'd flip straight to the style section of my fave teen magazines, loving nothing more than those pages where the price and store would be named for each outfit. My mum tells one of her favourite stories about me when she took me to London for the first time when I was about nine. We lived about two hours away and I'd always wanted to go and experience the bright lights of a big city. Apparently, she pointed out Buckingham Palace and said 'That's where the Queen lives', only to be met with my reply, 'Okay, but where are the shops?' At least I'd already decided I wasn't into the monarchy, I guess.

To some degree, all of that could be put down to the consumerist interests of a girl in a small town without access to the 'cool' shops. Maybe I was just pulling a Kelly Clarkson, growing up in a small town and wanting to spread my wings and learn how to fly. If you know, you know.

But clothes continued to play a big role in my life and my identity as I got older. I came of age at a time when, broadly speaking, there were still 'teenage' sections in shops. Teenagers didn't wear adult clothes. They wore outfits that were somewhere between adulthood and childhood, and were just watered-down versions of adult styles — you know, miniskirts but with embellishments just juvenile enough that you were clearly still a child. It's wild to me nowadays seeing teenagers dress like a Grammy nominee just to go to non-uniform day at high school. Where are the hoodies and butterfly clips to match your blue train-track braces?! But, hey, I guess I probably wouldn't trade my crimped frizzy hair for having to grow up in the age of smartphones and social media, so I'll take it.

Anyway, there was something womanly to me about moving into adult clothes. Teenage ranges often capped out at age 14 or 15, and because I was always a bit on the chunky side, I probably moved into adult clothes a little bit sooner. This was where my relationship with the number on the label began. Fourteen years old, already indoctrinated into the cult of good sizes and bad sizes. Size 10: good. Size 12: Okay. Size 14: scary number. What happens after 14, you ask? Luckily my mum had those sizes covered. Size 16: mum's good size. Size 18: mum's okay size. Size 20: mum's scary size.

And, no, sizes 6 and 8 do not feature in this tale because, and I can say this with absolute scientific certainty, there is not a day I have spent on god's green earth that I have fitted into a size 6 or 8. Not even at birth.

So why am I yapping on about how much the size on the label mattered to me? Good question. I guess this paints an important picture about my relationship with clothes, and that distinction between being a fashion girl with a genuine interest in style and the art of clothing, and the girl I was: one with low self-esteem, a big ass for my age and a belief that clothes were my ticket to liking the way I looked.

The more I grew into adulthood, the more I relied on clothes to prop up my identity, my sense of self and my confidence — or perhaps it was more masking my lack of it.

In my mind, I could solve my problems by changing myself. If I'd been rejected by some guy I'd pedestalled as the best thing ever, it was probably because he didn't like the way I looked. Better get a new dress for the next night out. If I felt like I didn't fit in—which is something I've felt for most of my life—it was probably because I wasn't good enough. Better try extra hard to look *enough* tomorrow or try and be like that cool person I do deem good enough. If I admired someone, it was probably because I felt they looked better than me and exuded a confidence that I believed stemmed from that fact. Better go out and buy an outfit that makes me look like them.

There was something about the feeling of a new outfit that I loved. Something about the possibilities it presented, the way I could change how I perceived myself and, I guess, how others perceived me too. The important part here, though, wasn't the clothes themselves but the story behind them. Using clothing as a way to express yourself isn't, in itself, a bad thing—that's what fashion is meant to be all about, right? My issue was the fact that I felt broken somehow, that I had flaws I needed to fix, an undesirable body I needed to hide, and a performance I needed to put on.

Clothes felt like a costume I could put on to be someone else in an attempt to be anyone but me. Being able to change my costume meant I could change who I was. I would try to use clothing to be who I wished I was or to replicate people I deemed more worthy than me. What this meant was that I spent years and years escaping myself, trying to play dress up as someone else and forever living in this state of not only not being myself, but not knowing myself.

How this manifested in my life

Having this relationship with clothes and seeing them as a bandaid for my problems and my fractured sense of self meant shopping was a prominent part of my life and my personal finances. Before your mind jumps into 'confessions of a shopaholic' territory, picturing the classic female trope of trotting down the high street with bags stacked up each arm and a broken heart to match, that wasn't me. In fact, the often-used female stereotype of a chaotic overspender who just needs to max out her credit card after a bad day is so far from the truth for most people.

No, my unhealthy relationship with buying clothes was much quieter than that. There weren't really big shopping sprees or designer bags. It was a deep-seated belief that clothes would make me feel better, and maybe, if I could just get it right, clothes would eventually make me good enough. The right outfit. The right capsule wardrobe. The right jeans that would make my tree trunk thighs look thinner. The right dress that flattened my belly.

I'd often fixate on certain items, feeling like once I'd seen them, I had to have them. Again, not because it was genuinely an amazing piece that I loved. No, it was much more sinister than that. The 'have to have it' compulsion came from the idea I'd be crafting in my head. The idea that this was finally it. Finally, the pair of jeans I'd been looking for. Finally, the trousers that didn't make me hate my legs. Finally, the outfit that would make me feel like I was Andy Sachs walking into the office in *The Devil Wears Prada*, turning heads with her new look that meant she was now worthy of being seen. Every shopping trip was some kind of opportunity for sartorial metamorphosis as I shifted between versions of myself trying to find confidence.

In my first book, *Good With Money*, I talk about a concept I call your 'creative director': an inner beast that comes up with the most extravagant stories and meanings about things in our lives and our finances. Mine directed a lot of plots about my clothes, too. In my head, I wasn't buying a pair of jeans, I was buying a new pair of legs. I wasn't buying a dress, I was buying a new body. I wasn't buying an outfit, I was buying a new personality. Standing in a store, a week out from payday and only $37 in my bank account, all rational thought would fly out the window. I needed to have this thing. I'd either pull money from any savings I'd attempted to accumulate, or chuck it on a credit card and vow to pay it off next payday.

Then would come the promises of being 'done'. 'I'll just get this and then I'm done', I'd tell myself. But I was never, ever done. There was always more. Always something else that gave me that feeling, that whisper of possibility. I could be a different person for $54.99.

It was the same for much of my 20s, whether that was at university in the UK or living and working in Melbourne, Australia, where I ended up after starting a long-distance relationship with my now-husband.

While buying lots of clothes for nights out as a uni student isn't exactly a unique experience — after all, you're hitting the clubs multiple times a week, you *need* those poorly fitting satin dresses, right?! — for me, it was this underlying self-erasure that motivated so many of my clothing purchases. Because I felt so deeply, completely, truly less than other people, buying a new outfit simply became a cycle of normalcy. It was a way I accommodated that constant feeling in my life. Made room for it. Gave it a home in my brain and my bank statement.

That created a cycle. Feel crap. Buy clothes. Feel better. Feel crap again. Repeat. Now that sounds pretty bleak, but really, the quietness of it all, the way it was just so deeply embedded in the way I saw myself, meant it just went unnoticed. It was my normal and the normal of so many others too. And because we weren't talking a Carrie Bradshaw–style Manolo Blahnik addiction at $400 a pop (we were talking fast-ish fashion purchases costing a few hours' pay at most), it became even easier to ignore. The amounts I was spending were, in isolation, so small that I didn't really consider the impact it would have on my finances, despite the fact my attempts to save were often trampled on by my latest insecurity and the new outfit I'd prescribed as a solution.

The effect of emotionally driven behavioural patterns on your bank balance is seldom discussed in depth in the personal finance world. In fact, that was a big reason I wrote my first book *Good With Money*, because breaking out of those behavioural traps was what finally helped me turn my finances around. My relationship with clothing was linked to my relationship with money but was also its own beast. I did a lot of work on my spending habits, which you can read about in *Good With Money*, but this co-dependency with clothes really lingered. I'd gotten so much better from a financial sense but, ultimately, clothes were still my Achilles heel. While I wasn't spending money I didn't have anymore, nor chucking things on a credit card to deal with later, I was still always a victim to a great item of clothing. That connection between my relationship with myself and using clothes to remedy that was still there, lurking beneath my otherwise well-developed financial confidence.

The decision to turn it around

I think the fact that I'd made so much progress with my finances but still couldn't quite kick this clothing thing really came to a head in 2022. The two years prior had been spent bouncing in and out of lockdowns where I, like many people, bought clothes online despite having absolutely nowhere to go. Unfortunately, my affinity for red wine and cheeseboards during lockdown also meant that my waistline expanded with every day we spent inside, so most of the clothes I'd bought didn't even fit by the time I could actually wear them.

Then we hit 2022, the first year without a lockdown, which meant adjusting to what we came to call the 'new normal', and grappling with who we were after two years of life being somewhat on hold. I went into lockdown an ambitious, bushy-tailed 29-year-old and emerged a burned-out 31-year-old with more question marks about herself and the meaning of life than ever before.

I spent that year reinventing myself over and over again. Grappling with my new dress size and an ever-present craving for confidence meant I leaned on my enjoyment of buying clothes as an emotional soothing technique.

That year, I also went all in on my side hustle as a freelance writer and content creator, and I hoped that leaving a job I was struggling with would help improve my sense of self-image.

This change in career path and work normalcy sparked a change in identity and a craving to be successful that lent itself perfectly to my attempts to buy my identity. The job I'd left before going into self-employment full-time was a pretty toxic environment, and my confidence was left shattered for quite some time. That, combined with the identity shift of being newly self-employed and making this big bet on myself, plus the vulnerability that comes with going out on your own and not 'quantum leaping' (to quote my least-favourite girl bosses) to exponential success created a breeding ground for my clothes-buying compulsions to reactivate. Despite what the girl bosses will tell you, diving into self-employment is *tough*.

I've lost count of the number of times I've heard someone say, 'Once I quit my job and went all in, I was making three times my salary within the first year'. Yeah, didn't happen to me, gang. Still waiting for that magical day. I'll keep you posted.

I'd see other businesswomen in matching pink suits or minimalist beige outfits, and equate that to their success. If I looked the part, I'd be the part, right? I developed this belief that if I could dress the part, cosplay as the confident, knowledgeable, expert business woman, that would be the difference between adding up whether I'd made enough to cover my expenses that month and thriving in self-employment.

Safe to say I'd had enough of the hold clothes had over me. I was sick of always buying clothes and never having anything I felt good in. I knew I was too reliant on the dopamine of having an online order delivered, and I wanted to do something radical to change it. Enter: the idea for an experiment.

There were a lot of my behaviours in 2022 that led to me wanting to commit to a full year without buying clothes. Here are some of them:

∞ Several bursts of listing things online. Ahhh... my favourite revolving door. I'd decide in some frantic surge of motivation that I was going to change my life and clear out my wardrobe because, of course, if I sell stuff online for a bit of cash I can use the fact that I'd cleared out space in my wardrobe as a solid excuse to buy more stuff. Oh, and because I made some money selling the old stuff, it feels like it's free. Classic.

∞ I bought a Bella Freud striped red top in one of my many attempts at being the Pinterest-y capsule wardrobe girl. I thought, for some reason, that buying a fancy brand of yet another striped top would make a difference to the fact I was never going to look like that chic ideal. It didn't.

∞ My camera roll shows me how much I was clinging to this idea of wearing high-waisted jeans and a baggy preppy shirt because that was a style I loved so much on slimmer influencers and a couple of people I knew personally. The proportions are all off on me, and I never looked the way I wanted to, but that didn't stop me trying and trying to replicate the look!

∞ I bought a Zimmerman jumper at a sample sale that I didn't even want, but just wanted to buy something. Honestly, that has got to be one of my brain's great betrayals. Luckily, I sold it online for almost what I paid for it, but I honestly have no idea what I was thinking. Zimmerman doesn't even carry my size, so it didn't even fit right.

∞ I bought a matching blazer and shorts set from Country Road in *purple* (do not ask me why) and kept it even though it didn't feel quite right and I wasn't sure where I'd wear it. Janet from Footscray really lucked out on Facebook Marketplace the day I set that one free, let me tell you.

∞ I bought several items in green, which offered up a smorgasbord of mistakes. Firstly, I do not really wear green. I don't particularly like green. But, of course, that didn't stop me. I ended up with two green tops because I'd liked them in black, a green shirt because I'd bought it in pink (for the record, I don't like pink either) and a green dress because, drum roll please, they didn't have my size in the colour I wanted. *Give me strength!*

∞ I bought a pair of black wide-leg trousers that were a solid 6/10 (fine but nothing special), but I bought them because (ready?) they fit. Were they exactly what I wanted? No. Were they available to me immediately? Yes. Bingo! That's all my brain needed.

∞ I bought an incredible red dress that I got from Net-a-Porter on sale, which was actually one of my better purchases as I still have it and still wear it. But to prove just how misguided I was at this point, after the novelty had worn off, I convinced myself I didn't like it anymore and tried to sell it. Sigh.

∞ I bought a pink cross-body bag, which, in and of itself isn't too bad (despite the small fact that I don't like pink), but I distinctly remember the weekend I bought it. It was one of those times I just wanted to *buy* something. I knew I shouldn't have bought it—not because it was expensive (I think it was $38)—but I just had that craving to give someone money and get something in return. It now serves more as a piece of home decor than it does a bag, as it hangs on the end of my clothing rack, unused and unsold, despite its long-term listing on Marketplace. Spare a thought for it.

Basically, I was in a pattern of very clunky buying. I'd buy nothing for a while, largely by avoiding going to the shops or because nothing online triggered my desire to replicate the style of an influencer living in a loft apartment, then I'd buy several things at once, kind of out of nowhere. I got into the habit of ordering a few items at once online (which is really dangerous for racking up the notches of your total items purchased in a year, by the way). Something about the thrill of having several items in a package to tear open was so exciting to me. Multiple possibilities, a treasure trove of dopamine, so many chances to reinvent myself all packaged up into a squishy bundle lobbed onto my doorstep by a postie.

A lot of my purchases of this kind would happen when I shopped the sales. I was an absolute sucker for a really good sale. I'd find myself looking at one specific item, and thinking 'I'll just see what else is in the sale'. If the prices were particularly attractive, I'd then race through the site throwing things into my cart with reckless abandon, with more consideration for the price than the actual purpose of the item in my wardrobe. That's how I'd end up with stuff in the wrong colour, or in a size that wasn't quite right but with a price tag I couldn't say 'no' to. Once I was done on my supermarket sweep–style binge, I'd open the cart, look at the total, maybe remove a few items until the price was something I could gag down, and then check out.

I came to realise that I've shopped this way for much of my life. Single-item purchases would drip money out of my account one by one, but I was often enamoured with the idea of a multi-item sale spree. Shopping in this way caused so many problems:

∞ I'd end up with stuff I hadn't thought through properly—accelerating my journey to regretville.

∞ I'd buy based on price or perceived saving, rather than whether it was what I actually wanted.

∞ I rarely said 'no'—I'd buy in a colour or a size that wasn't quite right, and vow to try and make it work.

∞ It would be more about the dopamine of the order arriving than actually building a wardrobe of things I could truly wear.

∞ It left me no room to understand what I wanted or needed in my wardrobe.

At one point in my life, I'd whack these kinds of splurges on my credit card for an extra layer of avoidance, but even when I'd got out of debt and sorted my money stuff out, I still found myself in the same emotional cycle of buying when it came to clothes.

Creating the Project

Around the time I started to seriously consider taking radical action to change my relationship with clothes, I was, like everyone else, emerging from the dystopian lockdown period of the pandemic, during which I turned 30; discovered you could order cases of wine on the internet; worked a full-time job and two side hustles and, therefore, missed out on the down time some people experienced; gained weight; lost weight; and, of course, tried to reinvent myself more times than I can count. And with that came clothes buying. Nothing illustrated our wacky relationship with clothes like lockdown. We couldn't leave the house for more than an hour a day but did that stop me ordering clothes online? Absolutely not. And I know I wasn't alone in that.

Turning 30 during lockdown threw my identity into question in a whole new way, so I'm really unsurprised that clothes were my soother during that time. The transition from your 20s to your 30s is one of those big ones in life. Some dread it. Some throw a big party. Some get Botox. I found myself facing the questions of, Who am I at 30? Who do I want to be as a 30-something? Clothes were once again an outlet for my attempts to understand myself.

Stripped of my ability to actively start ticking off a pre-30 list (though I guess I'll never know what I'd actually have done if I had that year back), I began engaging in some sort of 'claw back reinvention'. I figured if I could just emerge from lockdown a totally different person, a totally upgraded version of myself, it wouldn't have all been for nothing.

It was reminiscent, in a way, of the feelings I'd have during summer school holidays. That big chunk of time away from everyone you know, time away from being perceived, judged, ranked in the brutal social hierarchy of a public high school. I remember wanting to return to school different somehow — prettier, thinner, cooler, more confident. Of course I never did, but that didn't stop me longing for my big transformation.

Clothes were always at the forefront of that transformation. If I could just wear the right clothes, I'd be different ... right? This trapped me in a mindset of putting anything 'new' on a pedestal. Regardless of whether it was cheap, expensive, brand new or second-hand — if it was new to me, it was better than my existing wardrobe and I simply had to have it.

Halfway through 2022, I fell out the door of my friend's shed, smacked my head on a pole and broke the fifth metatarsal bone in my foot. Eight stitches in my forehead, a misdiagnosis and a long recovery meant I was hobbling for three months and in a moon boot for two more. As a result, I gained weight rapidly, which, as a child of the 90s, has been deeply ingrained in me to mean something very, very bad. Remember my 'scary size' I mentioned earlier? Yeah, we were way past that.

Weight gain is tough as a woman. You find yourself unable to fit into your usual clothes, so you need to buy things that'll fit. Because we're taught that weight gain is bad and must be temporary, we tend not to buy with a long-term mindset. We buy something that'll 'do for now', because, of course, if you're worth anything in this capitalist patriarchal world, you'll lose the weight eventually, right?

If you don't lose the weight, whether that's because you remain injured or unwell, or perhaps — and I hope you're sitting down for this earth-shattering piece of information — you're just not meant to lose it, you're quickly swept up into one of the most dangerous states for a woman's finances: the state of 'almost'. This mental holding pattern keeps you feeling like you're not quite enough, not quite where you want to be, not quite who you need to be. This state leaves us buying things with the assumption that we'll change eventually. It leaves us looking in the mirror and believing that what we see is bad in some way. It leaves us open to any fix or remedy anyone wants to sell us, whether it's an outfit we feel slimmer in, or some contraption or concoction they cooked up in the diet culture laboratory.

I'll talk more about the state of 'almost' on page 31, but in 2022, I was right there in the thick of it. Buying clothes to fit my bigger body, my body image taking a battering, and basically in limbo when it came to my wardrobe.

It was quite a visceral feeling. Seeing a piece of clothing I wanted and deciding whether to buy it had me like a mouse in a trap. Wriggling my way out, despite knowing exactly how this would end, I'd start engaging in the mental gymnastics of why I should get it. How it was unlike anything I'd seen before. How I'd better get it because I'm unlikely to find anything else like this in my size. How it's low in stock so it'll sell out soon. How it's a staple that'll 'complete' my wardrobe. Except it never did. I swear sometimes I'd just buy the item to relieve myself of the psychological hoop-jumping. Nobody ever talks about the weight of decision-making in such a consumption-obsessed world.

And so, in October of 2022, moon boot on, stitches out, scar emblazoned on my forehead and absolutely sick to the back teeth of the Harry Potter jokes, I started to seriously entertain taking a year off buying clothes. I'm not entirely sure where I got the idea or how it first entered my mind as a possibility, but the more I thought about it, the more I was sold.

Initially, I wasn't sure how much I spent on clothes in a year, but I was certain there was a chunk of money to be saved if I withdrew completely. When I went through my transactions (yes, manually, statement by statement, totting up any transaction that looked to be from a clothes store), I realised I'd spent somewhere in the region of $5000 to $6000 on clothes that year. The idea that by changing just one category of spending I could release five grand back into my budget was enough to convince me. I was all in. What I didn't know at the time was that I'd gain so much more than money.

I'll admit I waivered, though. Despite becoming more and more obsessed with the idea of a full year's break from clothing consumption, seeing an outfit I loved or one of my favourite style influencers popping up with their latest affiliate link did rattle me. I'd think ... do I really want to do this? *Can* I even do this?

As with most pursuits of change, the exciting bit is always the planning. It was one of those commitments that felt like a great idea when I was sitting at home at night with no temptations, nowhere to be and nothing forcing me to do anything just yet—we've all been there. You know, when the idea of a 6 am gym session sounds so appealing the day before you actually have to do it.

But unlike the hours I'd spend dreaming of the person I'd be if I drank celery juice and went to Pilates three times a week for a year, this one really stuck. Even when it came to crunch time, to the purchase that would be my last, I was still all in. I was ready to stick to something, ready to be challenged, ready to see where it led and ready to plug the financial leak that lurked in the back of my wardrobe next to the moth repellent.

What I didn't know then, though, was what lay ahead of me. To be honest, I expected to finish the year with a sense of completion I hadn't felt for a while (thanks to the treadmill of adulthood that begins once you graduate school and doesn't really stop until you retire), and perhaps a chunk of money in my bank account that I could use for something that mattered to me more than a poorly manufactured fistful of polyester.

I finished the year with both of those things plus so much more that I can't wait to share with you in this book. Are you ready to come on the journey through the year with me?

Preparation

To be honest, I'm not altogether sure where I first got the idea for the no-buy. All I know is that it percolated in my brain for several weeks as 2022 drew to a close. With every week that came and went, I became more and more enamoured with the idea; though the closer it got, the heavier the commitment felt. The challenge of it all excited me and scared me at the same time, which, if I'm honest, is kind of embarrassing to admit. The fact I was *scared* of not being able to buy clothes for a year made me feel like such a privileged little brat... which frankly just spurred me on.

As 1 January loomed, despite being more and more certain of how good it would be for me, I doubted myself. I've often been that person who makes grand promises of completing something big, who vows to start some big transformation on Monday or declares the first day of the year as the start of something. Problem is, I've also been the person who backs out of those promises.

I've lost count of the times I'd start some big endeavour, only to fall off the wagon after a couple of weeks or months. A year felt like such a long time. Despite my certainty that I should and could do it, the question of 'what if I fail' kept lurking at the back of my mind. Nonetheless, I persisted with my plans and listened to the part of me that felt that something genuinely was going to be different this time.

Truthfully, preparing for the year was tricky. I focused on setting myself up for success. I asked myself what I could do to minimise my chances of falling off the wagon, so I addressed a few key areas of my wardrobe to mitigate practical problems, and got clear on what my rules would be, and why.

In the final week of 2022, I ordered a pair of cream jeans and three black T-shirts from Marks and Spencer. I already had a black pair of jeans and figured that, if push came to shove, having a simple jeans and T-shirt option would mean I could never pull the excuse of not having anything to wear. Other than those things, I resisted buying too much else under the umbrella of 'to wear if…' because I was conscious that, if I really wanted to experience the changes I said I did, pre-buying stuff to maintain a feeling of newness in my wardrobe was most definitely cheating.

Wishlist items

I had a few things lurking on my radar towards the end of the year, including a work bag from July (which I still have and love to this day!), and about four items I'd been eyeing off in stores during my visit to the UK. This included a pair of wide-leg cream trousers, a pinky-red midi-dress with long sleeves, a pair of straight-leg trousers and a cream jumper with an open collar.

My logic here was to get that craving out of my system. I knew all too well the allure of seeing something and visualising myself wearing it, and I really didn't want that to be what derailed me. However, knowing what I know now, all four of those items were wrong for me. I shouldn't have kept them, and I wouldn't buy them again if I were to go back in time. In fact, each of those items would teach me a lesson during the year ahead, I just didn't know it yet. But more on that later.

The rules

When embarking on a year of change, it's important to have specific guidelines for what you're doing and why. Not buying clothes is simple enough on the surface, but I was conscious that my pesky little brain would run into grey areas.

Does activewear count? What about merch? Are accessories considered clothes? Can I buy shoes? What if something needs replacing? What if I don't have something to wear for a specific occasion? How about costumes? What if I gain or lose weight?!

While you never know what a year will hold, I was fairly certain I wasn't going to become a marathon runner *and* a band groupie *and* get invited to a black tie event *and* a cowgirl-themed costume party *and* rip a hole in every item of clothing I owned all in one year.

As for the weight thing, I had no plans to lose weight, and I'd have been frankly floored if my chunky-since-birth body had suddenly decided it was going to become the weight-dropping kind. Gaining weight was a more legitimate concern for me, given my track record of being able to inflate a few inches from merely smelling a croissant.

But I knew I was sitting a little above my body's usual set point (firmly chunky and equally funky), so I wasn't too concerned about *significant* weight gain during the year ahead. I also had a fair few things in my wardrobe that could withstand a few extra kilos. Bless up the return of the wide-leg trouser, long may it reign.

While I knew there was potential for weight gain or cowgirl-costume-shaped curveballs, my approach was to simply focus on trying to not buy clothes at all and deal with any obstacle if and when I came to it. If I gained weight, I'd set out a new plan as needed. If I needed a ballgown or a cowgirl costume, I'd assess my options. Rent, borrow, make an exception — it would be a case-by-case basis. Spoiler alert: no ballgowns or cowgirl outfits were required. We're home and dry, Stetson-free.

The only exceptions I opted for were accessories and shoes because I didn't feel I had a consumption issue with those things. I'm no Carrie Bradshaw in the shoe department, and rarely bought bags, belts, hats, scarves, etc. I knew I'd have to be careful not to cheat by treating myself to shoes or accessories simply because they were 'allowed', but I was up for the challenge of buying these more mindfully. Accessories can actually help you get more wear out of the clothes you have, so I was open to experimenting with these in the absence of new clothes.

So, I was locked in. One year. No clothing purchases. Just me, my existing wardrobe — flaws and all — and a lot of determination.

What about ...

Now, at this point, I know you're going to have all kinds of questions. People always do when I tell them about the Project — and even more questions begin to bubble around the more they contemplate doing it for themselves. What about thrifting? What about underwear? What about borrowing clothes from my sister? What if my wardrobe spontaneously bursts into flames and all I'm left with is my cat pyjamas and a pair of undies I've had longer than my last relationship? What do I do then?!

Well, first let me say: that's entirely up to you. The best advice I can give you at this point, when your mind is playing ping pong with questions and excuses and what ifs, is to really dig deep on what patterns of behaviour you're trying to change, and what kind of outcome you want.

Here's where I stood on many of the fringe areas of clothing consumption for my Project.

Thrifting

Thrifting wasn't allowed. I know, I know ... I'm a masochist. But, trust me, I come bearing good reason, so hear me out. Shopping second-hand is a great alternative to buying new.

It's often cheaper, and it's better for the planet. Big up that circular economy. But, for me, it was one of the biggest traps for my inner clothes-obsessed consumerist goblin.

I find thrifting highly enjoyable. I got into it a few years ago and quickly became enamoured with the slowness of it, the fact I could spend a day browsing, hunting, fishing for treasure, and come away with a few wins and barely a hole in my bank balance. But that environment also isn't conducive to mindful consumption. In fact, it became my playground for overconsumption with a clean conscience.

Every purchase could be justified. No reason was strong enough to battle my brain's platter of reasons why I should get whatever shiny thing I'd found.

The prices weren't usually enough of a barrier, and because things were so cheap, the uncertainty of sizing wasn't enough of a barrier either. I couldn't employ any of my usual mindful consumption techniques, like time delays or saving up for something, because the genuine scarcity of thrifting supply means if I didn't buy it, someone else would happen upon my treasure and steal it out from under me. The ever-present ability to just re-donate the item back to the very store I'd paid a few bucks for it the first time left very minimal room for discerning consumption. And while this type of consumption wasn't leaving as much of a dent in my bank account — though it certainly does add up faster than you'd think — it was contributing to a broader cycle of buying. That mindset I mentioned before of putting anything outside of my own wardrobe on a pedestal, well, this mindset thrived on thrifting, and kept my wardrobe working like a revolving door of expired dopamine.

So if you are thinking about taking a break from buying yourself, take me as a cautionary tale when you're assessing whether to allow thrifting. If you're a very occasional thrifter, or you're particularly discerning about buying second-hand and you'd be happy for your current consumption patterns in that area to stay as-is, allow thrifting. Be my guest. But if you relate to the pressure cooker of not being able to walk away from something because of its price, rarity, how cheap it is compared to its RRP or just the thrill of the hunt, you might wanna leave it out.

Clothes swapping

Despite swapping, either with friends and family or at dedicated events, being a great way to refresh your wardrobe without spending money, I didn't allow swapping during my Project for a couple of reasons. Primarily, I don't have many (any?) friends that are the same size as me, so I wasn't exactly turning away a long line of people offering up their outfits for me to swap. I could've attended a clothes-swapping event, but, to be honest, I wanted my year to be all about working solely with what I had. It's not that I didn't want to try these ways of changing up my wardrobe without buying—in fact, since completing the Project I have gotten more into swapping. As rules for the Project went, though, I knew I had enough, and I wanted to challenge myself to wear my wardrobe without the psychological relief of newness. Swapping felt a bit like I'd be cheating my way to a clean sheet, without actually learning to exist without the thrill of something new.

Renting clothes

I've rented clothes in the past and actually really enjoyed it. While a lot of clothing rentals are reserved for formal wear or one-off outfits, I once had a subscription to a rental box that allowed me to rent three items per month that were much more everyday casual or workwear. It was fantastic. I could try new clothes without having to buy them and keep them. I even found it kind of helpful for processing that novelty factor—by the time I was bored with an item, it was time to send it back. You can probably already tell where I'm going with this—that was the exact cycle I wanted to break. I wanted to see my clothes as more of a marriage than a fling, and renting only served to uphold that fling mindset. Alas, it was a 'no' from me.

If you need underwear

Alright, listen up. Underwear *always* comes up when I'm talking about the Project, which honestly astounds me given most people's underwear collection is a hole-ridden museum of ill-fitting bras and knickers with the gusset hanging out (or maybe that's just me). And yet, when I propose we skip out on buying clothes for a hot second, everyone's crying out *'but what if I need underwear!?'* Honey, you've probably owned the bra you're wearing since Taylor Swift released *1989*, what the hell are you worrying about?!

In case you hadn't guessed from my facetious sarcasm, underwear was allowed. In fact, I encourage you to buy some underwear at some point during your Project. Not immediately, but at some point during your allotted time away from clothing consumption. Go get fitted for a good bra, clear out your underwear drawer, and get yourself some fresh panties, the kind you want to reach for.

We wear underwear every single day. It's the one item of 'clothing' that we consistently guarantee we'll not only wear, but actively rely on to live our lives comfortably. And yet it's the item we give the least respect. Why?

It's just further proof of the hold clothes have over us. I can't tell you the number of times I've browsed bras or underwear, grimaced at the price (however reasonable that price may be), decided not to bother, and then gone and dropped the exact same amount, or more, on a jacket or a dress the next week without a second thought. Maybe it's because underwear isn't seen that we respect it less. Unless, of course, it's 2002 and you've got your lace girl boxers peeping out the top of your low-rise jeans—but, hey, that proves it, right? The only time we care about underwear is if it's seen by others. The only time we give underwear respect is if it serves to change the way we're perceived.

Anyway, bottom line. *Underwear is allowed.* That's the only rule I'll prescribe as universal. Everything else is up to you. Except this. Buy the fucking undies.

If something breaks or wears out

Another question I'm often met with is an exasperated 'What do you do if something wears out?' Really, this is up to you. I decided to take it on a case-by-case basis. If something broke, I'd assess at the time how badly I really needed to replace it. If, for example, my only coat happened to burst into flames in the middle of winter (highly likely, of course) leaving me with no outerwear at all, sure, I might replace it. But if one of my approximately 16 black tops shrank in the wash, I'd just live without it.

If you need a ballgown/bridesmaid dress/costume/ any other rarely worn specific item

And the final question you might find whirring around your brain is this: What if I'm faced with an event for which I genuinely have nothing appropriate to wear? I hear you. What if, in one year, you're invited to walk the red carpet at the Golden Globes, *and* a fancy dress party that requires you to dress like a member of the BeeGees, *and* your friend who has never had a themed birthday decides to have a purple-only party, *and* Harry Styles invites you to dinner on the basis that you must, and he means *must*, wear jeans in a specific shade of ecru. What will you do then?

Look, first thing I'll say is you're probably going to encounter fewer curveballs than you think you will. But, even if you do get hit with one, don't let the risk of a difficult invite stop you from trying the Project. Just take each occasion, if and when it arises, on a case-by-case basis. If you genuinely need something you don't have, deal with that when the time comes. Maybe Harry Styles will be flexible on the ecru jeans thing, you never know.

When it comes to a project like this, people often crave hard and fast rules. They want answers for every eventuality. And I get it. We want to understand how we can get a clean sheet.

But, I promise you, the best way to get the most out of this Project is to cultivate self-trust. Don't set yourself strict, binary rules. Instead, decide on the mindset you want to have for the Project, and the outcome you're working towards. From there, the answers will come to you naturally. Rely on what you know about yourself and your spending habits. On some level, you probably know what your vices are, what you always reach for as a pick-me-up. Trust that you'll be able to recognise when your brain is trying to bend the rules, or when a question of 'is this allowed?' jeopardises your intention for the Project. Self-trust will serve you well, not just during the Project, but afterwards too.

Alright, rules locked in, plans laid. Let's start at the beginning...

JANUARY
The beginning

Style actually isn't as easy as it's sold to be, but it's profitable to sell the idea that looking good is simply a combination of the right items.

Waking up on 1 January 2023 on day one of my commitment to not buy any clothes for the year felt ... well, in all honesty, I didn't really feel any kind of way about it yet. I could sit here and tell you I felt all kinds of personal development–adjacent words about starting a year-long journey of self-discovery, but I'll spare you the overinflated self-improvement speak. Frankly, at this point, I didn't really know what I was in for. In fact, I was simply sitting with the fact that it was time to live out the year I'd been planning.

There's something so interesting about how much we, as humans, love to plan for change more than we love to execute change. If I had a dollar for the number of times in my life I've flirted with who I'd be if I did yoga every day, or if I got up at 5 am, or if I decided to study some fancy-schmancy degree at night school ... Let me tell you, I love inserting myself into inspirational movie montage sequences, speeding up the effort it takes to follow through on your promises and adding an upbeat soundtrack. Damn, it feels good. I've lost count of the number of times I've watched the Elle Woods law school montage in *Legally Blonde* and immediately felt like applying to Harvard or climbing Mount Kilimanjaro. Reading textbooks on a Stairmaster? Sign me up.

The reason these give us all the feels is that they romanticise the work that goes into getting an outcome you want. They skip over all the hard bits, the painful alarms, the Stairmaster thigh burn, the things you miss when you've got your nose in a textbook. Most importantly, they skip over the self-doubt and the wobbles and the backslides and the almost giving up. You don't see the self-doubt in the montage because the outcome has already arrived.

For the months prior to 1 January, I'd been in montage mode. Excited. Ready to meet the person at the end of the sequence. But that first day of 2023 was the day it actually started to mean something. It was the day where all the exciting stuff dissolved into accountability. Alright bitch, you've started. You're on day one of 365, and you're not gonna get that 'new outfit' feeling for one whole year.

I had to start thinking seriously about how I was going to approach this, and what I'd need to do to actually make it through the year without thinking I had to have something. If I'm honest with you, writing that sentence feels quite vulnerable, because I know so many people could easily go a year without buying clothes, easily see nice things and know they don't need them. People who maybe haven't bought clothes in years because they're simply not ruled by their appearance in the same way I had been for so long. But, in all seriousness, it really felt like I was going cold turkey on some kind of addiction. There was a sense of fear there that the pull of wanting something would be so strong I wouldn't be able to say 'no' to it. I knew that feeling so, so well. The feeling of seeing something great and feeling compelled to get it. Feeling like I'd be missing out on something if I didn't get it. Grappling with the price or the stock levels or chasing it halfway around the country on stock checks if it wasn't available at my local store.

Being so early in the year, the one major thing I lacked at this point was momentum. I needed to focus on making progress through the first month so that I had something to lose. If I got tempted too early,

I'd find myself in the danger zone of thinking I could just get this one thing and then start fresh in February. Knowing this about myself, my first strategy was to minimise my exposure to things that would likely put me in that state of temptation. I combed my social media and cleaned up my feeds with the unfollow and mute functions. *Unfollow* for the ones I felt made me feel worse about myself, and *mute* for the ones I knew I enjoyed taking inspiration from and would want to return to one day. Then I checked my email inbox for any marketing emails and unsubscribed from any I thought might get me to click.

With my digital environment primed for savvy spending, I made it my mission to avoid the shops. At the time, I lived near one of Australia's largest shopping centres, which made it all too easy to find myself popping into a clothes shop while I was over there running an innocent errand, like going to the chemist or grabbing something from Aldi.

Tip: *Committing to a calendar year was additionally helpful for scaffolding that all-important 'something to lose' mindset. While I knew I needed to start making headway so I wasn't tempted to start again next month, the idea that this was my one shot to have a clean full year to complete the challenge did, in part, help me stay the course in those early days. While I could always start again in February, my brain was very keen on the calendar year approach, which in itself gave me something to lose if I slipped up. You can definitely do the challenge at any time, and for any length of time, but using date containers like a calendar year or a calendar quarter, or your birthday to birthday year, can help hold yourself accountable and build early momentum.*

To embrace or withdraw?

I knew a big part of making it through the year without buying clothes was going to be wearing what I already had. The way I saw it, there were two ways of doing this: I could either embrace the challenge of finding satisfaction with my existing wardrobe by getting creative, building new combinations and trying new things, or I could withdraw from trying to look good, and just wear jeans and a T-shirt on repeat. Both have their benefits, so I tried a bit of both. In fact, both became part of my toolkit.

I made sure I had my go-to outfits locked in my mind for days when I didn't have the energy to try and look good, or perhaps when I didn't feel I wanted or needed to. Jeans and a jumper or T-shirt, wide-leg trousers with any manner of basic black top, and a simple stretchy midi-dress that wasn't exactly what I wanted it to be, but would absolutely do. I locked these in my mind so that when I felt rushed, overwhelmed or under pressure, I wouldn't tumble into a vortex of wanting to 'grab a few basics'. The withdrawal approach lays the foundation to not *need* any clothes.

The other side of the equation, the embracing it side, lays the foundation for not *wanting* any clothes by replacing the dopamine and creativity I got from new things with the things I already had.

To my surprise, being creative with my wardrobe was actually … fun. I thought I knew what was in my wardrobe, and I realised that I had a belief that every time I wanted to buy something new it was because what I already had wasn't good enough. But, I can honestly say those first few weeks of digging in my wardrobe, pulling out things I hadn't worn for ages and trying new combinations to see if they worked were so much fun. I had absolutely no idea how much I was mentally writing off items in my wardrobe simply because the novelty had worn off.

I'd look at an item on a hanger and feel utterly uninspired by it, only to put it on and remember just how much fun it was to wear. I couldn't believe the disconnect between what I thought I owned, and what I just hadn't taken the time to properly wear. This was the first lightbulb moment of my year: *We don't try on our stuff enough.*

If you do one thing after you put down this book, open your wardrobe and treat it as though it's a whole shop personalised to you, and everything's free. Grab things off the hangers like you would in a real store, and try them on with the curiosity and excitement you would if you were shopping during a 30 per cent off sale.

You'll be surprised by how much fun you can have by getting creative with what you've got. You might find old things that hold memories, you might uncover things you'd forgotten you had, but you'll almost certainly realise that you can start to see your clothes differently — and this is where the change starts to happen.

You might remember me saying earlier that I was stuck putting all new things on a pedestal, always seeing newness as better than what I already had. The beauty of a commitment like the year-long Project is that you become willing to change your beliefs, and that's what happened when I was able to get curious and creative with my existing wardrobe.

As January wore on, I realised I'd need to use both the embrace strategy and the withdrawal strategy to make it through the year. It wasn't a case of one or the other, though I dare say you could probably struggle through simply wearing the same few items over and over again. That said, I don't think you'd have as much fun, and knowing what I know now, I don't think I'd have learned as much about myself as I did. Leaning into the creativity aspect and really getting to know my clothes was the first step in a series of learnings about who I am and how clothes have been part of my identity.

Making it through the first month was exciting, but somewhat daunting. The month was enjoyable, and I was making headway on my Project, learning new things and wearing clothes I thought I hated. At the same time, I was aware that I'd only scratched the surface. I was one-twelfth of the way through, and the vastness of a year was starting to dawn on me. I was starting to realise this was going to be a Project about myself, just as much, maybe even more than about consumption.

The urge to purge

In the early weeks of the Project, I fought an urge to clear out my wardrobe. I don't know if it was a hunger to make rapid progress (classic me) or just a need to feel like I was *doing* something — most likely both.

I'm a product of modern self-improvement culture after all. The idea of settling into a challenge centred around abstaining from a behaviour for an entire year didn't exactly satisfy my dopamine-deprived existence.

I forced myself not to, because I suspected my overzealous clear outs played a role in my fractured relationship with clothes. I wasn't sure what yet, but I'd done one too many back-breaking trips to the donation bin to know that my wardrobe purges weren't always entirely innocent. In the past, I'd used a clear out as an excuse to add more to my wardrobe, masking my desire for newness with the illusion of being a ruthless minimalist. I'd got such a thrill from donating or selling things, proclaiming 'if I haven't worn it in a year, I won't wear it', only to eventually replace those poorly fabricated mistakes with near identical ones.

Cataloguing my clothes

Have you ever heard of the 80/20 rule? It's used in a lot of contexts, but the most relevant here is this one: you wear 20 per cent of your clothes 80 per cent of the time. To be honest, if you'd asked me if I thought that was true before I started this Project, I'd have said 'no'. I'd have been adamant that I wore more of my wardrobe than that. But, barely a month into the year and I'd already been slapped around the chops with just how flippant I'd been with my wardrobe.

I actually had no fucking idea what the hell was hanging in my wardrobe despite being able to rationalise that I needed another pair of black trousers like an absolute pro. I decided early in the Project to start cataloguing my clothes. I figured if I had a visual log of not just what I owned, but what I wore, I'd be more aware of what I had and could start to build that feeling of having enough without the need for new.

There are several apps you can use to catalogue your wardrobe, but I personally opted to simply take a photo of what I wore each day and add them to an album on my phone. I know the apps have fancy whizzy features like *Clueless*-style outfit creation and cost-per-wear data, but here's the thing with me: I can tell you with absolute certainty that I'd have used the app for a week and then forgotten it existed. I need there to be as few steps as possible, as minimal friction as possible and as little chance of me losing any memory of starting it as possible in order to follow through on something like this.

With the photo approach, it was an action I was perfectly used to doing (whipping out my phone to snap something) and it only took a couple of seconds. As for adding the photos to the album, I usually did this while killing time on public transport or while waiting in a queue for something. God forbid I give myself *two* instructions to follow at once. Nonetheless, if you have a brain that's more capable of basic executive functioning than me, get stuck into the apps. The ones that have been recommended to me endlessly are:

- ∞ Whering
- ∞ Indyx
- ∞ Stylebook.

After a couple of weeks, I felt a distinct sense of satisfaction about my library of outfits I had banked up, and it spurred me on to fill it with more. It was immediately refreshing to be browsing images of outfits on *my* body, and with things I already had, having been so used to scrolling endless troves of influencer bodies and fashion-forward lookbooks as my way of engaging with the fashion industry and with style as a whole. It also exposed me to the fact that I so rarely reflected on the degree to which I liked my outfit, or how I felt in it, or which ones made me feel good about myself or bad about myself. I was quite binary with my view of my style. I either liked my outfit or I didn't. No real nuance, no understanding of why or where I was going wrong. Each day I got dressed was a roll of the dice rather than something I was doing with intention and knowledge about myself and who I was and what I was expressing in my outfits. Building out my own little inspo feed of outfits I could repeat or reimagine became the beginning of a new way of getting dressed, and I was hooked.

In the zone and splashing about with endless dopamine from discovering forgotten treasure in my wardrobe, I bounced into February hungry for more lessons about myself and my style. I guess, at this point, I kinda thought it was going to be easy … but I'll let you be the judge of that later!

The stories hanging in our wardrobes

What I've come to learn through doing this work, with myself and with so many people in The Wardrobe Project, is that so many of the things hanging in our wardrobes have a story to tell. The path they took from hanging on a rack to hanging in your wardrobe says so much about your buying habits, from the way you were feeling when you bought them, to the expectations you have of how you want to look, to the comfort zones you've carved out in your self-image.

While each item we own has its own unique backstory, together they form our buying behaviour. As a result, patterns start to emerge that group together the things we own into categories that reflect these stories. I've listed some of the most common I come across below. You might recognise some of your wardrobe in this list.

∞ *The greatest hits:* The absolute cream of the crop, you wear these on high rotation and wish every item in your wardrobe was as spot on as this.

∞ *The almosts:* Pieces that were almost there but not quite. Maybe you loved the idea in your head but not in reality, maybe there's something not quite right about it, maybe you lust after similar versions of it because there's something missing.

∞ *The shots in the dark:* Things you bought as a complete guess that turned out to be better than expected. A dress you grabbed last minute for a funeral. A piece you picked up when you forgot something you needed that ended up being one of your most worn pieces.

∞ *The grabs:* The impulse purchases that you bought thinking they'd be great, but weren't.

∞ *The duplicates:* Things you own that are all remarkably similar, or the things you bought in another colour because you liked one you already had.

∞ *The fantasies:* The pieces you bought to be the person you wish you could be. That ultra-slick, polished, confident, unflappable you that only ever exists in your head.

∞ *The ghosts:* The pieces that haunt you, hanging unworn in your wardrobe despite once being something you loved. It might represent a past version of you, a previous iteration of your life or maybe even a size you wish you could get back to.

∞ *The postcards:* The pieces that evoke memories, happy or sad, that are hard to get rid of because letting them go would mean letting go of a part of yourself.

∞ *The guilties:* The pieces you spent too much on to get rid of, despite never actually wearing them or feeling good in them.

∞ *The workhorses:* Those rinse-and-repeat pieces that aren't anything special, but are always reliable.

∞ *The fixables:* Those things that will be perfect once you take them to the tailor to be fixed or fitted. Every clear out you promise yourself the same thing … and yet, here we are.

∞ *The drama queens:* Those high-maintenance pieces that evoke instant nausea with their complicated care label demands. Handwash only? What is this, 1950?

∞ *The alter egos:* Those things you bought that just aren't you. Maybe they feel too bold, too youthful, too trendy. They differ slightly from your fantasies in that they don't follow that typical 'I wish I looked like this' pattern. Instead, they're wildcards that come out of left field.

∞ *The placeholders:* Those jeans that don't quite fit right. The work trousers you vow to one day update with the perfect pair. The coat you bought in a pinch that you hate having to wear on every cold day. These are the things we buy while we wait for the right thing.

∞ *The strangers:* Those pieces that make you say 'why do I even own this?' They may hang unworn in your wardrobe with the tags still taunting you.

∞ *The one days:* Those pieces you save for 'best', that you reach for and eventually chicken out of actually wearing for fear of being too overdressed, or spilling something on it, or maybe even being seen. Yep, you'd be surprised how often we fear being seen looking diggity damn hot.

We have a tendency to view our clothes and our style as one homogenous 'thing'. I don't know about you, but I've lost count of the number of times I've fantasised about overhauling my style, or dreamed of what it would be like to go on one of those makeover shows and get a whole new wardrobe, as though my style and confidence in myself would be easier if I could just find the right clothes. But the collection of clothes we own forms a complex tapestry of who we are. Our wardrobes hold insights to our insecurities, our self-perception, our lifestyle, changes we've undergone in our lives, and even our emotions.

We can learn a lot from the stories our clothes tell us, and being open to the granularity of why we've bought what we've bought, both in an emotional sense (I'm looking at you, fantasies, alter egos and ghosts) and in a logistical sense (I'm looking at you, duplicates, placeholders and workhorses), we can understand ourselves better, and learn to experience our clothes, our style and our self-image differently.

Because when we really think about it, style actually isn't as easy as it's sold to be. Stylists spend time curating the seemingly effortless looks we fawn over, and celebrities have experts helping them look good. For retailers and advertisers, though, it's profitable to sell the idea that looking good is simply a combination of the right items. As though it's like pulling the lever on a slot machine and getting the same symbol three times in a row for the jackpot. This idea is what keeps us buying. On top of our obsession with trying to get the right combination to the padlock that's holding our style hostage, we seldom consider that maybe there's more to our style than just the clothes.

Okay, it's at this point of the book I start giving you homework. You can use these exercises to try and extract the learnings I've shared from my own experiences for your own wardrobe.

Tasks: Your wardrobe story

Task #1: Wardrobe story audit

To kick off our practical wardrobe work together, I want you to start thinking about the stories your clothes are telling. Which of those categories had you going 'OMG, that's me'? Follow that thread into your wardrobe, and spend some time getting curious with your clothes and exploring which categories they fit into. Can you find a duplicate? What about a greatest hit? Any *almosts* in there? See if you can categorise at least ten items using our categories list to get an idea of where you're indexing most.

Then, whenever you pick up an item of clothing you own, consider which category it might fit into based on its back story. You'll notice a major shift in your understanding of and connection to your clothes once you start viewing your clothes through these lenses.

Task #2: Purchase pathway mapping

Now we're going to really delve into the stories behind some of our items, and step ourselves back through the purchase process to see what was really going on.

I want you to take three items of clothing you own and plot out the journey they took to end up in your wardrobe. We want to

(continued)

really get into the depths of the thought processes, emotions, feelings and motivations for why you bought this item, what you intended it to add to your life, the purpose for which you bought it and the context surrounding the purchase itself.

Think about how you felt when you saw it, what your mind told you about this item, how you pictured it in your life (if you did at all) and whether any part of your self-image or identity came into play. Were you trying to be someone you're not? Were you trying to 'fix' any part of your image? Did you wish you'd look a certain way when you wore it?

Then think about the purchase process itself. Were you calm and mindful or urgent and anticipatory? How were you feeling when you bought this piece? Did that change as a result of the purchase? Were you soothing or avoiding? Think about how you feel about the item now. Which of our categories do you think it fits into, noting it may fit into more than one?

Complete this exploration for the three pieces you chose from your wardrobe, and then sit with the results. Are there any commonalities? Do you feel more aware of some of your buying patterns? Is there anything you could learn about your style or spending challenges from these pathways?

Chapter summary

- ∞ Style isn't as simple as it's sold to be. When you let go of the idea that the right items will equal style, you open yourself up to the deeper meaning.

- ∞ You may feel the urge to ruthlessly clear out your wardrobe when you feel overwhelmed by getting dressed. While it can provide temporary relief, it means you miss out on the learnings that are hiding on the hangers.

- ∞ Cataloguing your clothes can help you make sense of what you have and give you options to refer back to.

- ∞ Everything in your wardrobe tells a story about your relationship with clothes and how you buy. Using wardrobe categories to differentiate between items can give you a deeper understanding of why you have the clothes you do.

- ∞ Using pathway maps can help you understand how you buy and the route things took to end up in your wardrobe. Commonalities between these pathways help you form an understanding of your buying style and the emotions surrounding it.

FEBRUARY
The mirror to myself

Fashion is about conveying who we are. But what happens when you're not actually happy with who you are?

If there's one thing I'd begun to observe by this point in the challenge, it was an unfamiliar sense of quiet. Peace. A lightened mental load. I had absolutely no idea how much space clothing consumption was taking up in my brain, but there was a noticeable lightness to the idea that no matter what I saw, no matter how much I liked someone's outfit, no matter what sale emails I got, no matter how good the spend and save offer was at Country Road—the answer was just 'no'. I didn't have to make any decisions about whether to buy or not, it was decided for me.

On the surface, that sounds pretty restrictive, right?! I'll admit, I wondered if I was indulging in some sort of masochism. What maniac gets a thrill from denying themselves?

Then I thought about what it's really like buying clothes as a woman. You see something you like, you look at the price, you consider it. You think about it. And think about it. You search for it on other websites to see if it's cheaper elsewhere. You look around for another photo from a different angle. Maybe it's out of stock, so you check the 'find stock in store' feature with the precision of someone developing a life-saving vaccine. You engage in the mental gymnastics of whether you need it. You manufacture excuses, reasons you should get it, endless ways you deserve it. Then you order it (or maybe you find it in store) and try it on. Then you've got to assess whether you keep it, what it goes with, whether it's what you expected. If it's not, you've got a whole other decision to make. And that's just the practical part.

Add on the emotional layer of the ways you think it'll make you look, what it will add to your identity. You flirt with the version of yourself you wish you could be, and begin craving the dopamine you know lies on the other side of the purchase. Maybe you're imagining how other people will perceive you in it, where you'll wear it, how it'll make you feel. And then we have to ask, does it fit? Why is it pulling at my thighs like that? Shouldn't this size fit me? I wish I looked like the picture. Maybe it's not as nice as I thought. Maybe I'll size up. Oh, the next size is out of stock. What now?

When you put it like that, it's really fucking exhausting, right?

Each time we consider a clothing purchase, it's like a mental escape room just trying to decide whether or not to buy it, and the only way to find the exit is to engage in the mind games of sizing, fit, shape and budget. Once you're out, it doesn't matter whether you bought or not, it's only a matter of time before you see something else that's kinda the same, but somehow different, that traps you all over again

This palpable sense of peace that I started to experience so early in the year made me really question the way we're taught to engage with shopping, consumption and the fashion industry as a whole. The very act of consumption stipulates that you're trading resources for a return. In the case of fashion, you're trading money for clothing. Money for creativity, joy, self-expression, art, texture, shape, comfort and a ticket to the world of 'style'.

The peace I felt just one month into withdrawing from the circus of clothing consumption started to show me just how much the fashion industry was taking from me, and how much I'd fallen for the lie that I was the one gaining. If I feel so good as a result of not having, what convinced me to spend so many years obsessed with acquiring more?

Back in my wardrobe, February was a month of revelation. I was in the groove of snapping a photo when I felt I was serving a certified *look*, and I was replacing the dopamine I'd previously got from *newness* by creating circular novelty in my existing wardrobe. Everything was rocking along nicely. I really thought it was just going to be a case of rinse and repeat of what I'd already been doing.

It was once I'd settled into the year that I started peeling back the layers of what I was working with.

Seeing my clothes in a way I'd never really seen them before highlighted the mistakes I'd been making. Patterns were emerging in what I was observing in my wardrobe, and I was able to step back and see the story that my clothes were telling. What I'd thought was a collection of clothing was actually a museum of my insecurities.

Meeting my 'fantasy self'

There's really something to be said about taking away your vices. A wise friend of mine always says: 'When you take away your vices, what you're left with is your life.' Cutting off access to new clothes left me with nowhere else to look for validation, dopamine, novelty, confidence or the currency of self-esteem but myself—and that really taught me the meaning of what my friend meant. When I took away my source of confidence, what I was left with was a clear picture of just how much I was relying on outsourcing my identity to consumption.

While I was finding a solid (and surprising) amount of enjoyment from my existing wardrobe, I'd begun to notice the pieces I reached for more than others, the ones I avoided and the ones that told the most important stories.

I was living out the 80/20 rule, realising how much easier it was to reach for the same 20 per cent of my wardrobe over and over again. Generally, my 20 per cent consisted of the 'better' purchases in my wardrobe: the things that fit fairly well, that were purchased more neutrally or out of necessity, or sometimes just random luck. A dress I'd got on sale and unexpectedly worn to death. A great blazer that worked with almost everything. But when I dared to examine the 80 per cent, which you're kinda forced to when you commit to the Project, that's where it got interesting. There was one factor that united so many of my wardrobe mistakes: I was buying for somebody I'm not.

When I stood back and looked at what my wardrobe was telling me, what those lesser-worn pieces had in common, what the *almosts* and the *strangers* and the *alter egos* shared, I saw a life I didn't lead, a body I didn't have and a style that I'd copied off Pinterest.

My fantasy self would wear sleek tapered trousers and matching jackets. She'd trot about in heels, light on her feet and dainty in her movements. She'd have shiny, glossy hair that was never out of place. She'd show off her long, slim legs in high-waisted skinny jeans and a crisp white shirt with a low messy bun. She wore basics with such elegance. Impeccable posture, flawless jaw line. Feminine. Elegant. And a word that we'll unpack at length in this book: polished.

For all the things she was, there was one thing she wasn't: me. None of the things I admired in her stemmed from anything I truly was. Her feminine daintiness didn't mirror the space I took up, or the bold playfulness of my personality. Her slick demeanour didn't reflect my dry, acerbic humour. Her mile-wide thigh gap certainly didn't match my wobbly thighs and dump truck ass (two things I've since learned to love).

I was starting to see how my entire relationship with clothes was fractured. How I was erasing myself, rather than embracing myself. Fashion is about conveying who we are. But what happens when you're not actually happy with who you are? What are you expressing when you identify as someone who isn't good enough? When you exist in a body that society considers wrong? When clothes become your way of hiding your flaws and trying to be who you think you should be, you're left conveying everything you're not. This incongruence is bound to be uncomfortable, and I was realising I'd felt that discomfort for most of my life. I was stuck on a hamster wheel of wanting to 'express myself', but not for who I really was, but for who I *felt safer trying to be*. In many ways I knew my fantasy self, while uncomfortable and unhelpful, better than I knew myself.

The outfit in my head vs on my body

A big way my fantasy self played out in my buying habits and style choices was this constant disconnect between outfits in my head versus outfits on my body. The image of my fantasy self was so strong that I could conjure up an image of what I wanted to look like in an outfit so easily. I'd then replicate that, either with clothes from my existing wardrobe or clothes I was buying, and instantly be disappointed.

Oftentimes I'd try to force it, convince myself that I did look like the image in my head, try to shove confidence in the way I looked down my own throat, but something always felt off. I'd catch myself in a shop window—you know, doing the subtle head turn pretending you're looking into the store but you're actually looking at yourself—or see myself in a photo someone had taken. I was so familiar with this huge gap between what I'd tried to look like and what I'd actually looked like that it felt as though style was this game of moving goal posts.

I think this disconnect comes down to a few things. First, glossy images on product pages and social media. I'm clearly a fashion marketer's absolute dream because a good image can make me want an item instantly. When these images triggered my desire to imitate my fantasy self, I'd slide into the vortex of buying and expecting the product to look like that on me.

Second, I think, as women, we've actually been conditioned over many years to see a distorted view of ourselves at any given time. I spent years trapped by body dysmorphia (when your view of your body distorts your true size and shape), convinced I was substantially bigger than I actually was—and this is complete proof that just because we're looking in a mirror, doesn't mean we're really seeing ourselves clearly. When we don't really see ourselves, we can't really know ourselves. And that's why our fantasy self provides such psychological comfort in many ways, because we can easily see them represented in the media we're consuming and the lives we're admiring. It's almost easier to pretend to be someone else than it is to meet who we really are.

Meeting my fantasy self was a necessary but somewhat painful step on my journey. While I'd started to unlock the mistakes I'd been making, I wasn't quite sure where to go from there. I had ten months to go and a wardrobe filled with things I suddenly saw in the cold light of day as entirely wrong for me. If I was going to start dressing in a way that expressed my real self, I needed to get to know who that really was.

What I'd begun to learn was that style on a page isn't the same as style in real life. Whether it's a professional commercial photoshoot or an influencer sharing their latest haul on social media, that view of style is so one-dimensional. Mirror selfies and exceptional lighting don't express clothing in the way it's worn on a real body in real life. When the train was cancelled and you had to jog to the replacement bus service only to find the air conditioning was broken and you're now flustered. When you were eating your packed lunch at your desk in corporate hell and spilled a bit of last night's curry on your blouse. When you haven't slept thanks to your child's unexpectedly early first tooth coming through and you've still got to pull it together with the dress you didn't have time to get dry cleaned.

We have to learn to see style differently, outside of the curated and the commercial, and in our real lives. And that looks different for all of us. We all lead our own lives and we all have different routines, rituals and audiences for our outfits.

Signs your fantasy self is tapping your card

Do you relate to the idea of a fantasy self? If you did, I've got some tasks for you to help tease that out a little more, but for now, let me share with you some signs that your fantasy self might occasionally run away with your wallet.

∞ *Buying pieces to create a specific look.* This is a trap so many people get stuck in when following trends. We buy things that go together in one specific context, to create one specific outfit, only to then feel stuck with nothing to wear and, therefore, chasing newness, because, well, we don't have anything to wear except that one specific outfit! Trends often stir up a part of our fantasy selves that makes us want to replicate, imitate or take shortcuts to the way we want to look.

∞ *Buying pieces that go with one specific thing.* Oh, the number of times I've tumbled into this one! Buying a top that'll go really nicely with a specific pair of trousers you own, only to never wear those two things outside of their silo.

∞ *Buying pieces to mirror the style of other people.* While your fantasy self is just a concept, we anchor that fantasy to people we see in real life, whether they are people we know, follow or just admire from afar. We then use their style to gain proximity to our fantasy self and get that hit of dopamine we love so much.

If anything on this hit list exists in your wardrobe, welcome to the fantasy self club. Don't worry, by the end of this book, you'll be ready to break up with them once and for all.

The 'almost' trap

The presence of our fantasy self creates a difficult set of conditions in which to engage with fashion in a healthy way. Earlier I questioned what happens when we're trying to express who we are but end up expressing who we're not, and that juxtaposition creates what I like to call our state of 'almost'.

As women, society benefits greatly from us being kept in this state of 'almost'. Think about it. We're always one commercial solution away from everything we think we're supposed to be. The perfect outfit, the perfect capsule wardrobe (more on that on page 87), the perfect skin, the perfect weight, the perfect erasure of ageing. The ever-moving goal posts, by design, keep that state of 'almost' familiar and, to a degree, comfortable.

While comfort zones are, in theory, places of comfort, what they are more often than not are places of *familiarity*. That familiarity might actually be inherently uncomfortable, but its familiarity is what makes it a comfort zone. We might feel deeply uncomfortable with the fact we're raised from a young age to measure our worth in line with the size on the label of our jeans or consider cellulite or an absent thigh gap some kind of moral failing. But the idea that we're just one solution away from being good enough is so familiar that, after a while, we become our own worst enemy. We get such a rush from each time we play the societal slot machine of 'will this be the product that fixes me', that we keep coming back for more. Despite all of our experiences telling us that the cellulite cream never works and the perfect dress isn't perfect for long, we're still somehow addicted to the fight. Addicted to trying. Addicted to one more round of camel blazers, blue jeans and Breton striped tees in the hopes of landing on that elusive capsule wardrobe.

The state of 'almost' spans so many areas of womanhood, it's no wonder we get stuck in its revolving door when it comes to our sense of style. I was raised by Trinny and Susannah's *What Not to Wear* (look, it aged terribly, but I stand by my love for Trinny) and magazines with shoppable editorials that promised ways to dress for your body type or 'look one size smaller'. The style confidence we craved, and the identity it would allow us to embrace, was always found on a rack somewhere. It felt as though buying the right thing would be the key to feeling good, never mind what was going on in my head.

As I unpacked the idea of the fantasy self more, I began to untangle just how misled I'd been over the years. I realised I'd been completely and utterly missing the point of clothes and fashion. Instead of seeing them as a way to express myself, I saw them as a means to an end. A way to acquire the feelings I wanted. A way to try on other people's identities and see which I liked best. The dopamine hit I'd been getting from the excitement of buying something new, and the potential step closer to the confidence I craved, was being misattributed to real confidence, creativity and joy. In fact, it was just a temporary rush from the experience of buying, and the potential for it to ultimately close the gap between who I was and who I wished I could be.

The break from buying was already teaching me that this process obviously didn't work. Stepping back exposed just how much of a cycle I'd been stuck in. It seemed so clear to me now, I just couldn't see it when I was in it. Of course you're never going to feel good about your style when you're just replicating other people. Of course you're never going to feel like you've got enough clothing if you're treating every symptom of your low self-esteem with a purchase. Each time a new symptom pops up, you need more to plug the hole in your identity.

So I'd begun to see where I'd been going wrong. I wasn't expressing myself, I was erasing myself. If I was going to change the way I bought, I'd have to get to know myself better ...

Tasks: Confronting the fantasy

Okay, the fantasy self is one of the meatiest themes of this book, so I've got a few exercises here for you to start exploring yours.

Task #1: Picture your fantasy self

As you've read about my fantasy self, you might have seen flashes of what your fantasy self looks like. Our fantasy self can be:

- an elevated version of how we see ourselves; for example a slicker, more elegant, more expensive or polished expression of what we like to wear
- the opposite of how we see ourselves; for example, tall if we're short, slim if we're thick, flat chested if we're part of the big titty committee...you get the idea

(continued)

- a version of ourselves with all of our 'flaws' reversed; for example, high cheek bones, thick shiny hair, cellulite-free and perfectly proportioned
- the very image of someone we admire, like an influencer, celebrity or someone you know.

Usually, our fantasy self stems from a few or all of these areas. They might be like you in some ways and differ from you in others. You might visualise your fantasy self in a specific outfit or a specific setting like a workplace, or you might even have a few different visuals of what your fantasy self looks like. Spend some time fleshing out your fantasy self, and identify the key traits they possess. When we have a clearer view of who we have on a pedestal, we can better work on separating our true selves from the fantasy we wish we could be.

Task #2: Audit your inspiration

The next task is about where your fantasy self shows up in your life, and countering that with some healthier sources of inspiration. Now let me be clear: the fantasy self isn't all bad. There are parts we can keep, and parts we might be better off letting go, but we'll come to that later.

For now, I want you to think about the media or content you consume that upholds your fantasy self. It might be the influencers you follow, the magazines you read or even the TV shows you watch. What we want to do is give you some space from this fantasy ideal, so you can explore your style and your identity independently. You need room to discover who you would be if you weren't trying to be your fantasy self.

I'd encourage you to mute, or unfollow, anyone who upholds your fantasy self ideal. It's not forever, it's just for a while so you can experience style outside of that silo. What I'd also encourage is broadening your inspiration pool. Whether you're a TikTok scroller, Instagram devotee or Pinterest pinner, try to add in five new accounts to your feed. Opt for people with some similarity to you. Whether that's lifestyle, body type, height, size...anything. This is going to give you a wider lens through which to view style potential.

Task #3: Lifestyle pie chart

Your final task, for now, is something called a *lifestyle pie chart*. I learned this from my friend and sustainable fashion stylist Jenna Flood when she was teaching for The Wardrobe Project group program. The idea is to deepen your understanding of how you live your life, so we can build a sense of style around that.

Many of us have a fantasy self who is actually living a fantasy lifestyle, too. That might be because we've gone through a life transition, like becoming a parent or entering a new decade, or it might be part of our long-held views of what constitutes style that sees us dressing like we're Miranda Priestly's assistant when actually we're taking our toddler to soft play. Trust me, those toddlers' heads won't turn if you walk in wearing the infamous Chanel boots.

For your lifestyle pie chart, draw a circle and section off a portion of it for each context in which you live your life. Think about the roles you play, the places you go, the parts of your identity that come out when you're getting dressed. Maybe you're a mum who's at home 40 per cent of the time, an executive at work 40 per cent of the time, a runner or beachgoer 10 per cent of the time, and a lover of art galleries and fine dining 10 per cent of the time.

For each portion, write a few sentences about the types of clothes and styles that are best suited to those contexts.

(continued)

Keep this in mind when you're getting dressed or working with your wardrobe over the coming days and weeks—you might find that you're actually buying most of your clothes for your 10 per cent, leaving yourself with nothing to wear for your 40 per cent, perhaps indicating that you haven't embraced that part of your identity fully—which may be especially true if that part of your life is new to you.

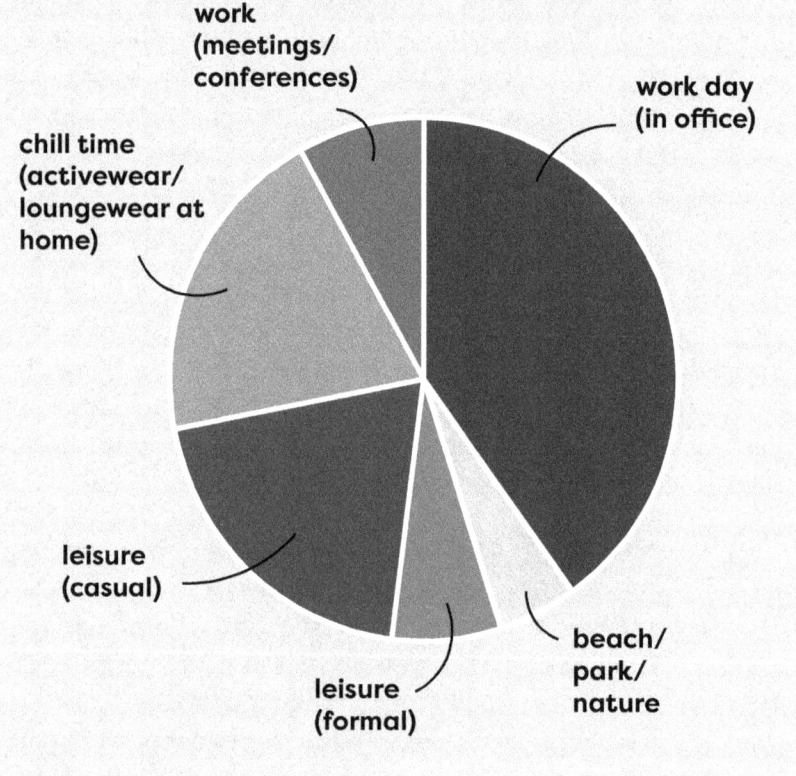

Real people

Doing this kind of work on our self-image via our wardrobes is deeply personal, and it can bring up a lot of emotion. Sometimes it can feel like we're the only ones who have experienced these things, but so many of our experiences are shared. I want you to feel held by this book and the learnings within it, so I have enlisted five participants from my Wardrobe Project group program, who have generously shared insights into some of their challenges with style and self-perception at various points throughout this book. Let's meet our five friends and hear about their relationship with clothes and their fantasy selves.

Jo, 50s, living in New Zealand

'I was rebuilding myself, and my wardrobe was a key focus on that journey. And boy, did I build . . . '

When I was younger, buying clothes was about trends, I think, but also, as someone who has always been plus size, fashion was not something that felt entirely accessible to me. Even just a decade ago, plus-size 'fashion' was either incredibly cheap, poorly made with no regard to actual body shape, or was extraordinarily expensive designer muumuu-type garments, just with extra flounces of fabric to 'disguise' our lumps and bumps. So, while I tried to dress well, I was still entrapped in the 'covering' mentality, and making do with what I could find in my size.

In my mid-40s, I exited a dysfunctional relationship. I was often criticised, demeaned and humiliated for how I chose to present myself, so I embarked on an 'I'll show him' journey (despite having no intention of him ever physically seeing me again—but it made sense to me). I had found Instagram and influencers, and a whole world of plus-size fashion that was well made and designed. I was rebuilding myself, and my wardrobe was a key focus on that journey. And boy, did I build . . .

I did amass quite the wardrobe of clothes, but I still wasn't feeling entirely how I wanted to feel: confident, stylish, unique, good enough . . . The Wardrobe Project (which I did twice, just to reinforce the information) was the missing link for me . . . I was still chasing my (or maybe his) fantasy me.

Amy, 30s, living in the UK

'I was buying for my old life and my old body, rather than who I truly am.'

My relationship with buying clothes has always been chaotic, problematic and often frantic. From the moment I had a full-time job and regular pay, I had an unhealthy relationship, and borderline obsession, with buying clothes. Importantly, the obsession has been with *buying* rather than the clothes themselves.

I'd often order things in multiple sizes or colours, often spending over £150 at a time. I was in a horrible cycle of purchase high—disappointment—stress and shame—cheering myself up with a purchase high, and so it began again.

Once shopping apps were in my pocket, I would often scroll websites and buy due to boredom. I was also buying for every time I had somewhere to go, as I felt I would only look okay if I was wearing the *perfect* thing, which inevitably would never be found in my own wardrobe.

I can often get fixated on the idea of something, so if there's a sale or I think something is about to sell out, I can go into 'must have it whatever the cost' mode and pull money from savings or use buy now, pay later to get it. That's when it becomes frantic and all sense leaves my brain.

My fantasy self still spends her life at boozy brunches, on girls' holidays and spends five days a week in an office. In reality, all my friends now have children and the time I get with them is limited. I work from home 60 per cent of the time and the rest of my time is generally spent with my partner, and walking our dog.

My fantasy self still has the energy, occasion and time to fake tan and style her hair, while my real self only wears make-up two to three days a week now. My fantasy self needs a lot of holiday clothes, tons of co-ords and outfits to wear out for drinks—so I was buying them for her, but my real self was never wearing them. It meant I pretty much always felt I had nothing to wear because I was buying for my old life and my old body, rather than who I truly am.

Lizzie, 30s, living in Australia

'My fantasy self became the mum who doesn't look like a mum.'

I have always and continue to love shopping. Shopping (in my head) has been there for me in good times (hello celebratory shopping!), or sad/stressed times (aww feel bad, let's go spend money!)—because of this, it has been a fairly strong constant in my life from as soon as I had any expendable income.

My fantasy self has definitely evolved over time and really heavily relies on social media and types of advertisements. Social media allows you to curate your own feed to follow accounts that you directly align with—and for me, a lot of them are mid-size influencers who are in their style/consumption era. Seeing clothing on bodies that resemble my own has honestly encouraged me to shop more.

Especially since becoming a mum, I follow a lot of fashion influencers who are bucking the trend of looking like a 'mum' (because, for some reason, this is a bad thing?!). Essentially, gone are the days you do drop-off in your comfies. Now, you're in a put-together outfit. My fantasy self became the mum who doesn't look like a mum, but is kicking ass at work and home—essentially, signing up to become an impossible standard.

Olga, mid- to late-30s, living in Switzerland

'Trying to be forever young is a pressure of its own.'

I'm a mother and an office worker during the day and a music and video games fan in the night. My salary affords me my needs and even some fashionable wants. That already made my purchases quite erratic, and there was also an emotional component of 'I grew up in a modest-income family, and the wealthy girls in my school made fun of my old dresses, so I can now *fight back*'. So I actually spent way more money than I would like on impressing the demons in my head, not even the actual people whom I could possibly try to blend with.

I could buy pretty much anything — from a high-end luxury boutique item to a second-hand store or an outlet mall find — and I felt like '*OMG, I am obsessed*'.

I also bought quite a lot of stuff out of loyalty, be that a store discount program or just an affinity for a rock band that I wanted to support by buying yet another concert T-shirt, even if I already had 13 concert shirts. The very fact that my purchases were emotional and erratic ruined a lot of fun and replaced it with guilt and regret about wasting money and time. It was borderline addictive, and I am actually glad that I got out before getting completely hooked on these behaviours.

I definitely encounter the fantasy self quite a lot, but it has more to do with lifestyle than body image. I do have a problem with realising that I have a teenage daughter and a day job, so I do need clothes for 'mundane' everyday wear.

I go to a lot of rock concerts and goth parties, so a significant part of my wardrobe consists of 'going out' clothes, which are quite provocative and countercultural nature. I end up buying for the 'teenage rocker girl' fantasy self a lot, but way less for the everyday me who needs to buy potatoes and toilet paper (and sometimes I even dreaded this 'old and boring' version of myself). Trying to be 'forever young' is a pressure of its own.

Rebecca, early 50s, living in the UK

'*I began a decades-long cycle of buying things because they looked great on other people.*'

I grew up wearing hand-me-downs or clothes from jumble sales as there was *no* money. I was never cool and always felt shame. As soon as I started earning money at 16, I started throwing it at new clothes. To be able to buy new and trendy clothes (finally, not hand-me-downs!) when I wanted made me dizzy. But I had no idea what suited me. I can remember putting some things on and somehow feeling that they felt more 'me' than others, but that was probably the extent of my analysis.

I wasted so much cash on trendy pieces that did nothing for my shape or proportions, and so began a decades-long cycle of buying things because they looked great on other people (or a shop dummy) so surely they'd look great on me too. But I'd find myself avoiding picking them out of my wardrobe because actually, when I wore them, I didn't feel great at all. I'd be tugging at a top that was too short on my long torso or walking around in a trendy short, flared skirt, which looked fabulous on the girls with long, slim limbs but with my short, thicker legs, I felt dumpy and inelegant. Still, I didn't actually understand why, and no-one was telling me or helping me out.

When I was old enough to get a credit card, things got even worse. So began the debt cycle it would take me 22 years to break away from. But even after the debt was sorted, I still hadn't got very far on the style aspect. Okay, I'd progressed from frilly mini-skirts, but I was still wasting really hard-earned money (that should have been going into a pension scheme, might I add) on items I'd end up giving away or selling for peanuts. I wasn't learning from my mistakes at all; it was complete madness.

I've gone through most of my adult life dealing with a wide range of emotions: disappointment, despair, anger, bitterness, envy … all bundled up with an already low self-esteem (bordering on self-hatred). Eventually things got a bit out of hand. I won't go into detail. But I have also spent good money on counselling, which I highly recommend.

Learning about what suits you—with your very real unique body shape and proportions—might sound trivial to some, but for me, it has introduced much more self-acceptance and a much healthier mindset. A bonus is I now have more money to spend on life, and that's definitely not to be sniffed at. I now need to work on forgiving myself for all the mistakes I have made in the past, including the financial waste.

Chapter summary

∞ Your fantasy self is an idealised version of yourself based on who you wish you could be.

∞ Fantasy selves are formed by insecurities, conditioning, the editorialisation of our lives on social media, and unattainable standards for women.

∞ There's often a disconnect between how you want to look in your head, and how you look in reality. When you cling to this ideal too much, you're developing a negative relationship with clothes that keeps you stuck in a buying cycle.

∞ Buying to create a specific look, buying pieces to go with one specific outfit, and buying to mirror the style of other people are all signs your fantasy self is driving your buying decisions.

∞ The 'almost' trap can keep you stuck in a buying cycle because you feel like the right purchase will solve your problems.

∞ You can combat the fantasy self by addressing who they are and what's feeding them. Fantasy selves are often upheld by the people you follow on social media, people you know and admire, or past versions of yourself.

MARCH

The steer into the skid

The allure of clothes promises an identity and an escape from the lives we lead, the bodies we live in and the way we see ourselves as a result.

I was steaming towards the first-quarter finish line, on a crusade to ditch my fantasy self and uncover more of what I liked, and so this month, I began something I like to call 'exposure therapy'.

March began my quest to build tolerance for temptation. I'd started to recognise how much easier the challenge was when I didn't have anything on my mind that I wanted to buy, and as I mentioned, this had been my strategy for smart spending on my money journey more generally. Reduce proximity to temptation = easier to spend less.

But with clothes being my Achilles heel, I knew I couldn't rely on not seeing anything I liked to protect me from buying. I wanted to develop a relationship with the clothes I owned that would be strong enough to squash the temptation from well-merchandised stuff in stores and curated content on social media.

My exposure therapy consisted of me taking myself to stores, browsing things I'd like to buy, indulging myself in the perils of merchandising, touching the soft silks and the lush leathers... and then walking away without buying.

Now if you're considering setting this book on fire/throwing it out the window/hammering your keyboard on a review site to tell the world the author is a maniac and shouldn't be trusted, I understand. Telling people that I did this has induced many a grimace and more eye rolls than I can count. Please, I beg of you, give me a chance to prove I'm not a sociopath.

The reason I did this was simple: curiosity. Curiosity was at the heart of this Project, and by March, I knew it was going to be more than a money-saving experiment. It was going to be something that profoundly changed my relationship with clothes and myself, so I faced that curiosity head on.

I went hunting for emotion. I went hunting for that feeling I knew would show up the second my beady eyes clapped onto a pair of black slim-leg trousers. I went hunting for the images my brain would conjure up of my fantasy self, to try to activate the hunger I'd feel to get closer to being her by acquiring whatever viscose creation fell into my path that day.

I remember the first place I tried exposure therapy. It was at a Country Road store in Sorrento on the Mornington Peninsula in Victoria. If you've been to that store, you'll understand why it was the epitome of throwing myself in the deep end. The store is simply stunning. It's got a sort of Hamptons feel to it, with timber decking at the entrance and green shrubbery lining the entrance walkway. It's one of their 'lifestyle concept' stores that invite you into the world of Country Road, which made it perfect for my mission, because not only did it house my fantasy wardrobe, but my fantasy home too. Cleverly, there's even a cafe on site, so you can sit among the pretty plate-adorned shelves and momentarily pretend the shop floor is your walk-in wardrobe and the plumply rolled fluffy tea towels are yours to dry your hands on. I didn't stay for coffee.

It wasn't long before a few things caught my eye. Autumn had just begun, so rich earthy woollens were draped over buttery leather skirts that skimmed the ankles of boots I could only dream of ramming my colossal calves into. A really gorgeous shade of expensive-looking lilac was accented throughout the store at that time, bouncing off the cosy beiges and elegant blacks of cardigans and coats that cost a week's rent.

And then, I felt it. The somewhat visceral sensation of *wanting*. At first, it was the general aura of being surrounded by beautiful things. It does something to me, for some reason. Beyond just clothes, it's like it truly sells me a better life, lets me believe that buying from here means I'm making my life better. Like fragments of what it means to live a life that aesthetic were available to me at $199 a pop. And I'd fallen for it so many times.

But it was a matching suit in a sort of darkish purple-y mushroom-y colour that gave me the whiff of my fantasy self. Bingo. That's what I'd been looking for. The matchy-matchy-ness of it gave this illusion of being so perfectly put together in such a way that it sends a message to onlookers. The wearer of this suit is not just sartorially immaculate, she is immaculate as a person. As though, if my suit matched, that would make up for the fact that, in general, I am a human tornado, blustering through life as inelegantly as possible.

When people mistake this commentary for needless self-deprecation, I remind them of how I came to break a bone thrice in my lifetime: once tripping over on the first day of high school, once by tripping at the post office and breaking my elbow of all things, and once by tumbling head first into a lamp post in my friend's garden. NB: On none of these occasions had I consumed a drop of alcohol.

See. Human tornado.

Anyway, we're back in the store, salivating over suits. I let my mind go to where it would often go: the fantasy. I let myself flirt with the person it thought I could be if I just wore this suit. If I drank my morning coffee from this pretty mug with COUNTRY ROAD emblazoned on the side. If I dried my dishes with that plush tea towel. If I slung this supple leather bag over my shoulder and went to work.

When I allowed myself to question that vision, I could see it more clearly. I quite literally could see myself moving through life that way. Living in the immaculate home, walking with immaculate posture, make-up sitting perfectly on my immaculate jawline—double chin nowhere to be seen.

The allure of clothes promises so much more than warmth and coverage. It promises an identity and, in many cases, an upgrade or an escape from the lives we lead, the bodies we live in and the way we see ourselves as a result.

I wandered around the store while I welcomed this feeling, probably looking a smidge conspicuous to store staff as I stroked the scarves, slung coats over my shoulders and practically drooled over the racks filled with possibility. As I began to get myself ready to leave the store and walk away from that feeling, I noticed a distinct sense of something akin to grief. I'd been doing so well on the challenge so far, it had felt almost easy. Now I was met with sudden awareness that I wouldn't get to buy into that lifestyle again for nine more months. I was somehow existing in two places at once. Even though I could, intellectually, see how delusional it was to believe that buying items would fundamentally change my life or who I am, I was still sitting with the feeling of wanting to do it. I guess it's a bit like right before you text someone you shouldn't after a couple of glasses of wine. You know it's not good for you, but you still want to anyway.

Thankfully, I am nothing if not a stubborn little bitch, and I wasn't about to give up three months of the challenge to buy something that probably wouldn't even fit me (nudging over the size 16 mark did make it easier not to shop at Country Road—can't sell to me if it doesn't fit me, mwahaha). I walked away, but that's not where the exposure therapy learnings stopped. I could, however, say with absolute certainty that outside of the challenge, I'd have found it hard not to give into the temptation. If I'd had the money available, and/or if there had been some kind of enticing sale on (ya gal loves a spend and save), I could have been easily swayed to buy.

Over the next few days, I noticed something else: the pull I'd felt in the store was entirely disproportionate to how much I actually wanted them. I realised my life was no worse without all those beautiful things that promised me so much just days ago. In fact, I'd all but forgotten about them by the end of the week. And yet I *thought* I wanted them in the moment.

That's when I could really see, in the cold light of day, just how much that feeling we experience when seeing pretty things isn't real at all.

The allure of looking 'polished'

In taking you with me through that exposure therapy browse of Country Road, I mentioned the suit that caught my eye, the one that perfectly captured my desire to look *put together*, slick, elegant, dare I say, *polished*, and I want to unpack that term a little bit more.

I have a theory that the universal pursuit of looking *polished* costs women billions of dollars. In fact, I've become somewhat fascinated with the term, policing it in people's conversations and picking at what they mean when they use it. I'll let you in on a secret: this book was originally called *Polished,* because it comes up over and over again in women's vocabulary around clothes.

In a survey I ran when researching for this book, 75 per cent of respondents said they'd had the thought 'this will make me look polished' when buying a piece of clothing. In fact, when I asked respondents which of seven buying motivations they most related to, 'wanting to look polished' scored the highest, closely followed by 'this will flatter my figure/hide my flaws'. Interesting. However, when I surveyed my social media audience on how often they felt they looked polished themselves, only 7 per cent responded 'often'. Another 48 per cent responded 'never', and the remaining 45 per cent responded 'sometimes'.

There's something about the term 'polished', and while we're at it, 'put together', that seems embedded in women's perceptions of themselves, particularly as it relates to clothing. It's conceptual, it's undefined, it doesn't have a clear meaning and, yet, we all somehow understand its subtext.

Synonyms for polished include: glossy, refined, smooth, accomplished, flawless — even *privileged* came up under the subcategory of refinement, which immediately makes me want to pull at the thread of the 'old money' aesthetic that's been deeply embedded in social media style culture for years, and really embraces the idea of looking 'polished' as somewhat of a status symbol. At the time of writing, #oldmoney had over 1 million posts on TikTok. Clicking on any of those posts will invariably take you to a video sharing tips on how to look 'expensive' or 'classy' or how to look like you're 'old money' when you are, in fact, hoping the zip doesn't break on your $39.99 Zara trousers.

While swiping through videos of slim white women wearing cream ensembles with ballet flats certainly captures aesthetic appeal, I learned more from the videos that promised to tell me why I *don't* look old money.

Apparently it comes down to fit (your clothes must fit well to look classy, I'm told), your hair (it must be styled, I'm told) and tone (you shouldn't wear black bottoms with a light top, I'm told. Keep it tonal).

And look, I guess I can't disagree. Whether we're packaging it as old money or polished or anything else, well-fitting clothes, styled hair and tonal pieces will generally look appealing to the eye. The thing that's not being said in these videos is this: you will look more expensive if you are thin. Thinness is at the centre of looking 'polished', and that comes down to the way we view size in modern society.

Now, of course, being thin is not a guarantee of polish. Many thin people yearn to look polished despite being arguably in much greater proximity to the possibility. This takes me onto my next observation around our obsession with looking polished: the erasure of signs of life.

Women have been ruled by a patriarchal set of beauty standards for a long time—and in recent decades, the commercialisation of our adherence to these standards has rapidly evolved. We can click and buy any manner of things that we believe will help us satisfy those standards at any given time, and algorithmic advertising has rolled up its sleeves and tucked right in. Recent reports of Meta serving adverts for beauty products to young girls who upload and subsequently delete a selfie tells you all you need to know in that domain.

There's something about the allure of looking polished that feels immediately incongruent with everything that makes us human. To look polished is to somehow look clean. Notice how there's no room for sweat. There's no room for that splodge of yoghurt you dropped while eating breakfast. There's no room for baby dribble. Creases are unwelcome. Comfort feels unwelcome. The backpack you have to wear to lug all your stuff to and from work on public transport is unwelcome. To me, it feels like life itself is unwelcome when trying to appear polished, and yet, the idea that we can all look put together and unflappable at any given time is still so appealing.

You're not going to look like the picture

Much of the polish we aspire to possess lies in the photos (and, more recently, videos) of clothes that we're exposed to. Whether that's from creators on social media, in commercial photography seen on online stores, editorial images from advertising campaigns or in print and digital media—the outfits always look more polished when we're viewing them in this way than when they're on a real human body living a real human life.

In some cases, these images are an outright lie. Clothes are often clipped, tugged, tucked or pinned into place to create the perfect shot, or smoothed in post-production, when in reality, they don't fit like that at all. But even without this manipulation of what clothing looks like, viewing clothes on ideal bodies in ideal circumstances creates an unrealistic expectation of what we're going to look like.

Just like in our pursuit of looking polished, we're aspiring to something that, broadly speaking, isn't possible. You can't look like a styled image when you're out living a real human life. Real bodies move, clothes crease. Real bodies run for the train. Real bodies carry a work bag and hope our soup won't spill. Real people have to wear flats because heels are completely and utterly impractical. Real people get blisters. Real people have to wear big period undies and hope nobody spots the visible underwear line.

One of the most freeing realisations you can have is that you won't look like the picture. The picture isn't real, and there's no room for what makes you human in the images we admire and try to live up to.

We've been so conditioned to view clothing in the context of how we see them advertised and idealised that we've forgotten how beautiful it can be to look human.

The more we chase the glossy idea of style that we see in photos, the more we create and uphold a cycle of perpetual failure, and that perceived failure serves to keep us buying more and more and more as we attempt to close that gap of 'almost' that we talked about on page 31. When we're hung up on looking like the picture, this gradually distorts the way we view ourselves in clothes and creates this disconnect between what we *think* we're going to look like and what we *actually* look like.

The rise in expectation along with the rise in dopamine as we anticipate a purchase feels good in the moment, but when we're met with the harsh reality that we don't look like the ideal we're holding in our heads, the crash happens. Suddenly we're flooded with disappointment, which serves as a breeding ground for our insecurities and all the ways we wished we looked different. That post-purchase state leaves us vulnerable to any future opportunity to feel good. It leaves us craving that feeling of anticipatory dopamine we get when we buy something new, meaning we're more likely to buy again in an attempt to get it right. Over time, these misguided buying patterns create an unhealthy relationship with clothes and a fundamental misunderstanding of ourselves and the way we look. The excitement and perceived joy we get from buying clothes is seldom true enjoyment; it's usually a cocktail of emotions and beliefs we have about ourselves and how we're perceived.

During my year of not buying clothes, I had the space to confront my lifelong pursuit of polish head on. So rarely did I try to look polished with what I already had—it was always something I was striving towards with my purchases.

Just like the 'almost' gap, I had developed somewhat of a comfort zone around pursuing a polished look. It was always something I saw as outside of myself, always something I tried to purchase and consume, never something I tried to cultivate. The thrill of thinking I could buy my way to that look kept me consuming, kept me wanting, kept me just dissatisfied enough with what I had to keep playing the slot machine.

I've talked a lot about how unhelpful it can be to chase this external sense of polish. How the glossy polish we see in commercial and editorial imagery, and even on curated social media feeds, does nothing but make us feel less than, and teaches us to view our human quirks as flaws (baby hairs, sweat, creases, movement).

I can't argue that any and all pursuits of polished are bad or toxic. Wanting to look polished or put together doesn't have to mean being someone you're not or aspiring to an unattainable ideal, and to be honest, most of us can't afford to withdraw from polish altogether due to the role our external presentation plays in determining our economic value.

A study by Wong and Penner (2016) not only confirmed that attractiveness is a predictor of salary, but identified that grooming (hair, make-up, clothes, etc) played a greater role in women's earning power than men's. Likewise, the well-documented cognitive bias known as the 'halo effect' explains that we are more likely to perceive something or someone favourably if our initial perception of them is positive. In this context, if you dress well and/or are perceived to be attractive, employers may be more likely to assume you have other positive traits too. It's clear that shunning the idea of looking polished altogether is simply not an option.

Curious about what the concept of looking polished meant to others, I asked my Instagram community what it meant to them to look polished. Here are some of the most common words/phrases that came up:

∞ Well tailored
∞ Put together
∞ Classy
∞ Formal
∞ Organised
∞ Neat
∞ Smooth
∞ Good hair
∞ Deliberate
∞ Elegant
∞ Conservative
∞ Nails, hair, make-up
∞ Simple
∞ Understated
∞ High quality
∞ Without imperfections
∞ Intention
∞ Well-fitted
∞ Cohesive
∞ Clean, pressed and neat
∞ Ironed
∞ Well-coordinated
∞ Smooth hair
∞ Well thought-out

Call me Carrie Bradshaw, but I couldn't help but wonder … If tailoring and proper fit is such a big part of looking polished, is that why it feels much more accessible to slim women than plus-size women, women with disabilities or those with physical differences? It's often much easier to find well-fitting clothes at a smaller size, with more options available. I asked people to send a photo of an image they thought represented polish, and there were some alarming similarities. Unsurprisingly to me, all but one of the images were of slim women. Many were also wearing beige/black/white/neutral outfits, which really demonstrates the level of conformity embedded within this polished ideal.

A select number of people, however, sent a photo of themselves that they felt looked polished—and this was where the real gold was. What I saw was real women wearing outfits that made them stand up tall, look confident and powerful, with small nods to the consideration they'd put into their outfits: a tuck of a hemline, a considered length of trouser, a necklace, a brooch, a bag. Some added context that they'd gotten a blazer tailored or a waistband taken in, and that better fit was what made them feel slick. What I saw wasn't perfection, but intention and personalisation. That's where we can reclaim the allure of looking polished, let go of the 'plastic' polish we see splattered across Pinterest and make it our own.

Whipped cream: An alternative to chasing polish

If you too have felt the pull of wanting to look polished, I present to you an alternative. I call it *whipped cream.*

Whipped cream involves taking two, five or ten extra minutes getting ready in the morning, and viewing your outfit or your presentation from the perspective of 'how can I add a little something on top?' It holds space for the very real biases that we're competing with every day, while bringing in intention and personalisation.

Your something on top might be running a hot brush through your hair. Putting a belt on. Changing your shoes to match the colour of your top. Dusting off that nice bag you don't use enough. Steaming your shirt so it's ultra crispy. Clipping on a brooch or a hair clip. Wearing that necklace you usually save for special occasions. Popping on some highlighter and a lip stain.

Whipped cream is also about noticing the minutiae of your clothes, and perhaps ways they can be better suited to you. Sometimes we don't need new clothes, we just need the ones we have to fit us better. Tuning into the finer details of your outfits can help you notice where something could be a better fit. A nip in the waist, a shortening of the hem, a tweak to the shoulders—a quick trip to an alterations shop can make all the difference to your clothes, and most importantly, make them more *you*.

The difference in this whipped cream approach is that it internalises the polish. It doesn't leave it outside of you to be purchased. It doesn't tempt you with fancy merchandising or a glossy editorial. It's a sense of polish that you experience in yourself, and that can be cultivated on the real you, not the fantasy you.

I found that by adding a bit of whipped cream to my outfits, and by bringing a look together without having to look outside of myself, I gradually changed the way I saw myself. It's such a subtle shift, but it's a quiet move away from being someone you're not, which, if you relate to buying for the person you want to be, is an incredibly important step.

 Intention unboxing: I want to buy because ... I want to look polished

That allure of looking polished or put together has long hung over my head, and it's a commonly shared experience. When we want to buy that feeling, we're often wanting to upgrade ourselves, our lives and our identities, and consuming is the easiest way to achieve that.

Often our idea of what it means to look polished or put together is some sort of cosplay of a life we think we want, or a life we've been conditioned to admire. Looking polished shares a lot of characteristics with looking successful, looking wealthy, looking clean, looking unflappable, looking like we're got it all and we're holding it all together with no signs of cracking. And when you think about it, that's exactly what we've been told we should be as women. We're supposed to be able to do everything and look after everyone—and we're supposed to be able to do it while looking like we've stepped out of a magazine shoot.

When we crave that feeling of looking polished, so often we're trying to live up to a standard and step into a life we, for some reason, value over our own. Dressing a certain way offers up a shortcut to feeling like we're improving or upgrading our lives and our identities, when actually nothing has fundamentally changed. Don't get me wrong, there's some truth to the idea that dressing a certain way can support personal growth and evolution of the self, but when we're regularly striving for this glossy aesthetic, there's probably something we're ignoring under the surface. Are we dressing as though we have it all figured out to hide the fact that we feel like we don't? Perhaps.

Whether we're buying clothes to look polished to mask an insecurity or simply because we're victims of an editorialised existence, there's still one gaping problem: often, we don't actually achieve the feeling of polish that we're striving for. That's where the cycle becomes so deeply problematic, for our self-esteem *and* our bank balance.

If wearing something a little bit fancy makes you feel polished and put together, hey, who am I to argue? Is there really anything wrong with dressing a bit nice and putting a message out to the world that you're nailing your life and your outfit? Probably not.

(continued)

After all, expressing the best of yourself is kinda what fashion is all about, right?

The problem comes when the thing we're trying to buy can't be bought. See, I warned you this wasn't a fashion book. Striving to look polished is fine ... if you actually feel like you're achieving it. When we're not, we're simply piling more shame on top of our already fractured view of ourselves. If we platform this idea of looking polished, and continually fall short of that ideal for whatever reason, we're doing nothing but wasting money and widening the gap between who we are and who we wish we were.

Task: Pinning down the polish

We've talked a lot about polish in this chapter, and I want you to think about what polish means to you. Conjure up an image in your head of what polished looks like in your opinion.

Now ask yourself this: was that an image of you or of someone else? If it's someone else—bingo! Here lies the problem.

I want you to spend some time auditing that unhelpful idea of *polish* you have in your head so that we can begin to step back from that unattainable ideal. Believe it or not, we can actually create a bit of a comfort zone around pursuing these ideals. Working with who we really are means adopting radical self-acceptance—and sometimes that's harder than striving to be what we're told we should be.

With the image of polish in your mind, write down the characteristics of that image. Note down anything you associate with your idea of polish, whether it's an item of clothing or a type of shoe, or an air of confidence or power.

Then for each item on the list, I want you to strike through the ones that make you feel shitty. Yep, plain and simple. If it makes you feel like you'll simply never be glossy enough to fulfil it, we're striking it through. For anything that you'd actually like to embrace more of in your style, circle it.

For example, let's say your idea of polish always involves heels, but you're simply not a heels kinda gal. Strike that baby through. We're leaving that standard behind, we don't need it anymore. But maybe wearing simple jewellery is something you associate with polish and is something you'd actually like to incorporate for yourself. Circle that, and consider adding it to your whipped cream routine we talked about on page 53.

When we separate the aspects of polish that work with us from those that work against us, we begin to base our self-image around who we are, not who we're not.

Here's the real kicker: we have to be our own polish. By that, I mean our pursuit of looking polished has to be based on who we are and what we already look like.

Sitting here now, over a year on from completing the 12-month challenge, the image in my head of polish is of me at my best. Me with my hair done and in clothes that fit me well. It's an achievable sense of expression, and it's a way of expressing who I am, rather than who I'm not.

Chapter summary

∞ Exposure therapy trips to meet your desire to buy clothes while saying 'no' is a powerful way to confront your buying behaviour head on. Over time, you neutralise the heightened emotions you associate with buying and build more resilience to temptation.

∞ You might be stuck in a trap of trying to look polished, but the clean, clinical nature of 'polish' is erasing everything that makes you human.

∞ Trying to look like the pictures you see online or on social media is keeping you stuck.

∞ Whipped cream presents a more you-shaped version of polish, that feels less like a chore and more like an extra sweet 'topping' to your look.

∞ Internalising your own version of polish, rather than externalising it by chasing impossible ideals, is key to detoxifying your view of what polished means.

∞ Establishing which parts of polish are achievable to you, and which just make you feel bad about yourself, can help you make this distinction.

APRIL

The resistance

It wasn't so much about what I didn't have, but about what I couldn't have. I'd never really realised how much value I placed on having the option to buy.

By April, I was deep into the challenge and, for the most part, loving it. That's not to say I didn't find myself thinking 'what the fuck have I got myself into' when confronted with an absolutely perfect camel blazer in my size in the sale rack for under $50. Realising I had eight months left to go was confronting, and April brought a change of season that rattled me more than I care to admit.

The perils of a change of season

April brought my first wave of resistance to the Project. The first three months had, in many ways, felt so easy. So light. The mental peace of not having to decide whether to buy, the endless treasure trove of free dopamine I was finding by wearing the forgotten 80 per cent of my wardrobe ... the learnings just kept on coming, kept on teaching me things and kept me engaged.

But by April, I hit a bit of a wall. The weather was starting to change, and I realised how much of a spanner this can throw into our sartorial choices, and by extension, how much of a trigger it can be to want to go and buy more stuff.

The first challenge that a change of season presents is unfamiliarity. When you've been dressing a certain way for several weeks or months, your brain is wired to dress for that climate. Suddenly, the idea of not sliding into a pair of sandals or throwing on your go-to summer dress on days when it's hot as balls feels completely alien to you. You know your thighs are going to humble you with their ability to start fire by rubbing together, and you find yourself questioning, *'What even goes with jeans?'* Where are my jumpers? I wonder if there'll be any money in the pocket of my coat that's been hiding at the back of the hallway cupboard for the last few months.

I hadn't expected the change of weather to present such a challenge, to be honest. But the unfamiliar territory of needing to dress for cooler weather left me looking outside of my wardrobe for guidance — and that sent me tumbling straight towards temptation.

Suddenly, the things I was able to see in stores or on social media and keep my distance from lured me in. Instead of proudly scrolling past, uninterested and ensconced in my Project, I felt a sudden pull. The excuse of 'maybe I need something' started to creep in. And my wardrobe, that had felt so abundant, so limitless, so full of possibilities, suddenly felt barren. I didn't know what to reach for. The outfits I'd been giddily photographing and adding to my album suddenly weren't so easy to refer back to anymore, and I found myself lusting after the wintry tones of chocolate brown and maroon, the wealthy-looking winter creams, and the supple leather on the rows of ankle boots that looked so much more appealing than the pair waiting to be dusted off at the back of my wardrobe.

I came to realise that a change of season is when we're most vulnerable to trends. Now, I'll be honest, I don't consider myself particularly bound by trends. I'm past the age of caring what's 'in fashion', which is one of the best parts of being in your 30s, I have to say. I think I thought that insulated me from trend-led temptation altogether. But it was the change of season that opened my eyes to the role of trends in our buying habits. While trends are ever-present, they thrive when we're looking outside of ourselves for signals on what to wear—and a change of season presents a perfect opportunity for our decisions to be hijacked.

Interestingly, I found that my lack of confidence around dressing for the changing weather meant I placed higher value on what I saw in stores. While I didn't seek out what was on trend, I still found myself responding to the things I was seeing. You can't really help but take notice of what coats are cropping up over and over again, or what colours seem to be adorning the windows of every store you pass on your way to the post office. In that time of confusion and dwindling familiarity with my wardrobe, the racks offered easy options, ready-made solutions to my 'What the hell do I wear when it's freezing in the morning and warm-ish by lunchtime?' dilemmas. New clothes represented simple answers to questions I frankly didn't have time to answer, and it was so tempting to just grab a few warm things to make the transition to cooler weather easier, or let a new trench coat do all the work for me. I suddenly became more aware of how much of my clothing purchases were driven by a craving for ease or simplicity, or by overwhelm with the task of getting dressed.

The curious case of trends

The thing with trends is that they're dictated to us by the fashion industry. If you've seen *The Devil Wears Prada*, you'll remember the iconic scene where Miranda Priestly tears Andy Sachs a new one by explaining how the specific shade of blue she was wearing trickled down from Oscar de la Renta's runway and into the bargain bin of a department store. Now most of us 'normal people' aren't watching what big fashion designers drop on their runways, but it's true that styles, colours, themes, homages and concepts trickle down from their collections to the stores we shop in.

It doesn't matter that you're a 30-something millennial scarred by the return of low-rise jeans and mesh tops—we're still told what's cool and what's hot. We might have the wherewithal to say 'no thank you' to diamanté-encrusted denim due to its MSN-messenger-adjacent legacy, but we're still fodder in the hands of the fashion industry when it comes to what colours are in season or the trouser style of the moment. During the autumn of my Wardrobe Project, expensive-looking camels, rich reds and winter creams lined the stores of my local shopping centre and tumbled out of influencers' parcels. Those were enough to leave me feeling like my existing winter wardrobe was somehow worse than these shiny new ranges in stores.

Since I was paying more attention to my urges to purchase than ever before, I was able to notice how I interacted with these trends. What struck me was just how quickly my opinion could be changed. Just how quickly the repeated exposure to certain styles or colours could reverse my initial dislike, and leave me wanting more.

The perfect example of this was the return of ballet flats. They'd been creeping back into style for a few years at this point, but during my Project, I recognised just how much my opinion was starting to shift. At first I was repulsed, vowing never to slip my gargantuan and annoyingly wide trotters into a pair ever again. But as I saw them more and more, I started to hate them less and less. And soon, that familiarity turned into something akin to a want. I didn't give in, because I wasn't about to give up my progress for a trauma-evoking ballet flat. But, the change in my perception was eye-opening.

This shift in perception is why we must be careful of trends. Whether you feel you're guided by trends or whether you prefer to shun them like I did, we're all still just consumers in a well-oiled machine. Our tastes are dictated to us, and the repeated exposure of something is enough to change the way we see it. Over time, as we see a colour or a style on more people of influence, as we see it expressed in more polished and aspirational ways, as we see it creep into the mainstream, we slowly close the gap between us and that trend, and it becomes more and more likely that we'll buy into it.

That's not to say we shouldn't buy into trends. Some trends, particularly colour-based ones, can be fun to play with, and when a colour you absolutely adore shows up in every store, it's not wrong to want to take advantage.

But my number-one rule with engaging with trends as a mindful consumer is this: if you say 'yes' to trends, you have to say 'no' to trends. By that I mean, it's fine to say 'yes' to certain trends, but you have to say 'no' to others in order to maintain your agency over your consumption decisions. When we say 'yes' to any and all trends, or we identify as being 'on trend' above all else, we risk having our decision-making processes hijacked and profited from.

I know that might sound harsh, especially if you personally do enjoy trends and you consider yourself into fashion as an art form rather than just a consumption activity, but I see trends as one of those things that capitalism has kind of ruined. We simply can't have trends for what they are without acknowledging the surrounding context, without acknowledging that the trend cycle has sped up dramatically in recent decades and without acknowledging that the faster trends move, the more money there is to be made, and the more waste we're complicit in creating.

We have to, at some point, draw the line and practise saying 'no' to the trends dictated to us, whether that's more obvious expressions like a shape or a style, or something more subtle, like a specific colour or shade, particularly when that requires us to buy more stuff. Trends manipulate our minds into putting newer clothes on a pedestal above our existing wardrobe, and that's when it can really cause an issue.

It's okay to just look ... okay

Moving through this point in the Project with a wardrobe that I felt wasn't quite equipped to handle the move to cooler weather really challenged the way I'd been thinking up until now. Until this point, I was finding so much enjoyment in mixing and matching my outfits, finding new life in things I hadn't worn before, and being quite pleased with how I looked, despite not buying anything new or relying on that hit of dopamine to make me feel good.

But with the change of season, I felt stuck in my attempts to like my outfit or put something together that delivered dopamine comparable to that of an online order. To be honest, this surprised me. I've always been a cold-weather gal. Must be my English blood. I'd so much rather be too cold than too hot, and, frankly, winter provides relief from the oppressive Australian heat and the sweat that comes with it. While everyone else groans at the clocks going back and the evenings getting darker, I'm the one giddy at the thought of being able to go for a walk without sweating, excited to feel the cuffed sleeve of my sweatshirt against my skin.

While the colder weather should have been easier for me, it wasn't. And I think that came down to two things. Firstly, I'd only known the Project in the context of the warmer weather, so my habits and instincts were based on sleeveless tops and minimal layering. Secondly, my winter wardrobe was much leaner. I genuinely had less on hand to dress with, which meant my reliance on novelty from new combinations was also challenged. I think this came down to the fact that the couple of years prior to the Project had been largely spent in lockdowns. Melbourne experienced some of the longest lockdowns in the world, and my weight had fluctuated up, down and sideways during those lockdowns. As a result, the cooler weather wardrobe I was left with was, in many ways, unsuitable and uninspiring.

What this phase of the challenge really forced me to accept was that we simply cannot look the way we want to look at all times. That might sound obvious, and I'm not by any means suggesting I'm able to love my outfit at all times (in fact, far from it), but there was a distinct discomfort when I didn't have the clothes I wanted and I couldn't just go and buy some. It wasn't so much about what I didn't have, but about what I *couldn't* have. I'd never really realised how much value I placed on having the option to buy, almost like it was a crutch I didn't know I needed. Staring down the barrel of an entire winter without being able to buy new clothes felt, for the first time, really quite difficult.

This was the first time I felt tempted to break the rules. I flirted with the idea of allowing myself just one coat. Or a couple of jumpers or a jacket.

A lot of people said I was being too harsh on myself. Too restrictive. They said I could surely get a couple of things to get me through to the end of the year and still benefit from the challenge. To be honest, they were right. I could absolutely still have learned almost all of the things I learned during the year if I'd gone and bought a couple of considered items. I even said at the outset that I wasn't trying to get a clean sheet above all else. I was trying to learn and observe. But it was something about the discomfort I felt during this seasonal shift that I didn't want to give into. I wanted to ride it out and make it work. I wanted to sit in the discomfort of not being able to consume. Not being able to buy that feeling away.

And I'm so glad I did, because that made way for the next phase of learnings that were waiting for me on this journey.

Task: Wardrobe Workout Method

When we feel a sense of lack in our wardrobe, it's easy to look outwards for things that will alleviate that feeling and get us closer to the feeling we want to experience with our clothes. By doing this challenge, I took that option away from myself and had to build that sense of range and possibility with what I had, which is what led me to create The Wardrobe Workout Method, and I want you to give it a try.

Step 1: Choose an item in your wardrobe that you want to get more wear out of.

Step 2: Describe the item and type that into Pinterest, followed by the word 'outfit'.

(continued)

Step 3: Browse the images that come up from that search result, and refine further if you want to be more specific. You can add more keywords like 'summer' or 'plus size' or 'holiday' to refine the results.

Step 4: Gather inspiration. The key here is not to try to replicate the images you're looking at exactly, because this can trigger the idea that you need to buy more clothes. It could also set off your fantasy self radar if any part of you wishes you could embody the style of the images you're looking at. What we want to gather here is ideas. Look at how outfits have been created. What colours, shapes, textures and combinations have been used? What layers or visual intrigue have they got?

Step 5: Set a timer for 30 minutes and try that item on with other pieces from your wardrobe, using the inspiration you've gathered to help you. Try on as many things as you can, even if you don't think they'll work together. We want to get creative here and try different things that you might not otherwise have considered.

Step 6: When you land on an outfit combination you like, take a photo of it and add it to an album or app on your phone to refer back to later.

Doing periodic Wardrobe Workouts, especially around a change of season, can help you build a feeling of possibility with what you have. It's not uncommon for us to visit a store and try on multiple items of clothing at once—all we're doing here is bringing that creativity into our own wardrobes for free!

Intention unboxing: I want to buy because ...
I have nothing to wear

Feeling like we have nothing to wear is one of the strongest examples of our wacky relationship with clothes, because usually when we say this, we're standing in close proximity to a wardrobe *full* of clothes. Rarely do we mean we have nothing to wear. We mean we have nothing we *want* to wear.

We misattribute the feeling we're experiencing to simply not having something, which is why it makes so much sense that when we think we have nothing to wear, we go and buy something new. Not having something can be solved by having something, right?

But what this does is create a cycle that's hard to break. If we solve the feeling of not having anything to wear by adding something that satisfies the need we have at that point in time, we're building out a collection of clothes that will forever be inadequate. Here's why.

When we buy with this intention, we get used to responding to that feeling by buying. We give credence to that feeling of not having something to wear, and enforce its truth by finding something to wear and buying it.

What kind of wardrobe are we building if this is the way we're buying? When we buy this way, we're not building out a wardrobe that works for who we are and how we live our lives. We're building out a wardrobe made up of individual pieces or outfits that make sense on that one given day that we buy it.

Sure, we might attempt to buy things that we can wear again, or buy something that'll go with other things, but those are secondary drivers of our decision-making. Our primary goal is to relieve that feeling of having nothing to wear.

(continued)

In a society where our clothes serve far more purposes than just warmth and utility, we know that we probably do have something to wear. Our job is to understand what the underlying feeling really is.

Having nothing to wear can mean I have nothing that:

- I feel good in
- doesn't make me feel too [insert insecurity here]
- is clean or ironed
- will make me fit in at the place I'm going
- makes me look slim enough
- hides me enough
- is on trend
- makes me excited
- makes me feel like I look good
- makes me feel good enough
- hides my belly
- makes me look young.

Next time you feel like you have nothing to wear, I want you to really interrogate the feeling underneath, and address that before you go and buy something based on the idea that that'll solve your feeling of lack.

Is the lack coming from your wardrobe or from yourself?

Task: The Wardrobe Calculation

Feeling like we have nothing to wear despite staring at a wardrobe full of clothes is one of the greatest style fallacies around. We can combat this by creating a perception of possibility with what we have and changing the way we perceive style. Instead of seeing style as something we should be able to pull off a hanger and achieve in seconds, we should see it as something we *create*. To be able to create it, we need to believe we have the resources to experiment.

In The Wardrobe Project program, I ask participants to calculate the number of theoretically possible outfit combinations in their wardrobes to remind them that they actually do have the means to experiment with their style without buying anything new. It looks like this.

The Wardrobe Calculation: (tops x bottoms) + dresses + jumpsuits = total number of outfit combinations.

For example, if you have 20 tops, 10 bottoms, 3 dresses and 1 jumpsuit, this equates to (20 x 10) + 3 + 1 = 204 theoretical outfit combinations.

Obviously, this doesn't take into account colour and print clashes, but it's more of a conceptual exercise to ground your mind in the potential that lies within your wardrobe.

The clutter factor

While we're talking about having 'nothing to wear', I'm reminded of a realisation had by many participants of my Wardrobe Project program about the role of clutter in our wardrobe woes.

Here it comes: sometimes you don't need to buy a new outfit, you need to do a load of laundry.

Ouch.

I know, it stings. I'm right there with you. I'm not the tidiest person in the world (never have been) and I can be honest and tell you that, at any given time, a good chunk of the clothes I wear are either stored in the dirty washing basket, hanging on a clothes rack somewhere or waiting to be put away post-wash.

So it's no wonder that when life gets hectic and I'm three weeks behind on laundry and wearing the undies I only reach for when all my comfy ones are nowhere to be found that I feel like I have nothing to wear.

Now, I'm not going to tell you to overhaul your life with some hectic laundry organisation schedule. Life is busy, and if you have kids, it's even busier. Laundry pile-ups are a fact of life. But be very wary of any cravings to buy clothes that happen when you feel overwhelmed and consumed by your household mental load.

Not only does buying something new solve the immediate need for something to wear, the act of spending and consuming gives you a hit of dopamine to feel temporarily in control of your overwhelm. The problem is, neither feeling lasts for long.

Honestly, sometimes it's just easier to take a big deep breath, keep your money in your bank account, shut the laptop and put a wash on.

Chapter summary

- ∞ A change of season can leave you vulnerable to temptation.
- ∞ Trends tell us what to like, what's cool and, therefore, what to buy.
- ∞ We often want to buy clothes simply because it's easier; it's a shortcut to that feeling of having something to wear.
- ∞ If you say 'yes' to some trends, you have to say 'no' to others to maintain your sense of agency over your decisions.
- ∞ *Feeling* like you have nothing to wear doesn't mean you *actually* have nothing to wear.
- ∞ Sometimes, the best thing you can do to quell your cravings to buy clothes is to put a wash on.

MAY

The classroom of my mistakes

If you learned to like ballet flats again, you can learn to like yourself.

By May, I'd started to settle into the cooler weather and pushed through some of the resistance I was feeling from the change in season. Getting over that hump really didn't take much more than determination, and that's the annoyingly unsexy truth about changing behavioural patterns. At times, you're having epiphanies left, right and centre, and the changes you want to see are just happening without too much effort. Other times, you're ready to throw the towel in altogether, and nothing but sheer grit will get you through. For once, my stubbornness was doing me a favour instead of getting me into trouble at work.

Luckily, I loved the challenge more than I loved the idea of new clothes, and I was starting to build my confidence in my ability to stay the course. A lot of this came down to doing more exposure therapy trips, and upping the ante a little bit by trying on some of the items I saw and liked. I know, I was playing with fire. But I wanted to meet that desire to buy in even more intimate detail, so by trying on the clothes, I could get even closer to the beliefs that would flood my mind as soon as I tried something on.

You might be reading this thinking, 'Has she completely lost it? Surely trying on pretty things is going to make it so much harder?'

Look, you're not alone in questioning whether I've gone completely off the rails. When I say I try things on during my no-buys, I'm regularly met with open-mouthed stares (or emojis on social media!).

I did think that trying on clothes would mean I'd start trying to justify why I should break the challenge, why one small treat wouldn't hurt. But, surprisingly, the complete opposite happened.

Trying on clothes I liked during the Project kind of felt like when you see a nightclub in the daytime. You know, when you have to go back and get your jacket that you left in the cloakroom because you tumbled out at closing time, 11 Jagerbombs deep and more concerned with finding the nearest chip shop than your jacket.

All the stories I'd usually tell myself about why I should get something or why the clothes were so different just weren't there anymore. It's almost as though the cold harsh light of the Project, and, therefore, the absence of the possibility of buying them, made it easier to come up with reasons *not* to buy. When the answer was a guaranteed 'no', my mind was more able to see that buying wasn't the best outcome available to me.

It got me thinking about how often we're unknowingly in a default 'yes' state. We might not think we are, but we're so easily swayed that maybe we actually spend most of our time existing a lot closer to the 'yes' than we realise. The mental peace I mentioned on page 25 suggests that we probably are. Are we so often unknowingly open to consumption that it feels noticeably lighter once we switch that off? And, once switched, are we insulated from many of the tactics used by retailers to get us to buy, and even the emotions that drive so many of our purchase decisions?

In many areas of our lives, there's often a gap between our attitude to something and the way we actually behave. We might think we're discerning with what we buy, what we add to our wardrobe and how much we think through our purchases before tapping our card. We might think we only buy what we need or that we don't buy on impulse—but we know intention doesn't necessarily translate to action. In fact, intention alone is rarely enough to completely influence behaviour.

It's a bit like when we hear stats around how many items of clothing the average person consumes, particularly here in Australia, where we are the worst consumers of textiles per capita. According to The Australia Institute, Australians purchase a whopping 56 items of clothing per year. The US came in at 53 items per year, while the UK fared slightly better at 33 items per year (clearly didn't measure this data when I was at uni, wow) and China came in at 30 items per year.

Most people gawk at the number relevant to their country, grimacing at how obnoxiously unnecessary it is to add upward of 30 items of clothing to your wardrobe per year. And yet, it's pretty easy to rack up a bigger number than you think. Most people aren't tracking the number of items that enter their wardrobe each year — unless they're doing some kind of controlled challenge like me, or they're on a particularly conscious sustainability or consumption journey. When women in my Wardrobe Project program went back and counted the number of items they'd purchased each year, they were astounded at just how far they'd underestimated that number. Even though we don't actually have any idea how many items we bought last year, we're always absolutely 100 per cent certain that that big scary shame-y number couldn't apply to us.

Unfortunately, the gap between our intended behaviour and our actual behaviour suggests we're probably closer to it than we think. I decided to reflect on what causes us to keep on buying, despite having already bought such a vast amount of clothing. In theory, if we've bought upward of 30 items the year prior, why would we need to buy 30 more? The answer was staring me in the face: we're buying the wrong stuff.

Buying mistakes I'd been stuck in

Unravelling that idea of what can happen when we're in a 'yes' state, a state of openness to consumption even though our intentions might suggest otherwise, got me curious about some of the unhelpful buying cycles I'd been stuck in. May was a month of discovery as I really leaned into understanding how I ended up with the wardrobe

I currently had, and what I could learn from the mistakes I made over and over again. I realised that if I could establish the mistakes I was making and the ways I was buying the wrong things, I'd stop feeling compelled to buy more and more over time.

Earlier on page 18, we talked about the story categories in our wardrobes — remember *the ghosts, the duplicates, the fantasies*? Those backstories can help inform the patterns of buying that we get stuck in. Some are more emotional, like the fantasy self trap that we covered on page 27, but others are more practical, like buying more and more of the same stuff we already have, or settling for things that aren't quite right. Here are some of the patterns I uncovered in my wardrobe, and that I've seen in others' too.

Buying something in every colour

∞ In my wardrobe hung a pair of black trousers that I also had in a stone-ish cream colour. I loved them in black. The cream was just okay. They showed my underwear line, and for some reason, despite being the same exact product, pulled more in the waist than the black.

∞ I also had a pair of black faux-leather trousers that, despite having their own issues, I wore a lot. I also had them in brown, which again, were an inexplicably different fit altogether, so they didn't get worn much.

∞ I had two of the best ever basic T-shirts — the Uniqlo U T-shirts, in case you're wondering. I had one in black and one in white. But I also had a slate blue, a teal green, and a sort of pinky-salmon colour. I rarely wore the coloured ones.

∞ I had a pair of wide-leg black trousers that I adored. I also owned them in a greyish taupe colour that I despised and struggled to style with anything other than a black top.

Do you see the pattern?! Once I liked something in one colour (often black), I'd giddily run out and buy it in another colour, thinking

I was making some kind of ultra-smart decision and capitalising on what I loved.

I'm going to give you a piece of advice now that I hope you'll remember for many years. If you ever utter the words 'I'm going to go and get this in another colour'—*run*. It's a trap. You probably won't like the other colour, and it'll just sit in your wardrobe and collect dust.

Copying or recreating a specific outfit

There are certain things in my wardrobe that I struggled to wear confidently outside of one specific outfit silo. Usually, this is a sure-fire sign that I'd bought it in a very specific context, like copying or replicating an outfit I'd seen someone else wear. What's really interesting, though, is often I'd have lazily thought about other things that the item could go with in theory, but never actually bothered to wear it with anything else.

Seeing someone wear wide-leg trousers with a specific type of shirt and then buying said shirt is all well and good in that one outfit context, but unless we actually integrate the item into other outfits, it'll always just be a one-hit wonder. I found this created friction in my style because it was usually an item that never seemed to go with anything, despite telling myself in my head that I'd considered its versatility (which is often just an excuse to buy things!).

Keeping something that wasn't perfect

Why I ever did this is so beyond me. There are certain items in my wardrobe that haven't ever been right for me. How do I know that? Because I bought them that way. I've made this mistake time and time again—either I'll try something on or order it online, and it won't be quite how I hope or expect it to be, but I'll keep it anyway because I like the idea of it so much. Or I try to convince myself I can somehow make it work, or it'll look different when my hair and make-up are done.

Trying to get yourself to wear things you don't love or aren't quite right is always going to keep you wanting to buy more. While we might get the dopamine hit at the time of buying, the loop doesn't ever really close.

A lot of this comes down to size and fit. As a jiggly size 16 to 18, stuff often doesn't fit me quite the way I hope it will. This was even more true when I was stuck in a toxic relationship with my fantasy self, because I was hoping things would hang off me like I was one of the clackers on my way to the office in *The Devil Wears Prada* (if you know, you know). Even outside of that fantasy self, clothes fitting well comes with a pretty low strike rate when you're plus size, partly because stores don't cater for curves well at all, but also because there's a greater variance in size and shape for us.

Regardless, it didn't stop me convincing myself that I could 'make it work'. If I got myself excited to buy something, or started creating a vision in my head of how something would look or fit, I'd start making excuses when it wasn't perfect. I think, in part, it comes down to having low standards in my wardrobe. Something about being in a body that's largely rejected by the fashion industry means we become accustomed to things not being a good fit, or things not looking the way we think they will because we've only seen them on a slim body. Recognising this pattern really helped me call myself out when something wasn't quite right.

Settling for something that's almost right

Ever go out looking for something specific, like a black jumper or a red cardigan or a pair of white jeans, and despite not being able to find what you want, you're so hungry to start wearing that item that you get something that isn't quite right and tell yourself it'll do? I had a few items that fell into this category.

I recognised this mistake both in my wardrobe during the Project, and in memories of items I'd owned before. Again, it said a lot about my attitude towards clothing and towards myself, as well as my buying patterns. This was proof of the urgency and pace that existed in my buying habits, as though, once I'd got the idea of an outfit or an item in my head, I had to get it even if it wasn't perfect.

Assuming things work together without checking

I mentioned earlier that I would often 'lazily' check that items would go with more than one thing in my wardrobe before buying them, and the most dangerous pieces to play this game with are absolutely, unequivocally neutrals.

I know, right, It makes no sense. Isn't the whole point of neutrals that they're, well, neutral? They go with everything?

Yeah, no. I learned the hard way during my Project that just because you have a wardrobe full of neutrals does not mean you have a wardrobe full of outfits. Who knew that not all blacks are the same. Not all whites are the same. And don't even get me started on creams, stones and beiges.

Several times I went to put outfits together only to find that the top I'd bought in beige actually wasn't the right beige for the rest of my wardrobe. Or tried to get creative with an item using my Wardrobe Workout Method, only to find that the basics formulas I found on Pinterest didn't translate to my wardrobe because the cream blazer that I'd hoped would go with the cream top actually didn't because the top was a cooler cream and the blazer was a warmer cream.

Buying things for one specific occasion

Having an event or occasion to attend is one of the most common reasons why we buy clothes. When we want to look nice, we invoke the shortcut of buying something we're excited to wear. The problem with this is we're then left with pieces we bought for that one specific context, in a similar way to when we buy to replicate a specific outfit. That item is then siloed in our minds, and we're less likely to want to reach for it for the next event. Plus, we've built up that behavioural loop of an event or occasion being a trigger to buy.

I recognised this in several items in my wardrobe, and saw my fantasy self in many of these pieces, too. Looking at them, I'd feel completely uninspired and wonder why I'd bought them in the first place. When I'd look back, I could so clearly see that they were a product of rushed decision-making when I need to find something that would work at short notice. I'd often settle for things that weren't right just to satisfy the need to have something to wear.

The outcome? A wardrobe that doesn't work

The impact of these consumption habits creates an environment where we're cornered from every angle. We have a collection of clothes that don't work together, don't make us feel good and don't allow us to express ourselves the way we want to, which leaves us looking externally for what we're not getting. The problem is, when we look externally, we buy more and more of the same.

I once interviewed Lauren Di Bartolo, founder of The Australian Style Institute, who told me about the reticular activating system and the role it plays in our style and shopping choices. Here's what she said:

Our brain is really at the centre of how we create our style, and we buy more of what's already familiar to us. Essentially, to not get overwhelmed—our brain is very good at cutting out overwhelm or anything that's unfamiliar to us. So we find more of what we already know. And, unfortunately, if we're not in a really great relationship with our body, often we're shopping for what we don't want or we want to conceal.

So what happens is you add together the looking for more or only being able to observe more of what you already have, and then you add on to that where your focus is actually going, which might be concealing your tummy or minimising your bust, and we're buying things that just don't suit us, or multiples [of things we already have].

Basically, as humans, we're just not great at buying well unless we really learn to. We know just how strong the emotional component of clothes shopping is. The chemical activity in our brains fires off our pleasure centres when we're shopping, giving credence to the term 'retail therapy'. Because of our fractured relationship with ourselves and our appearance, our lack of understanding of what we really look like, our conditioned habit of buying away our discomfort, and that craving for familiarity when we're overwhelmed, we're repeating the same patterns and amassing more and more stuff that isn't quite right.

The Project gave me the space to understand this properly for the first time in my life. No wonder I'd amassed a wardrobe full of clothes and still felt like I had nothing to wear when so many of my buying decisions stemmed from these unhelpful places.

Interestingly, while some items highlighted to me that I'd bought too impulsively, other items demonstrated that I actually just needed to ... well ... get over myself. There were things I thought I disliked going into the year, but in reality, the novelty of buying them had just worn off. Actually *wearing* my clothes properly for the first time, surprisingly, made me realise there were things I really did like — I'd just associated all of my positive feelings towards an item with the *buying* rather than the *owning*.

Looking at those things I found in my wardrobe that I did actually like more than I thought, I came to realise that they were strokes of luck rather than an actual understanding of myself, my body and my style. Being forced to work with what I had allowed me to understand not only why certain things *didn't* feel good but also why certain things *did*. For every style mistake I uncovered, I learned something from pieces I did like. Together, these lessons started to form a much clearer understanding of what my style really was.

Real people

To benefit from the learnings hiding beneath our mistakes, we first have to admit to them — and yes, that can be confronting. Sometimes it means articulating a behavioural pattern you haven't ever consciously addressed in the cold, harsh light of day. To make you feel less alone in your explorations of your mistakes, let's hear once again from our friends of the Project about the mistakes they uncovered in their wardrobes.

Rebecca

'Buying things because I like the look of an item thinking I could make it work.'

Mistakes I kept making were not taking into consideration my changing shape as I have grown older and my lifestyle has changed, still thinking I can pull off the things I could wear in my 20s when I was extremely fit and active and a UK size 8 to 10. I'm at least two sizes bigger now. But also, buying things because I like the look of an item thinking I could make it work … but then having nothing to go with it. Buying things off eBay thinking 'I'm sure that will fit', and then having it arrive only to go straight in the charity pile because it's straining across my chest or back and there were no returns.

Olga

'I'd rather buy now and make it work somehow.'

In the past, my biggest mistake was: 'Whoa, it's the final sale. The brand is so cool. I can't get a better price, and this will be sold out soon, so I'd rather buy now and make it work somehow.' Of course, it was a mistake. This is how I ended up with two pairs of jeans that are uncomfortably tight, three or so pairs of shoes that are painful to walk in, and at least one clothing item that I barely wear because it's white and dry clean only. No, I definitely should have thought about whether I could make it work before considering a purchase! I should probably have put the items I wanted in my wishlist earlier, so that I knew what I actually needed, and not impulsively wanted.

Amy

'When I get back to my old body … '

My biggest mistakes were keeping things that either do not fit or I don't like on me for 'when I get back to my old body'. Buying tons of clothes before a holiday that I wear once and then, by the following year, no longer like or fit. Keeping something because it's fine, rather than because I love it.

Lizzie

'If I lose three more kilos…'

I realised I was making mistakes like buying a new dress for *every* event: engagements, weddings, milestone birthdays etc. Buying clothing that requires too much maintenance (e.g., dryclean only, some knits, ironing). Buying inspirational clothing (e.g., clothing that will look *amazing* if I lose three more kilos), and clothing inspired by other women who look nothing like me.

Jo

'My biggest mistake was investing my self-worth into how I looked on the outside'

My most obvious 'mistake' was buying indiscriminately. I'd justify it by checking the refund policies, but shipping wasn't refundable. I was often paying NZD$30–50 just to try something on. This was amplified by some brands' fortnightly 'drop' cycles and the scarcity mindset that came with them. I *had* to buy it right now, or it would be gone.

I also fell into the trap of buying what looked good on others, hoping I'd look like that too. Discovering Instagram and all the influencers intensified this. Even people with my same shape and size body weren't a guarantee that something would suit me. But, really, my biggest mistake was investing my self-worth into how I looked on the outside, instead of healing what was going on inside.

Excuses we make to buy things

If you've ever cringed at yourself for the wild and wacky excuses you've made to buy clothes you don't need, get ready to feel validated. I asked my social media followers to share the most common excuses they've made to buy clothes, and there are some absolute gems. From the old classics like 'it's on sale' to creative curveballs like 'I didn't buy a train ticket to get laid so I bought clothes instead', you'll feel less alone after reading these.

Excuses we make to buy clothes we don't need

I've returned something so it's free money.

I was a big brave girl because I did something I didn't want to do (I'm 37).

If I don't buy coffee for a month it's basically free (but you still buy the coffee).

I don't think I bought myself a birthday gift this year (five months after my birthday!).

It fits so I have to get it (and three other colours).

It's on sale so I'm basically saving money.

Surely I couldn't not purchase the very essence of my being!?

I'm healing my inner child.

My horoscope said to do it (reality: my horoscope said something general and vague).

What if this is the actual thing that's been missing from my life?

Excuses we make to buy clothes we don't need

I didn't spend much the month before (so I can spend now).

After this I will feel complete and I won't buy anymore — promise!

I didn't eat chocolate while watching TV tonight so I deserve to buy a cute dress.

I got that refund back for that other thing in 1997 so I'll just use the money I saved then.

The planet is on fire, fascism is back and nothing matters.

I can resell it (and then hating my life trying to resell it).

I've paid for boring stuff so I need something fun.

I'm quite sure my 17 other pairs of black pants look nothing like these.

I ate at home this week so I deserve it.

I've got a new job so I need new clothes (it was work from home).

It doesn't count if it's from the op shop [thrift store] — I'm being charitable.

I've got a holiday coming up and there's no way I can wear the bathers I already own.

Snort-laugh worthy, these may be, but they're also proof that our relationship with clothing goes deeper than fabric and thread.

Lessons from items I've loved

Those items I discovered an unexpected love for had just as much to teach me as the items I didn't love so much. It's not just our mistakes that we can learn from — it's our successes, too. When we get curious about what's wrong and what's right in our clothes, we can gradually learn how to embed more of the good stuff, and less of the bad, in our buying habits.

- ∞ I have a shirt from Primark that I picked up completely randomly while in the UK because I needed something smart to wear. It must be six or seven years old, but I still love it and I still wear it. I didn't understand why until the Project. Turns out it has a very subtle drop sleeve that creates a shape I really like.

- ∞ I have a blue knitted skirt-and-top set that made me realise that compact knitted fabrics are great for my curvy body as they fit well and can withstand weight fluctuations — more on that later.

- ∞ A pair of black wide-leg trousers ended up being the signal to me that heavier fabrics are so much better for me than the wispy, light, delicate silks that I tried to wear for years, and always felt like they didn't look as good on me as other people.

- ∞ A cream knitted midi-dress that I actually wore to my wedding: I always loved it and I wasn't sure why until I styled it with other things in my wardrobe, and I could suddenly see that the knitted fabric and the longer-line midi length accentuated my shape so much better.

- ∞ A zebra-print shirt that I impulse purchased during a sale once became one of the first whispers of finding my real style. It's a caramel base colour with black animal print over the top, and it's a fairly standard-fitting blouse except for the sleeve, which balloons out just before the cuff. I'd never truly appreciated these tiny details before, but the bolder take on neutral colours, and the subtle extra shape on the sleeve felt so much more reflective of who I am than the obsessive attempts at curating a basic capsule wardrobe that you could pluck straight from Pinterest.

Speaking of the capsule wardrobe thing: we need to talk.

The capsule wardrobe fallacy

I know everyone's sick and tired of generational descriptors, but when I say I'm a millennial, I mean it. I listen to emo songs from my teen years on long drives, my heart pines for dial-up internet more than it should, the first three bars of 'Dynamite' by Taio Cruz transport me back to sticky-floored clubs and the taste of blue alco-pops, *Sex and the City* is my comfort show ... Oh, and I've been held in a chokehold by the idea of a capsule wardrobe since 2007.

I don't know quite what it is about our obsession with capsule wardrobes, but there's something universal about the way we've all tried and probably failed to curate one. It was Donna Karan who first pioneered the term as part of a campaign for her 'seven easy pieces' collection, which launched in 1985.

But it was 2010 when 'capsule wardrobe' took on the meaning we now associate with it. Fashion bloggers began editorialising their lives with outfit-of-the-day posts and capsule wardrobe round-ups, and soon the term 'capsule wardrobe' was synonymous with neutrals, basics and, of course, beige.

What comes to mind when you think of the term 'capsule wardrobe'? Probably a camel blazer and a pair of neat black trousers, right? Or one of those Pinterest pins with 24 items you *need* in your wardrobe to always have something to wear, usually featuring trousers in black, white and grey, a long trench coat and, invariably, a Breton striped T-shirt for a touch of Parisian chic.

A capsule wardrobe, at its core, is a considered collection of items that work together to create multiple outfits. I guess it makes sense that much of the way we view a capsule wardrobe revolves around neutrals, because in theory, neutrals all go together, making it easier to have less and wear more.

Well, aside from the fact I learned the hard way that not all neutrals go together and that there's a distinct difference between a warm beige and a cool beige (see page 79), the beige-ification of the capsule wardrobe idea was the point at which it became an aesthetic, not a wardrobe strategy.

When you think about it, you could have a capsule wardrobe of any colour, as long as those colours actually work together, and the items have been considered and well thought through. In fact, some of the people I know who have the most streamlined wardrobes actually don't dress in head-to-toe beige—they incorporate quite a lot of colour, and they use it well.

So why did capsule wardrobes become so synonymous with neutrals, and why is a capsule wardrobe more of a style than a strategy?

Honestly, I think it comes down to the ability to sell the idea. The rise of neutrals has coincided with the rise of ultra-fast fashion and the rapid consumption of apparel across the world.

Neutrals, basics, staples—call them what you want. They sell. Why? Well, firstly, they have mass appeal — colour tends to be more skewed to a specific taste, but neutrals can be appreciated by more people. But, more than that, the neutrals trend looks easy. Retailers aren't selling basics, they're selling simplicity. When we buy into the idea of a capsule wardrobe, we're buying the false idea that we're going to find the answers we've been looking for, or that getting dressed is going to be easier. We're going to finally have that all-important sense of timelessness in our outfits. We buy the idea that we'll need less if we just get this now.

But by buying what we think is simplicity, we're actually winding up with something a whole lot more complicated. Those flat lays of neutral basics, so glaringly simple, and exuding a sense of understated elegance that we all crave, are a head nod to our earlier discussions on page 47 about looking 'polished'.

Yet, it's not simple at all. For a start, basics are actually often the things that change in style the most. Wide leg, slim leg, cropped, full length, 7/8, high rise, mid-rise, low rise ... there are endless variations of basics that mean the timelessness we think we're buying into expires much faster than we realise.

Then there's the homogeneity of neutrals. As women, we all have vastly different body types, which means clothes are going to fit completely differently on each of us. We also have our own unique personalities, quirks, things we want to express about ourselves. The neutral, basic aesthetic doesn't offer much room for individuality, especially if we're operating from some commercial crib sheet of the 'ten items we need in our capsule wardrobe'.

The idea of a capsule wardrobe, or just neutrals as a wardrobe strategy more broadly, very cleverly hooks us into a hamster wheel of consumption by convincing us that we just need to find the perfect white shirt or perfect pair of jeans in order to be 'done'. Frankly, I've lost count of the number of times I've stood in line in a store with an armful of basics telling myself that I'd just get these and I'd be 'done'.

But we're never done. The goal posts keep moving, the styles keep evolving (yes, even the timeless ones) and the homogeneity of the aesthetic is rarely going to satisfy our need to feel good in our clothes. It's like we're so exhausted by trying to feel good in our own skin, that the idea of a capsule wardrobe is just appealing enough that we keep trying.

But there's always another basic waiting to tempt you. No matter how many black T-shirts you have, there's always another must-have. No matter how much you thought you nailed the neutral blazer, there's always more.

I had a realisation during the Project while overthinking my attempts at a capsule wardrobe in a level of detail reserved only for someone writing a book on the subject, and I want to share it with you here. It's one of those ones that changed my brain chemistry, and

I think it will change yours too if you relate in any part to the pull of a capsule wardrobe or the neutral aesthetic.

If the only time you engage with the idea of a capsule wardrobe is when you're buying things for your capsule wardrobe, you don't have a capsule wardrobe.

Look, I'm right there with you. I've been as much of a sucker for neutrals as anyone. But realising that I was so rarely trying to curate a capsule wardrobe in my actual wardrobe, and that the thought only crossed my mind when I was buying, was proof enough that something had to change.

Working only with what I had for a full year stripped back all the temptation of well-merchandised basics and laid bare all my attempts at finding that elusive capsule wardrobe. My mismatched neutrals and trousers I'd bought thinking they were the perfect pair, only to be dazzled by two other similar-but-somehow-different pairs a week later, were getting me nowhere, and I vowed from that moment to stop trying to buy into the capsule fallacy. It's not a capsule if I keep buying.

Instead, I knuckled down and committed to learning about the good and the bad in my wardrobe, in the hopes I could not just buy less, but want less, and as a result, buy better after the year was up.

While I've waxed lyrical for the last few pages about so many of the wardrobe mistakes I unearthed, it's important that I clarify here that, despite realising where I'd been going wrong, I didn't actually hate my clothes. While I was becoming more aware of the minutiae of why certain things were never quite right, or why I was always looking for more, having no other option but to just wear what I had actually had had an extremely positive effect on the way I saw myself. Even though I was wearing clothes that might not have been the best fit or might have been lazily acquired, I learned to like what I saw in the mirror when wearing them. Something about giving myself the grace to just look okay, and accept that my imperfect outfits were still perfectly acceptable, meant I could see myself in a way I never had before.

When we delved into the idea of trends, I talked about how the repeated exposure to new styles gradually increases our affinity towards the item—it's almost as though the same thing happened with myself. The more I saw myself, and the more I settled into just wearing what I had, the easier it became to find joy in my wardrobe and in the mirror, without relying on newness. As I broke down barriers to liking what I was wearing, I broke down barriers to liking myself. Almost like a trend that I once hated, the repeated exposure to myself gradually made me feel completely different about what I saw in the mirror.

If I had learned to like ballet flats again, surely I could learn to like myself!

I have this theory that buying clothes can be an avoidance tactic, a way of shielding ourselves from really seeing who we are or daring to discover who we are. When we're focused on the outfit, and what other people see, we don't have to face up to what *we* see. As a result, we think that if we can just look a certain way to others, we'll eventually like what we see as well. Almost like changing the label on a jar to convince other people of what's inside to avoid having to see what's inside for ourselves.

If we only ever change our label, and we never actually find out what's in the jar, there'll always be a disconnect. Doing the Project gave me the space to see what's in my jar—and I think this came down two key things:

1. Taking photos of my outfits and referring back to those photos meant I was my own inspiration. While I definitely got inspiration from others, like from Pinterest during my Wardrobe Workouts, the one consistent body I saw was my own. After a few months of taking my outfit pictures, I built up a bank of images of me, in my real home, in my real mirror—dust and all—living my real life. And that became my new measure of what looked good.

2. Spending more time putting my outfits together, doing my whipped cream (see page 53), and accessorising with my albeit limited collection of accessories meant I saw more of myself. I looked more intently in the mirror, but not for my flaws or things I needed to change—just looking for the sake of looking. Looking to like, rather than looking to avoid.

And so I have a challenge for you. It's called 'See yourself'.

Task: See yourself

I want you to take a photo of your outfit for 30 days in a row. It doesn't matter if you're at home in sweats or you're dressed up for a night out. If you wear multiple outfits during any given day, try and snap each one. We want to get a full photo diary of your outfits for 30 days. If you can, take the photo in the same spot each day, but it's not absolutely necessary. It just helps for visual cohesion when we look at them all together.

Each day, add your photos to an album on your phone. At the end of the 30 days, you'll have a collection of images of you wearing your clothes—and I can almost guarantee that the way you see yourself will change.

I'm not talking 'change your life in 30 days' shit. Don't get excited and start daydreaming of being a completely different person—I know what your brain wants to do, because mine does it too. I'm talking a subtle shift in perspective.

Here's something this Project taught me about change. It's quiet—and that's really unfamiliar to us. We want change to be loud. We want the movie soundtrack and the big crescendo. We want never-the-same change. We want the transformation porn of before and afters. We want a smoking gun, a magic bullet. That's how it is in the movies. The glow-up montage and the turning heads as she becomes unrecognisable.

But in real life, when it comes to meaningful change, the biggest changes are the quietest ones. It's not the flip of a switch or a line in the sand. It's a moment when you realise that you feel a bit different. You see things a bit differently. You see yourself a bit differently. The pull to fix and change and tweak isn't so strong anymore, your flaws aren't the first thing you see, you're less open to being told of the latest must-have or quick fix.

Commit to seeing yourself for 30 days, and you'll feel a seed of acceptance start to grow.

Chapter summary

∞ Just like repeated exposure to trends can change your perception of styles, repeated exposure to yourself can change your perception of how you look.

∞ If you're only ever interested in a capsule wardrobe when you're buying things, you don't have a capsule wardrobe.

∞ Your reticular activating system is the part of your brain that keeps you hunting for the familiar, which is why we buy more and more of the same.

∞ The neutral, minimalist capsule wardrobe aesthetic is trying to profit from your craving for ease—when it's actually a whole lot of complicated!

∞ Not all neutrals go together!

∞ Buying a specific outfit for a specific event, occasion or outfit risks leaving you with a wardrobe you don't really want to wear.

∞ Patterns in our buying mistakes and our buying successes can help us buy better.

∞ If you like something in one colour, don't immediately go and buy it in another colour!

∞ We often buy more than we think we buy, because our intentions around clothes don't match our real behaviour.

∞ We're often in a default 'yes' state when it comes to consumption. Flipping the switch to a 'no' state, and exploring the things we think we want while in that state, can help you come up with more reasons not to buy than to buy.

JUNE
The shift

For the first time, I wasn't trying to be anyone else, I was just trying to be more me.

Almost at the halfway point, June felt like it brought a sense of achievement in itself. Six months of sticking with my commitment, and so many lessons already learned about my wardrobe, my buying patterns and, of course, myself. Why is there always a lesson about myself lurking at every stage of growth?

At this point in the Project, I took up sewing as a creative outlet, which deeply challenged my desire to be good at everything immediately. I was not, and I have the wonky hems to prove it. Sewing was something I'd wanted to return to for years. My gran was an avid seamstress, and we used to sew together when I'd go and stay with her in the school holidays. I'd set myself a goal at the start of the year to be able to sew a piece of clothing, and I'd finally mustered the energy to give it a crack. It felt like the perfect skill-based goal to master as part of my year-long challenge, as it forced me to slow down and engage in a creative pursuit that occupied my dopamine-hungry brain.

June is also my birthday month (shout out to my fellow psycho Geminis), and so I was braced for resistance at not being able to treat myself. I'm not a big birthday party person, so I tend to be less concerned with wanting to get something to wear to an event or celebration, but the treating myself aspect was my biggest threat. Birthdays often have us questioning our identity, whether we're where we want to be in life, whether things are how we pictured them and how we stack up to our peers, and for me that's often prompted a hunger for a clothes splurge.

Buying clothes as a means of celebrating myself has been something I've engaged with for a long time. I think, in many ways, I struggle to feel things or experience my emotions fully—especially when something good happens—and so I counter that with the quick hit I can get from adding to cart. It's the same whether it's a new job, a work win, a birthday or any kind of good news or achievement.

It's as though I want to feel happy and loved and at ease when celebrating something, but in reality I feel anxious, lonely and a bit numb. Some of that comes down to my social circles and family background, especially when it comes to birthdays. I didn't have those big family celebrations for my birthday, nor a big social circle with gaggles of friends gathering to celebrate with me. I'm a much more introverted, one-on-one type of friend, which doesn't lend itself to a big birthday dinner or party. That's not to say I even want those things, but more that I've always felt like a bit of a failure for not having them. I've gone to some people's birthdays where a table of 20+ people show up and say such lovely things about the person whose birthday it is. Despite the latter part, in particular, being my idea of hell (please don't praise me to my face, I'm too awkward and don't know where to look), it's hard not to wonder if there's something wrong with you if you don't have a big group of lifelong friends with an ever-pinging group chat and those public birthday collage posts on social media. Something about buying myself a new outfit fed me the feelings of celebration I craved in just a few clicks.

But by early June of the Project, I started to observe something I'd never really recognised in myself before: there wasn't really anything I wanted. I didn't even realise it until my husband's family asked me for a wishlist. (They're generally the only people who buy me gifts and, as a rule, we provide a list when we're the recipient so things aren't being bought for the sake of it.)

Stumped, I was instantly curious. There was just nothing I could think of that I wanted. To be clear, as I set out in my rules, I wasn't going to allow anyone to gift me clothes, so there was no opportunity to add clothes to my wishlist—but that wasn't even really the crux of it. I rarely had clothes on my birthday list anyway, so it wasn't the absence of a want for clothes that left me with an empty wishlist. I found myself in this tension between my muscle memory of buying as a means of celebrating myself, but with no real want for anything specific.

What I think had happened was that I'd effectively stepped off of the material treadmill. By consciously and deliberately cutting off my ability to self soothe with buying clothes, that same level of disconnect bled into other areas. There was nothing I wanted, and that was unfamiliar territory.

The unfamiliar territory of not wanting anything

I found it quite jarring to be in a state of not wanting anything. As humans living in the modern world, perhaps more specifically in the consumption-driven Global North, our desires and ability to consume serves a purpose for the system we exist in. We're conditioned to want more and more and more so we keep spending more and more and more. It serves capitalism for us to always want something. So to be in a position where I couldn't think of a single material thing I wanted felt extremely unfamiliar.

So many of the things that are marketed to us revolve around making our life better. Whether that means making it more aesthetically pleasing, removing friction from otherwise irritating tasks or changing the way we're perceived by others, most hedonic purchases carry some kind of improvement to our lives. Clothes are no different. When we buy outfits, it's so rarely about the utility of the item itself, and much more commonly driven by the emotional benefits that come from buying into a certain lifestyle or identity.

The concept of hedonic adaptation refers to the idea that humans can find short-term bursts of happiness or enjoyment from things, whether that be material things or experiences, but will eventually return to a baseline level of happiness after the thrill has worn off. Over time, this can mean we have to consume more and more and more in order to keep accessing the same thrill.

When we look at it from the perspective of spending for life improvement and to acquire a specific identity, it makes sense that the more we buy, the more we feel compelled to keep buying. This feels in direct conflict with many of the beliefs we have about clothes, most notably the idea that we can buy our way to an end point — like the capsule wardrobe, for example.

The more we buy, the more we'll keep needing to buy in order to feel as satisfied. The fact that I stopped buying, and subsequently stopped feeling the desire to consume, not just in the clothes category but in other categories too, suggests that consuming less actually does more for our sense of contentment than acquiring another nice dress.

I knew at the start of this Project that the way I was buying clothing wasn't making me happy. But I hadn't quite expected it to lead to such a shift in my attitude to consumption more broadly. If anything, I thought not buying clothes would mean I spent more on other areas, but overall, I spent substantially less on material things during the year.

There is some research to suggest that we can combat hedonic adaptation by embracing two shifts:

∞ spending on experiences, which provide more lasting joy than material things

∞ spending across a wider variety of things rather than on the same select categories.

Given that clothing was one of my highest hedonic spending categories, it makes sense that decentralising that spending contributed to my reduced desire to consume overall.

I noticed I became more mindful across other areas of my spending, and there was much less urgency in my spending decisions, which was a mainstay in the way I'd consume clothes ordinarily. The more I thought about it, the more I considered that urgency could be an important indicator of a mindful versus a mindless purchase decision, regardless of whether it is related to clothes or any other category.

Urgency as an indicator of mindless buying

When I took up sewing as a means of getting creative and being more mindful with my clothes, I was confronted once again with urgency. I found myself frustrated at how long it took to construct a garment, even an easy one like a simple midi-dress. I had to stop myself rushing ahead to the good bit and had to practise slowing down, letting clothes not be something I could click my fingers and have exactly the way I wanted.

Looking back at how I'd come to buy many of the items in my wardrobe, so often there was a rush. A craving to be satisfied. A need, even. Frantic, somehow, even if I hadn't literally purchased the item in a physical rush. The rise of next-day or even same-day delivery has only served to amplify that urgency — I've been known to pay for express shipping when I could easily wait, or go and pick something up in store because I simply *must* have it now so I can get the thrill faster.

I noticed this sense of rushing to the good bit, whether that be the dopamine rush I'd get from buying, the thrill of novelty and wearing the item for the first time, or the sense of excitement I'd get from buying into a piece of the lifestyle or the identity I so deeply craved.

When we buy clothes, we're often responding to one of the following.

Emotional soothing

This taps into that age-old idea of retail therapy, where buying nice things makes us feel good, and allows us to either avoid an emotion we're experiencing or acquire one we're craving.

When I'd buy clothes after a bad day, or when I felt down about the world, or overwhelmed with work, it would be a fast experience. I'd have browsed and checked out in fairly quick succession, almost rushing ahead to get the hit of dopamine I craved and the excitement of something to look forward to.

Expressing ourselves to others

Many of our clothing consumption decisions come down to the way we're perceived by others. We might buy brands to communicate a message of affluence. We might buy into a trend in an attempt to belong. We might buy into a certain style to try to associate ourselves with the lifestyle it represents.

Buying to fit in with a group I deemed more worthy than me, or buying for a specific event where I'd want to look a certain way for certain people, again, felt urgent. I'd feel like I needed to find something, perhaps getting frustrated when I felt I couldn't find anything that would make me feel the way I needed to or communicate the right message.

Feeling good about ourselves

Sometimes we buy to prove something to others, but other times we're proving something to ourselves. Buying to hide our flaws, look slimmer, look like someone we admire or to cosplay a sense of confidence or worthiness are all common motivators. Of the women I surveyed, 68 per cent agreed that buying clothes can give them a boost of self-esteem.

Buying to feel good about myself often involved my fantasy self that we talked about on page 27. There was sometimes an element of wanting to transform myself or reach that lofty ideal when buying like this. This, too, was fast, with a sense of urgency in my attempts to look the way I wanted to giving way to lazy buying decisions or 'making do' with something that wasn't quite right just to experience the feeling sooner.

Retailer tactics

Our spending decisions can also respond to marketing tactics. Often coupled with another motivator from this list, we may buy clothing in response to the way it's sold to us, whether that's using scarcity or exclusivity to drive demand, strategic merchandising decisions or even brand collaborations or extensions. Retailers use what they know about our buying decisions and the way clothing relates to who we are in order to capitalise on why we want to buy, and they align product ranges to the emotions and expressions we want to experience.

Retailers and marketers benefit from urgency and rushed decision-making, so when they can foster rapidity in our spending decisions, we become well-dressed cash cows.

Now, it's not wrong to feel positive emotions when buying, or to feel excitement at the idea of buying clothes, nor am I suggesting that we can eliminate the chemical activity that happens in our brains when transacting altogether.

It's about differentiating between fleeting thrills and lasting enjoyment. I'd been stuck only experiencing fashion and style through the lens of consumption. Style and shopping are not synonymous, but it serves capitalism well for us to struggle to separate them.

The Project gave me the space to experience joy in clothing outside of consumption, and it felt completely different. The thrill of the see-want-buy sequence is loud, but it wears off quickly. The thrill of deeper self-expression and feeling good in your clothes is much quieter, but longer lasting. The latter doesn't leave you needing more and more hits over time—it leaves you needing fewer.

Task: Observing urgency

It's one thing to understand that we often buy with urgency, but it's another to experience it in your own life. Over the next week, I want you to observe any experiences you have with this sense of urgency and impulsiveness that we've explored in this section. Maybe you see something you love on a social media influencer and you want to add it to cart immediately. Maybe you spot a piece of second-hand treasure and just can't settle until you find out if the Depop seller accepts your offer.

When you observe urgency in real time, take a pause. Ask yourself:

- What emotions are underneath this urgency?
- What stories am I telling myself about this item?
- How does it feel to consider missing out on this item and walking away?
- What is this urgency trying to achieve?

Simply stopping to take note of the leaps your mind is making can help you calm down and allow your rational mind to step in.

The human behaviour element of fast and slow fashion

I think we can all agree that the emergence of fast fashion has contributed to our fractured relationship with clothes over the last two decades. As so many parts of life have become unaffordable, cheap fashion has become more affordable than ever. Thanks to the make-fast, make-cheap, sell-fast, sell-cheap model that fast fashion thrives on, quick-hit clothing purchases offer the perfect cocktail of emotional relief and illusion of control over our lives and our happiness.

When we talk about fast fashion, typically, we're referring to a production and retail model. The part we often don't look at is the behavioural component that that model has created. Clothes aren't only made fast, they're consumed fast, worn fast, loved fast, hated fast and eventually discarded fast, too.

Arguably, fast fashion is now as much about human behaviour as it is about retail. The model itself turned us into fast consumers, to the point where it's no longer clear whether supply or demand is the issue. Don't get me wrong, supply is absolutely a huge factor—after all, the supply came first. Experts have estimated that between 10 and 40 per cent of garments produced don't get sold and end up in landfill, brand new and never worn.

But, equally, fast fashion is now a $150.82 billion industry. It's estimated to reach $291.1 billion by 2032, and it has maintained a compound annual growth rate of around 10 per cent for the last five years. The demand is absolutely there.

With slow fashion, on the other hand, clothes are made slower, with more care for materials and craftsmanship (craftspersonship?!) to extend the life of the clothes. Slow fashion is made to be worn; fast fashion is made to be discarded.

Outside of the fast and slow fashion production models lies our own human behaviour. Regardless of what we're buying, whether it's true fast fashion or the most sustainable piece ever made, hand-crafted by kittens in cotton spun from the dreams of a unicorn, if we're buying it with a fast mindset, we're still not going to get far.

Slow consumption is just as important as slow production—and what's even better, it's completely within our control. The slower we train ourselves to consume, the less demand we're giving to fast-fashion models. Over time, this signals a collective move away from what big corporations want us to consume, and puts our purchase decisions back in our hands.

Slowness fosters creativity

Something I started to recognise was that, when we consume from a place of urgency or impatience, it often creates a rapid dopamine run-off. When all the emotion and all the experience is stuck in the actual consumption and not the wearing of the item, we don't really have the space to enjoy our clothes fully. The Project slowed me down to the point I had no choice but to create the feelings I was used to getting when buying with the things I already had.

Slowing down and exploring why I liked the things I liked, and what was lurking in my purchase mistakes, opened me up to a whole new idea of my style. It struck me one day when I was drinking an espresso con panna (espresso with whipped cream on top) and feeling oh, so cosmopolitan. I looked at my coffee and thought about how it reflected my style.

For so long, I'd tried to dress like an iced latte. Creamy, classic, beige, white, simple, smooth, laid back, light, considered. My fantasy self was polished and slick and effortless, just like that iced latte.

But my espresso with whipped cream—classic, but with a bit of extra sparkle, and a bit bolder and sharper than the iced latte—suddenly felt so much more me. I can be quite loud when I'm comfortable, but I'm also an introvert. I use humour in the way I communicate, I'm often goofy or silly, and I'll happily swear. I'm curvy and jiggly and, on a good day, I was starting to be really proud of that.

That was the seed of me discovering my own style. I wanted to keep aspects of the neutrals in a way that worked for me (heavy fabrics, flowy fit, longline midi length) but I wanted to accentuate my curvy body, not try to hide it. I wanted to be able to be bolder, maybe even smarter, and with a little extra *something*, whether that be a bright shoe, a bold accessory, a sleeve shape or an element of colour or print. Sort of... basics with 'benefits'.

I was so familiar with yearning to be that fantasy self plucked straight out of Pinterest, that I didn't know any other way. I knew I wasn't the kind of person who wore bright prints and patterns—it just didn't feel me. In the past I'd also tried to embrace feminine, floaty, delicate styles, too, but they didn't feel like me either.

This conceptual idea of basics with benefits, with that visual anchor of my espresso with whipped cream and how I felt when drinking it, was the beginning of me realising how I could take styles I admired and make them more me. For the first time, I wasn't trying to be anyone else, I was just trying to be more me.

∞ ∞ ∞

As I looked ahead to the second half of the challenge, I sensed a bit of a shift as I began the downhill run to the end. Being close to the halfway mark felt easier, like victory was closer or something. For the first time, I started to think about life after the Project, and what my game plan would be when I was back in the big wide world of buying again. Did I trust myself? Would I just go back to my old habits? Would I be banging on the door of my local shopping centre at 9 am on New Year's Day, waving my credit card and begging someone to sell me something?

These questions got me thinking a little more deeply about what I wanted the outcome of my Project to be, and how that had changed since the outset. I started this challenge with the intention of spending less and interrogating why clothes had always been my weakness. I hadn't realised that it would change the way I saw clothes forever.

Something about buying again, albeit in six months' time, felt dangerous. But I was conscious of not cutting off my nose to spite my face. I've done enough fad diets in my time to know that over restriction rarely ends well. I knew there were things I wanted to replace in my wardrobe, and learnings I wanted to implement with better buying.

At this point I started a saver in my banking app called 'Style Icon'. I set a weekly transfer of $30 into that saver, and turned on my bank's round-up function so that every time I tapped my card, it would round the transaction up and add an extra $3 to that saver. It made a $5 coffee cost $8, but it meant my savings climbed pretty quickly without too much effort. My intention for this money was to hire a stylist to help me replace some of the key items in my wardrobe, and fill a couple of gaps I'd identified. Plus, I figured if I had a professional helping me, I'd be less bull-in-a-china-shop and reduce my risk of rebound.

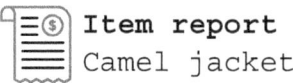 **Item report**
Camel jacket

Purchased from

Lee Mathews

How I came to own it

Ugh. I've been putting off writing about this one, as it's one of my biggest purchase regrets of all time. Don't get me wrong, it's a gorgeous jacket. I bought this at a time when my identity and my relationship with myself was really quite rocky. I was in a job that was all wrong for me — and I was all wrong for it, too, which really didn't help the ol' self-esteem. Turns out failing every single day makes you feel like shit. Who knew?

Anyway, to be completely vulnerable, I bought this jacket because someone I admired shopped at this store, and I felt like buying this jacket was buying a piece of everything I admired about them. Lee Mathews clothes are beautifully made, and you can really feel the quality in the pieces, but they just weren't me. Looking back now, I can see so clearly that I was buying to feel like I was a part of that brand and that I was somebody who would shop there, because that's who I wanted to be. A lot of the pieces are quite a structured, boxy fit, and they look incredible on the models — but that's the kind of style that would suit my fantasy self, not my real self.

The RRP on this jacket was around $650, but I managed to get it half price. Unfortunately, it hung in my wardrobe barely worn for over a year. The arrival of spring, however, presented the perfect opportunity to finally wear it. And it taught me some stuff.

The verdict

I shouldn't have had to force myself to wear this jacket. I avoided wearing it because I knew it wasn't right for me. The length was all wrong, and the back had a sort of pleat that fanned out in a really nice angle, but being a jiggly gal, it just threw my proportions all off. I'd bought it with my fantasy self in my head. Tall, slim, athletic and what 90s fashion commentators would call 'leggy'. It wasn't that the jacket looked particularly bad. It just highlighted that I was trying to be someone I wasn't.

What frustrates me is I kind of knew this at the time I bought it. Wearing it in the context of the challenge allowed me to actually face up to what I'd been trying to forget: that I spent over $300 on a jacket because I liked the idea of it.

Lessons learned

If you have any doubts about an item before you buy it—don't buy it anyway. I did this often with fantasy self purchases. I'd be so in love with the idea of it that I'd keep it even if it wasn't right. It sounds ridiculous to write that down on a page that will be published and read by (hopefully) thousands of people, but it's true.

Length and proportion (of both an item and your body) plays a huge role in how something looks and how something feels. This was my first experience of recognising what would have made the jacket a better shape for me, which was the beginning of my understanding of how to buy better and buy for who I really am, not who I wanted to be.

Chapter summary

- ∞ In a consumption-driven society, not wanting anything is not only unfamiliar, but uncomfortable. Stripping back my layers of 'want' shone a light on how much I was relying on consuming to feel the way I wanted to feel.
- ∞ Urgency is a common factor in mindless or unhelpful spending decisions. From emotional soothing to retailer tactics, there are so many reasons we buy clothes we don't need. Urgency underpins so many of the decisions worth changing.
- ∞ Fast fashion is both a production model, and a behavioural model. We can't control how clothes are produced, but we can control the demand we place on those systems by changing our behaviour.
- ∞ Consumption might be fast, but style is slow. Resist the temptation to rush your style and allow slowness to foster creativity.

JULY
The breakthrough

I allowed my body to become part of my style, rather than an obstacle to it.

I welcomed July with glee because it meant I'd officially surpassed the halfway mark and was on the downhill slope to bring this baby home. I'm not entirely sure how I felt at the prospect of having six more months to go. On the one hand it was very much 'Yeehaw, over halfway, I can do it!' and on the other hand it was a case of 'Six months feels like six years'. That pesky illusion of time, right?

The finish line felt both painfully far away, and somehow I could touch it. I'd also gotten to that point where you feel almost comfortable in a situation you thought you wanted to get out of, like the last day of high school when you realise it's all over and you're about to be gobbled up by the big wide world.

I felt safe in my Project cocoon, so while I yearned for the sense of accomplishment for completing the year, I was comfy where I was for now, in a rhythm of not buying and for the most part, not feeling tempted to. There was a small grumble of resistance around the mid-point of the year, though, as I'd learned so much about my buying mistakes that I felt eager to rectify them and see what it felt like to buy better. To not just accept any old dopamine-enshrined thing into my wardrobe and actually hunt down the things I really thought would add to my style.

Nonetheless, I persisted with what I'd set out to do. I decided to tug more at the thread I'd begun to unravel around finding a sense of style that's more me and less plucked-from-a-sea-of-beige-on-Pinterest.

From beige iced latte to punchy espresso

July was all about getting playful. I tried new things, rolling the dice on anything I thought could give my outfits that little extra bit of flare to pair with the more simple, classic bases that I'd previously tried to wear in isolation. I tried wearing belts over blazers to create shape and structure, I added the shoulder pads I'd previously removed back into a vintage blazer. I dug out a one-shoulder top I'd previously written off and played with angles. I wore curve-hugging midi-dresses in the daytime and wasn't afraid to appear 'overdressed'. I guess, to some degree, I dressed a little bit smarter, and let go of trying to always be the casual cool girl.

At first, I thought I was just getting creative with shapes and wearing some things I hadn't previously, but what I was actually doing was allowing myself to be seen. I was showing off my body rather than hiding it. I allowed myself to attract attention by erring on the side of overdressed. I wore things a little bit special even if the situation didn't require it—a heeled boot, a white jean with a creamy top for a tonal, rich aunty look. It was subtle, but it felt empowering. It felt like I was finally starting to find my own style, and more than that, I was okay with the fact I wasn't going to find it overnight. In the previous chapter, I talked about urgency and how it's such a hallmark of mindless consumption. The beauty of having this style shift in the safety of the Project was that I couldn't run out and buy a bunch of new stuff to reflect my changing style. It was slow. The freedom I gave myself to be a little bit bolder, try that slight style shift on for size, and get it wrong at times, was meaningful. It's kind of crazy what you're able to discover about yourself when you're not buying the answers.

Looking back, I think at this point in the challenge was when I really came home to my body. I'd spent most of my life in varying degrees of toxic relationships with my body. Growing up a little bit bigger than everyone else, I allowed the late 90s and early 00s diet culture to make me believe everything about my body was wrong, and that it wouldn't be right until I was thin.

While I think the entirety of the year did wonders for my body image, it was the point at which I allowed my body to become part of my style, rather than an obstacle to it, that something really shifted.

I'd been better with my body in my 30s than I had in my 20s, but to be honest, really, until this Project, I still deep down harboured this idea that one day my body would change. One day I'd be thinner, or one day I'd get back on the wagon of trying to lose weight. Something about the vastness of the time I spent unable to buy my way out of insecurities finally allowed me to see my body for what it is: me.

I think style is different when you exist in a bigger body. You always have to try harder if you're plus size, almost as though people think you look bad unless you prove them otherwise. Clothes fit differently when you're plus size. Curves often oversexualise styles that look casual and relaxed on slimmer, smaller chested women, and make you look somehow 'too much' for the outfit.

Integrating my curves into the way I pursued my style, and, for the first time, not seeing my body as something I needed to change was so refreshing. Being willing to be seen and perceived as a curvy woman with no intention of shrinking herself was unfamiliar, but the very fact I felt not just able to do it, but excited to do it, was a testament to how much I was benefitting from not buying.

Task: Select a style anchor

Landing on my espresso con panna style anchor marked a significant shift in my relationship with clothes and the beliefs I held about style—and myself. Why? Because it was the first time I'd approached my self-image from a place of embracing myself and working with who I really am.

(continued)

I want you to start seeking out your own style anchor—an external *thing* that you feel a visual connection to, something that represents you and how you'd like to express yourself. It might be a plant or something from nature, a destination like a city or town, or even something more conceptual like a building, a drink or a food item.

A dear friend of mine used to refer to her style as 'fairy bread' because she loved expressing herself through playful colours and punchy accessories. [For anyone not familiar with fairy bread, it's an Australian kids' snack of white bread topped with butter and sprinkles.]

The benefit of anchoring your style and how you express yourself to something you connect with is that it's personal to *you*. For whatever reason, you identify with that thing and you feel it reflects part of you that you want to express. It gives you a lens through which to view styles, colours, shapes and outfits, and you get to decide how you use your anchor in your wardrobe. It might be through a colour, it might be an attitude, it might be something you can't even quite describe. The point is it makes sense to *you*, and isn't something that's dictated to you by somebody else.

Your style anchor can also support you through changes to your style as time passes. That fairy bread friend's style evolved over time as she incorporated more neutrals into parts of her life as a lawyer. As a new part of herself developed within, she was able to express that by anchoring to a cup of coffee, and building that new era of her style in a way that fitted with the way she wanted to express herself.

Having enough and being enough

This next phase of the Project got me thinking about the link between having enough and being enough. It sounds ridiculous, but I genuinely don't think I ever fully appreciated that *having* does not equal *being*. When I'd try to buy that confidence, that polish, outsourcing the identity I wanted to clothes hanging on racks, I never fully grasped that while I could have the items, I couldn't be the person. That fantasy version of myself was really driven by this belief that if I had the right outfit, I'd be the person I wanted to be.

When we buy clothes, there's something inside us that's activated. Something that compels us to look outside of ourselves — how we see ourselves, how someone else sees us or an emotion that we want to avoid or acquire. Insecurity is often present when we're in this state, which creates a void that, in that moment, clothes are able to fill. However, it's only a temporary fix.

With the vastness of clothing availability now, whether at your local shopping centre, thrift store, online retailer or even social media account, it's easier than ever to find something to soothe the wound that's opened up.

If we're feeling anxious and we want to avoid that feeling, the dopamine and novelty of something new will set us right for a while. If we want to acquire a feeling, like excitement or hope, we might browse the stores online and lock in something to look forward to in three to five business days. If we're trying to fit in or impress someone, we'll browse endless troves of things that align us to that group. If we're feeling vulnerable in our body, or with the way we look, or with where we're at in life, an endless array of artefacts of a better life and a better identity are presented to us. We can copy someone else and buy into their life, or we can create a whole fantasy of our own and buy into that.

When we buy the item, we get that giddy feeling. The thrill. The excitement of possibility, the rush of dopamine, the belief that maybe things aren't so bad after all, the anticipation of what our lives will become, who we will become when we wear this thing.

That positive emotion that we experience is real—but only in the moment. The problem is, we misattribute that positive feeling to having reversed the emotion, filled the void, taken control of our identity or bought into the fantasy. We think we've achieved what we wanted to achieve because it feels good.

Eventually, whether after a minute, an hour, a day or, if you're lucky, maybe a week, the good feeling wears off, and what you're left with is the same version of you that you were before, just confused, a little bit poorer and more vulnerable than before.

What's happened here is we've mistaken *having* for *being*. We think that if we have all the right things, we will *be* all the right things. But it doesn't work that way—and there's nothing wrong with you if you fall into this trap. It's how we're conditioned to consume. If we attribute *having* with *being*, there's no limit to the number of things we can be sold.

But it doesn't serve us to think this way. The only way out of this cycle is to disconnect *having* from *being*.

We all want to have enough, whether that's in a capsule wardrobe or the perfect little black dress. We buy our way to trying to complete our style as though it's a game with an end point. But the game is neverending—the only thing that breaks the cycle is actually *being* enough, and you have the power to decide your *enoughness*. As Edlinger et al. notes in the 2021 study 'Enoughness: Exploring the potentialities of having and being enough',

> *Enoughness celebrates singularity: it is what it is, simply for what it is—not for what it is not, nor for what it could be. This is the acknowledgement of an intrinsic value that is not subject to any standard but its own. It is a value that arises from within a subject rather than being created and assigned to an object.*

Being enough means finding your intrinsic value outside of objects or externalities. Its singularity speaks to that sense of quiet we talked about on page 92. Enoughness is not loud and urgent, it's quiet and present. It doesn't need to be acquired, it doesn't need to be purchased.

It's not often that we address the link between having enough and being enough. Living in a patriarchal, capitalist society, so many of our consumption decisions are motivated by trying to be enough. Standards for what women should be are ever-changing, keeping us trapped chasing moving goal posts, and purchasing the things we're told will get us there. That's what tricks us into equating *having* things with *being* who we want to be.

We can't wait until we've satisfied all of society's standards to feel like we're enough because—*spoiler alert*—we'll never satisfy them all. Instead, we need to decide within ourselves that we are enough, so that we don't feel compelled to buy our way to being.

The link between having and being goes both ways. When we start to feel like we *are* enough, we start to feel like we *have* enough. And when we feel like we *have* enough, we can start to feel like we *are* enough.

We can use this link to our advantage. Deciding that we have enough is effectively what we're doing with The Wardrobe Project. When we say 'no' to more, we're signalling to ourselves that we have enough, and this halts our reliance on consumption to feel good.

Giving yourself the space to exist in the unfamiliar state of not relying on more and more and more to feel the way we want to feel is where change can start to happen. It's where you can start considering that maybe you don't need a new outfit to feel confident, maybe you don't need to try and be someone you're not.

After just six months of doing the Project, I was already proof of this. Deciding that I had enough gave me the space to see that I was enough, and because of that, I felt so much less desire to buy into the fantasy self I'd clung to for so long.

Enoughness has a lot to do with acceptance. It's not self-love. It's not even really liking yourself—though this is a term I use often, including on the cover of this book. I've always preferred the pursuit of liking yourself, because it feels more realistic than to 'love' yourself. But acceptance always comes first.

It's unrealistic to go from being insecure to loving yourself. Sure, it sounds good on social media, but for so long I felt ashamed that I couldn't flip that switch and just suddenly love myself. I understood the idea but I couldn't make it stick. That's because it's not a switch to flip. It's a gradual shift in perspective. First you begin to accept yourself—that's the being enough part. Then, over time, as you settle into being enough, you'll start to find parts you like — and that's where you start to discover your own sense of style outside of consuming.

Finding confidence outside of buying

Buying my confidence was something I relied on deeply. I didn't know confidence in my appearance outside of a new outfit or a very specific set of circumstances, and even then, it was shaky. The belief that confidence can be bought, that misattribution of that feeling, keeps us stuck. We have to practise confidence outside of consumption in order to set ourselves free. Here are a few things to try to sprinkle extra confidence into your life without having to spend a cent.

Stand up tall

Seriously, posture and pose make such a difference — not just to the way you look, but the way you feel. We're so conditioned to shrink ourselves and stay small that we often hide ourselves in the way we stand. Try standing up a little taller, especially in the mirror, and see how your perception of yourself changes.

Accessorise

I've mentioned my new-found appreciation for accessories before, and they can be a great way to boost your confidence without needing a new outfit. Accessorising prompts you to think about what vibe you want to convey with your outfit, and how you can express yourself through finishing touches to pull the outfit together.

Whipped cream

Speaking of finishing touches, remember whipped cream from page 53? Taking an extra two, five or ten minutes to add whipped cream to your outfit can boost your confidence, both from the outcome and the extra intention.

Look at images of yourself and neutralise them

If you're one of those people who sees a photo of themselves and either instantly looks away or fixates on their flaws, I need you to try this. Find a photo of yourself that you want to pick apart and just sit with it. Look at it. Look at yourself. Then I want you to focus on neutral or positive observations, either about you or the photo itself. What looks good in the picture? What looks fine in the picture? Do the flaws your eyes bounce to even really matter?

Have you ever heard the idea that your first reaction to something is your conditioned reaction and your second reaction is your true perception? Often our instant thoughts on how we look in a photo are negative because we're seeing all of the flaws we've been conditioned to fixate on. When we allow that emotional flooding to pass, and we look at the photo with a kinder, more gentle context, those flaws can fade, and we allow ourselves to see our humanness underneath.

Mirror affirmation

I've got three mirrors in my house and on all of them you'll find a message in the top right-hand corner. One says 'you are fucking fabulous', and the other two say 'I look phenomenal today'. Remember, confidence is all about self-perception. Put this book down right now and go and write yourself a note and stick it to your mirror. For the next week I want you to say it out loud every time you look in that mirror. You can whisper it if you need to—but make sure you say it. You'll be surprised at how it can very gradually change the way you see yourself and the thoughts you say to yourself about how you look.

Overdress

I have a theory. The idea that you can be overdressed serves to keep women from taking up space—especially plus-size women. When you're in a bigger body, feeling like you're too dressed up for where you are can trigger feelings of vulnerability, as people often pass judgement on what it means for a bigger woman to be so visible.

Regardless of size, though, overdressing is such a myth. Sure, there are some objective clashes in clothing and context—a ballgown isn't the most efficient outfit to wear to childcare pickup (though I deeply endorse this level of audacity if you want to give it a try)—but daring to wear something a little fancier than you might otherwise can be a power move.

Create something without buying

There's a sense of satisfaction that comes from creating an outfit from your existing wardrobe and replicating that same hit of excitement you get from buying without the dent in your bank account. To build your confidence outside of buying, challenge yourself to put together a new outfit each week or each month that you haven't tried before. Remember the Wardrobe Workout from page 65? Schedule in 30 minutes each month to add a new outfit combo to your rotation.

Ask people who care about you what you look good in

When was the last time you asked for compliments? Look I'm not gonna judge you if it's been ages because, frankly, I relate. Compliments can feel icky enough, let alone when you're asking for them, but there really is genuine value in asking people who love you what you look best in, or how they'd describe your style. People who love you don't see your flaws the way you do. They don't cast their eye to your chunky knees that have plagued you since year 9 (could not be talking about myself here). They just see you for you, and when you serve an amazing outfit, they see you shining.

As you get more playful with your wardrobe, talk about it! Ask people if there's an item of clothing they think suits you, or a colour or a shape. Share your thoughts with them, too, if they're interested in building their confidence. Seeing ourselves how others see us can help us shift into a much more confident mindset.

The therapy of spending

In my first book, *Good With Money,* I dive deep into our spending habits and how we can optimise them for a happier life and simpler money management. If you haven't read that book (please do, after this one!), I want to quickly talk you through a bit more of the deeper meaning behind spending more generally, not just in the context of clothes.

Spending is one of the most fascinating human behaviours in my opinion, because it expresses so perfectly the irrationality of our brains. People treat money as though it's mathematical — which in a way, it should be. It's numbers. One plus one equals two. But when humans are controlling the money, that's where things go awry.

The way we spend our money is deeply personal, and it's not uncommon for us to conceal our spending habits from others, or act like we have it all figured out when we actually don't. If you skew more on the spending side of the spender-saver spectrum, as I do, you might wonder why you find it so easy to spend money and so much harder to save money. Or why you spend money on non-essentials when, mathematically, you know you shouldn't. Or why you set a goal to save money but end up dropping $100 on a new jacket a week later. Where did all that motivation go?!

The good news is, you're not alone. In any book, space, program, podcast or piece of content created by me, I can promise you, you are safe and welcome as your spendiest self. No judgement, just support.

On that note, I want to share with you a few common reasons why people spend that have nothing to do with frivolity, carelessness or greed. You might feel shame for being a spender or for having spent money when you should've saved it, but it's just not as simple as that. Spending can be a coping mechanism or a response to financial wounds.

Spending can offer control

Spending is a behaviour that makes us feel in control of our emotions and the situation around us. It's an easy trigger to pull to get an outcome we want, such as satisfaction, dopamine and enjoyment, albeit temporarily. Many spending behaviours are an attempt to gain control when we're feeling overwhelmed by other things in our lives, including our finances.

Spending can feel safe

Spending can be more familiar to us than saving, and often that familiarity keeps us in a comfort zone that might not feel all that comfortable. Comfort zones aren't comfortable because they're necessarily good for us, they're comfortable because they're familiar. The comfort is psychological.

If you regularly spend money too quickly and then struggle to make it to payday, or struggle to achieve the goals you set for yourself, it might be because you feel safer doing what you've always done than doing something different.

If you have past memories of losing money, of money causing conflict or of money being at risk, perhaps from your childhood or a significant event in your life, it can feel safer to spend it than save it because the familiarity is more comfortable than facing the wound it activates.

Spending can be sabotage

Often our money habits become deeply embedded in our identity. It's common for us to struggle with our finances for years, and as a result, internalise the idea that we're 'bad with money'. Any time you pursue improving your money habits and try to confront that identity, self-sabotage offers a way to escape friction between those two states and return you to the familiar safety of what you know yourself to be.

Spending can be avoidance

Spending also offers an escape through avoidance. Avoidance of:

∞ addressing your goals—if there's no money to achieve them, you don't have to start working towards them
∞ other stressors, financial or otherwise—if you're spending, you're otherwise occupied, both emotionally and financially
∞ things that trigger you—if spending makes you feel better about yourself after a bad day, it serves as a way to avoid dealing with the underlying cause of that bad day.

Spending can feel like self-care

A lot of spending behaviours are a result of misattributed feelings of care. In a world where we're less cared for than ever and, in many cases, saddled with generational trauma on an individual level, spending offers a quick way to feel as though you're caring for yourself.

In my survey, 48 per cent of women agreed that buying clothes cheered them up after a bad day. In reality, self-care on a financial level requires a holistic view of spending, saving and investing in one's life and future, but it's easier in the moment to treat yourself and call it self-care. Again, no judgement here. Similarly, if spending is something newly available to you, it can act as self-care by healing wounds of being unable to afford things in the past.

If you're keen to do more deep work on your money habits directly, I'd love it if you read *Good With Money* once you've finished *The Wardrobe Project*.

 Intention unboxing: I want to buy because ... I can afford it, so why not?

Back on page 43 I talked you through my first exposure therapy trip where I'd seen things that I'd have considered buying if I'd had the money, and of course, if I weren't doing the challenge. I want to touch on that argument around being able to afford the clothes that we lust over.

I'm no stranger to whacking an item of clothing on a credit card when I really shouldn't be spending. It was a mainstay of my spending behaviour prior to sorting my finances out. In fact, in my university days, I had a store card (which was like a credit card for shopping at that store specifically), and I used to put clothes on it on a Tuesday (because the best nights out were Tuesday and Wednesday) and then

---

(continued)

plan to pay it off on Thursday when I got paid by my waitressing job. Planned being the operative word. I didn't always.

When we're stuck in these buying cycles, the need to change is more obvious. We're spending money we don't have, we're actively causing ourselves financial distress and making life difficult for our future self for something as unimportant as an outfit. In this situation, the incentive to change is much stronger.

But what happens when the money we're spending isn't putting us into debt? It isn't causing much financial stress, if any. Maybe, if we're lucky, it's not even taking away from our savings goals. What then?

I've worked with many women on their clothing consumption, all of them at different points on that financial spectrum. Some had no savings or were even in debt. Some were doing okay: they were still saving and/or investing and their clothing consumption wasn't sending them into debt. And some earned bloody good money and could genuinely afford the clothes they were buying without compromising on saving or investing or affording their living costs. With the latter two examples, I often ran into this same resistance.

I can afford it, so why not?

You might have even had this thought while reading this book. If I can afford the clothes I'm buying, does it really matter?

Good question. *Does it?*

Well, yeah, it kinda does. And I don't say that in a judgy way whatsoever. If you're reading this book, I'm willing to bet you've felt like you're stuck on the wardrobe treadmill just like I have. Maybe you relate to some of the identity challenges I've shared with you so far. Maybe you're sick of buying that perfect thing only to still be tempted by the next shiny thing. Maybe you still feel like you have nothing to wear despite staring into a full wardrobe. Those emotional cycles are exhausting. That's why it still matters. That's why being able to afford it isn't enough. Because you deserve better.

Has buying clothes ever really met your needs in the way you want it to? Has buying more ever got you to feel like you have enough? More isn't the answer to the confidence and joy we crave.

On top of that, I know I promised this wasn't a sustainability book, but this feels like as good a time as any to remind ourselves of the sinister context surrounding the clothes we consume. Clothes are often manufactured in horrific working conditions, workers aren't paid anywhere near a living wage, supply chains enable countless human rights abuses, and our overconsumption of clothing is killing the planet. In fact, according to The California Public Interest Research Group:

- we have enough clothes on the planet to clothe the next six generations
- 30 per cent of the clothing we produce isn't even sold, it's thrown away
- for every piece of clothing we bought in the year 2000, we now buy four
- 65 per cent of clothing is thrown out within 12 months of purchase.

When it comes to sustainability, the most sustainable outfit you have is one you already own.

In a Zalando study from 2021, Anna Granskog, a partner at McKinsey & Company, said:

If the global average lifetime of clothing increases from three to four years — closer to the upper end of the average lifetime currently — it would reduce emissions substantially.

(continued)

So while there's a lot to learn in terms of sustainable production, and a lot to unlearn in our current buying behaviour, you can still do something sustainable right now by wearing something you already have.

Reading about the fashion industry's impact on climate breakdown is a sobering reality check that'll probably flood your mind the next time you clap eyes on a cardigan from H&M or a jacket advertised to you on Instagram. But I'm in the business of human behaviour. I've made a career out of obsessing over why we do the things we do, why we act irrationally with our money and how we can change our behaviour. That's why I know that, on the whole, guilt, shame and anxiety-inducing statistics don't actually work long term. It works a bit, don't get me wrong. It's probably enough to get you to close your browser before checking out on that H&M cardigan. Maybe it'll even get you to swear off Forever 21 or Shein or Temu. But it's probably not enough, on its own, to contend with the deep emotional and psychological ties we have to the fashion industry as we know it.

The attitude-behaviour gap

An attitude-behaviour gap captures the human experience of holding a certain set of beliefs, attitudes or intentions regarding an issue, but failing to behave in a way that reflects those attitudes wholly and completely. We touched on this earlier on page 75 when exploring the connection between what we think we buy and what we actually buy, but it's extremely relevant when looking at the human behaviour around sustainable fashion.

The Sustainable Fashion Forum collated research from the aforementioned Zalando study from 2021, which captured some important snapshots of where these gaps are manifesting (which you can see illustrated on the following page).

60% of survey respondents said transparency is important to them

20% actively seek out information on a company's sustainability practices as part of the purchasing process

53% believe ethical labour policies are important

23% investigate what those policies are

58% believe they should understand the product, including the materials

38% regularly check the label for information

25% regularly buy second-hand

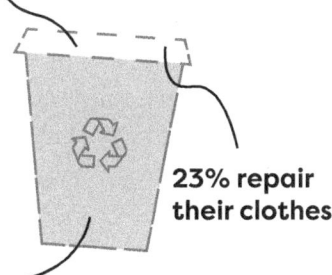

23% repair their clothes

60% of consumers say repair, second-hand and sustainable disposal are important to them

During the Project, I connected with sustainable fashion advocate and stylist Jenna Flood. Jenna was also doing her own year without buying clothes, so we shared a mutual newfound love of saying 'no, thank you' to clothes that tempted us. Jenna mostly shops from sustainable brands and second-hand stores, but still felt she wasn't consuming sustainably. Working in slow fashion gave her such an interesting perspective on her breakup with clothing consumption, and I want you to hear from her about the juxtaposition between the sustainability of the items she was buying and her actual consumption behaviour.

> *Jenna:* I decided to do a wardrobe freeze as I felt I was spending too much money on clothing. I was also working in a consignment-style store and I was buying and selling my clothing constantly. I was caught in a cycle I didn't know how to escape. It didn't feel sustainable anymore and so I wasn't really practising what I preached. I also saw Kate Hall, founder of Ethically Kate, doing a wardrobe freeze. When she first started doing that I was like, 'oh that's something I can never ever do'. But as she progressed through her year, I was like, 'okay, maybe I should start to think about this!'

> *Q: You're a big advocate for slow fashion and ethically made fashion. Do you think buying from sustainable brands/second-hand stores is enough, or do you think there's a human behaviour component as well?*

> *Jenna:* While it's fantastic to change where we buy our clothing from, shopping from ethical or preloved stores instead of fast fashion, we still need to consider what we are *actually* buying. We can overconsume in both places. When I first discovered ethical/slow fashion, I began to buy heaps of items from ethical fashion brands. I thought I was doing the right thing. I had replaced nearly all my wardrobe with these 'better' garments. But after discovering how much money I was spending, I realised that the best way would have been to just keep wearing what I already owned and replace what I needed with an ethical alternative. I thought my behaviours had changed, but in reality, I was still

using slow fashion like fast fashion. Buying, selling, buying again, selling again. My wardrobe was churning at a fast-fashion speed. It wasn't until later that I realised I had to change my behaviours rather than what I was buying.

It can be hard to reverse the need to buy. It was part of the reason I did the freeze; I was hoping to reset the need to consume. I wanted to better align my values with my consumption habits again. I did find my freeze really valuable in helping to do that but it does take a while to change those habits. I found that stepping back and giving myself space to think about the item or just to say 'no' (in the wardrobe freeze year) helped me to reset and re-examine my values.

I really do think there is the danger of overconsumption when it comes to the sustainability mindset and shopping second-hand. Many people overconsume because it is second-hand and obviously because it's cheaper as well. They will usually overconsume and buy more than they actually need.

I have seen this in action. I have seen people load up their carts in op shops and heard people say, 'oh, it doesn't matter, it's pretty cheap, I'll just buy it anyway and then re-donate if I don't like it or it doesn't fit'. I don't think that's the best mindset to have when buying clothing from anywhere because that's when you get stuck in an overconsumption cycle. Your wardrobe starts to fill up and you begin to have nothing to wear, essentially, even though you have a full wardrobe.

I think other methods where you can get 'free' or cheap clothing in the sustainable space also encourage people to potentially overconsume, unfortunately. Events like clothing swaps are susceptible to this. People want to get their value worth, even though it's likely a free event. I do feel this mindset at times, too. The feeling of not wanting to miss out because you didn't get a fair trade for your item or you might miss out on the good stuff. I love clothing swaps and encourage them to happen more, but we just need to be aware of what we actually need.

I do think that other sustainable activities like mending, renting, making clothing, upcycling clothing etc, aren't as susceptible to overconsumption due to the cost of time. It's hard to overconsume an item that can take a week to make!

Q: Do you think there is a gap between people's sustainability intentions and their actual actions?

Jenna: I do think there is a gap between people acting on their sustainability intentions and what they actually do in real life. It takes a lot of time and effort and, sometimes, money to act in a sustainable way, to buy ethically made items or to find the items second-hand—and sometimes we just don't have that time, effort and money. And in those cases, I think it's fair to take the easy way and to save ourselves the time and money to be honest. Even though I personally try my hardest to be sustainable in all areas of my life, sometimes it's just not possible. The cost is also a huge factor. Fast fashion is extremely cheap and sometimes we just can't afford the ethically made option.

It is also very hard to change your mindset to only seek out sustainable options. It's hard to change your habits. If you're used to shopping from a certain place, then you will automatically think about shopping from there. But when you start to change your habits in a sustainable way, it can take a while for your mindset to change. It can take a while for those habits to settle in so you may act on autopilot and head to where you should shop instead of seeking out a second-hand store.

Follow Jenna on Instagram at @ironicminimalist

Maximising my wardrobe

Given we've just talked about the most sustainable outfit being the one you already own, I thought it a good time to share some of the creative ways I've started maximising, customising or reimagining items to get more out of my clothes.

Wearing dresses as skirts

If you have a dress, you have a skirt, my friend. Just take a jumper or even a shirt over the top of your dress, and use a belt to bring in the waist to create the illusion of a skirt. This is also a stellar strategy for when trying to travel light.

Dyeing clothes

Honestly, if I've got a free Sunday and a twinkle in my eye, I'm mere minutes away from browsing the Dylon website. I love a dye project, and it's such a fun way to reimagine something you already have, correct a past purchase mistake or bring something back to life.

Dylon and Rit are both great fabric dye brands, and you can do a stovetop or washing machine dye job. I've revived old jumpers that were fading, rectified terrible colour decisions by dying a green dress black and finally turning it into something I'll reach for, and even embraced trending colours without having to buy anything new.

Changing the buttons

There's nothing like a browse of a button shop to get the creative juices flowing. I've recently got into switching up the buttons on otherwise simple pieces, like a black blazer, to make the item more personal to me, and to lean further into my espresso con panna style with bold elements. Buttons are also easy to change up, so you

(continued)

can completely reinvent the vibe of an item with a quick change of buttons.

Cropping, hemming, altering

If something wasn't right with a piece of clothing during the Project year, I couldn't just run out and buy something new — so I got comfortable thinking outside the box when it came to creating the looks I wanted.

Whether you learn to sew yourself or you find yourself a good local tailor, embracing alterations to your clothes can breathe new life into older pieces, and stop you always reaching for new every time something isn't quite right. You can change the lengths of things, turn longer jackets or tops into cropped versions, or bring in areas of your clothes to better match your body shape. Plus, you can often leave that excess fabric in the garment to let out later if you need to. YouTube has tons of tutorials if you want to give things a go yourself.

Accessories

I've always been a chronic under-appreciator of accessories, but the Project taught me the value of mixing up outfits with different accessories and creating different shapes and silhouettes with different extras. I allowed myself to purchase accessories during the year for this very reason. I was lucky I didn't go crazy — it would've been easy to overconsume on belts and bags because they were 'allowed', but I was really mindful and only bought a couple of things, like a cross-body bag and a scarf — both of which are still in my wardrobe now and are very well loved!

Stopping and considering my outfits more rather than rushing ahead to the excitement of new pieces or parcels arriving finally gave me the space to see the role of accessories in creating the looks I wanted.

Chapter summary

∞ Choosing a conceptual style anchor can help you find your style in a way that's truly unique to you and your perception.

∞ It serves a patriarchal, capitalist society for us to keep buying our way to feeling good—deciding to step back is a radical act of resistance.

∞ Buying clothes brings psychological relief from problems temporarily, but that feeling is misattributed to thinking that clothes are a real solution.

∞ When we feel like we have enough, we can open the door to feeling like we are enough.

∞ Overdressing, looking at images of yourself more often, neutralising negative thoughts, and straight up telling yourself you look fucking fantastic is a great way to find confidence within yourself—without the need for new clothes!

∞ Ask people who love you for an indication of what they think looks great on you.

∞ Spending is more than just a transaction or a frivolous treat. There's often a strong psychological comfort zone there that makes it harder to break out of because of the emotional relief it brings. But don't worry—it is possible!

AUGUST

The holiday and the three-year-old bikini

You don't go to work every day just to have a wardrobe full of clothes you don't even like.

August was a big month for me. I'd submitted the manuscript for my first book, *Good With Money*, that I'd been working morning, noon and night to finish, and I'd booked myself a week away in the Whitsundays with a friend (and without my laptop), a stack of trashy novels loaded onto my Kindle, and my three-year-old bikini. (Yes, I'd resisted the urge to go and buy new beachwear, and for that I expect a monument to be erected in my honour.)

The holiday was my first relaxing sun, beach and poolside holiday in years, so I was excited to spend the week in a bathing suit, the smell of sunscreen hot in my nostrils, alternating between glasses of crisp rosé and Coke Zero, and going hard on the hotel buffet.

But holidays and travel often present a tricky situation. Why do I want to buy an entire new wardrobe before I go away somewhere? Why is the allure of a new pair of sunglasses, a new hat, a new pair of sandals, new swimwear and maybe a nice dress to slip on for dinner so damn strong?

I saw a video on social media recently that said:

What was the most expensive part of your holiday?

The week before.

The video showed clips of the creator buying new clothes, accessories, luggage and performing all manner of ablutions from leg waxing to manicures.

It's a comedic look at how we prepare for travel, but once again, it tells an important story about the way we view consumption as a component of a broader experience. Buying up a whole raft of new things before a trip can come down to a few things:

∞ wanting to experience the holiday early

∞ feeling like we want to be a certain version of ourselves on holiday

∞ having an idea in our heads of how we want the experience to look

∞ feeling insecure about how we'll look while travelling.

The lead-up to travel is an example of what I call a spending runway, which is a very specific but financially dangerous behavioural pattern worth watching out for. Let me tell you a bit more.

Spending runways

A spending runway is the type of spending where one purchase acts as an instigator for a series of associated purchases. You buy one thing that leads to another and another and another, the spending behaviour gaining momentum each time you make another purchase, and making another even more likely.

Going on holiday is one of the most common spending runways people tell me about. They'll go out to get some sunscreen and maybe a hat that they genuinely need, and end up buying a new poolside cover-up, a bikini, a pair of sandals, three pairs of shorts and some protein powder for the diet they'll put themselves on when they get back.

Here are some other runways that might feel familiar.

The special event runway

You go out to buy a dress or outfit for something specific, and you end up buying the accessories, the jewellery, the bag and the shoes to go with it to complete the outfit.

The new season runway

You pop out to grab a couple of winter staples, and end up leaving with a coat you saw on sale, a pair of boots and a ski jacket in case you find yourself in Val d'Isère.

The fantasy self spending runway

Ah … our good friend the fantasy self is back again. Yep, she can put you on a spending runway too. If you find yourself buying an item that makes you feel like you're embodying your fantasy self, you're often more likely to buy other things related to that to extend the feeling and broaden your chances of achieving the outcome you want.

The 'it's a really good sale' runway

I've lost count of the number of times I've been caught out by this one. You're browsing a website that has a really good sale — like, really good. Pieces that usually cost over $100 are down to $30 or $40. You're high on the savings, and you feel like you've won the jackpot. Suddenly, the one item you were considering buying has evolved into a full cart and you're counting down the seconds until you can tear that package open.

The second-hand treasure hunt runway

Thrifters, this one's for you. You know how it goes. You're having an absolute corker at the thrift store or second-hand marketplace like Depop or Vinted, and the gems just keep on coming. Each thrill leads to a hunger for the next, and you feel completely unable to walk away from the treasure you keep uncovering. Before you know it, you're left trying to fit it all into your wardrobe and wondering when you'll wear the cat-print skirt that you couldn't walk away from.

∞ ∞ ∞

The key to spending runways is interception. Being able to spot when you're on one, or at risk of ending up on one, can help your rational brain step in and get you to walk away. The thing to watch out for is momentum. When is one purchase leading you to another and another and another? Are you feeling a 'fuck it' mentality creeping in? Do you feel yourself surrendering and vowing to deal with the consequences later? If you feel that domino effect start to take hold, remove yourself from the situation. Get what you need, and get out! It can feel hard at the time, but once you return to a more rational headspace, you'll thank yourself.

There's so much more to life and money than clothes

A hard pill to swallow is that there's just more to life and to money than clothes. I always tell people, you don't go to work every day just to have a wardrobe full of clothes you don't even like.

Take our holiday spending runway, for example. Rationally, we know that that money would be better spent on the experience of the holiday itself, but our emotional relationship with buying clothes is an extension of the way we view the trip.

Deconditioning ourselves from clothing consumption isn't easy — we know by now how emotional it is, and we know why it feels so good. But there's a level of self-respect that comes from reducing your clothing consumption so you can free up money for other things, and give yourself that space to have and be enough. For me, changing my relationship with clothes was about letting go of years of beliefs about myself, about money and about clothes themselves. I'll talk more about those beliefs on page 159, but for now, I want to take you through some of the things that have shifted my spending attention away from clothes and onto more meaningful things in my life.

Liking doesn't have to mean buying

The Project and everything I took from it brought back the possibility of liking without wanting. I grew up in the 90s, and came of age in the 00s when the internet was nothing more than a clunky question mark that existed inside those big box computers that only had about three functions (one of them being Solitaire, of course). Online shopping didn't exist, and our proximity to stuff was so much further removed.

I lived in a small town, so my exposure to the 'cool' shops with the 'cool' clothes rarely happened. If I saw something I liked, whether on someone else or in a magazine, that was where the story ended. No scan to shop, no tap for links, no pesky remarketing following me around for the rest of the week.

Now, of course, it's pretty impossible to avoid the latter part—the internet, and now social media, is deeply embedded in our lives. I wouldn't be writing this book if it weren't. But the part where we admire without immediately entering a decision about whether to consume—that part we *can* cultivate.

Don't get me wrong, it's hard. The world has become shoppable, but that means there's no relief from all of the emotions that come with shopping. That mental peace I told you about right at the beginning of the Project? That comes down to the clutter that's removed from your mind when you don't dance with the purchase-driven decision-making that's asked of us on a daily basis.

Pay attention to how easily you consider consuming, and the distance between seeing something and owning it. Notice how your entire focus can be hijacked by the allure of something you didn't know existed five seconds ago.

I was once watching an episode of *MasterChef Australia*, and I saw one of the hosts wearing an incredible maxi dress. I pulled out my phone and, for the first time ever, used Google Lens. Google Lens allows you to reverse image search an item in a photograph. Basically, it detects the item you've taken a photo of, and searches for identical or similar versions of that item via online stores. It's really quite remarkable.

So I uploaded the photo to Google Lens and in less than three seconds I had a list of four or five retailers selling this dress. I couldn't believe it. In the space of a minute, I'd gone from watching a cooking show to feeling like I wanted to drop $250 on a dress. It was so interesting to observe, within the safety of the Project, just how easily my state changed. From watching a comfort show, to admiring someone's outfit, to being three clicks away from owning it.

Of course, being eight months into the Project gave me the advantage of being in a default state of 'no', so I shut my laptop and got back to yelling at the telly for someone to plate up their red wine jus. But I'd be lying if I didn't feel resistance in that moment, as though it was almost muscle memory that liking could lead to buying.

At that moment, I could almost see the two outcomes of my behaviour playing out like a movie in my head. In one version, I add the dress to my cart, punch in my card details and check out. In the other, I take a breath, think to myself 'that's a nice dress, but liking doesn't have to mean having', and close the tab.

I thought about the version where I do buy the dress. What would I have given up with that decision? That $250 could have been:

∞ an incredible meal out somewhere fancy with nice wine
∞ a night in a new hotel I'd had my eye on
∞ freedom from the financial stress of needing a new tyre
∞ two visits to my incredible osteopath when I throw my back out
∞ a session with my psychologist
∞ a flight to visit a friend or visit a new city
∞ a spontaneous 'let's go this weekend' when a friend texts me about a new movie or exhibition
∞ 50 coffees at my favourite cafe along my walking route
∞ five visits to the infrared sauna
∞ so much fabric for sewing projects!

When I thought about what my impulsive decision would cost me beyond just the numbers, the stakes were suddenly so much higher. By finding something that meant so much more to me than clothes, I was able to intercept that craving to buy clothes and neutralise it with something else. The hunger for clothes is a fire burning, and thinking about those other things extinguishes that flame, calms everything down, and halts the see-want-buy sequence that we're so programmed to repeat.

In those moments, when we're emotionally flooded, filled with all the fandangled ideas of how this dress is going to change our lives, and the promise of dopamine hangs in the air, we have an opportunity. Give into the quick hit, or bring to mind all the other things that money could be spent on. This financial behaviour technique can help counteract the emotional pull of the clothes we want to buy, and help bring the more rational part of our mind back into the mix.

Task: Establish your 'benchmark' spend

I want you to spend some time thinking about what your 'benchmarks' could be when you next find yourself tempted to buy clothes. How much do you tend to spend when you shop for clothes, not just on each individual item, but per order or trip to the shops?

If you often chuck a few things in your cart and check out at $100, what else could that $100 be spent on? Brainstorm a list and keep adding to it as you think of things.

Then, next time you feel that familiar urge to buy new clothes, bring each of those things to mind and give context to the decision you're about to make.

This technique effectively exposes you to the consequences of your spending, which we so often override when making impulsive decisions. It breaks you out of 'now' thinking and helps you enter 'future' thinking.

Values-based spending

Values-based spending is something I talk about a lot in my first book, *Good With Money*, as a way of calibrating healthier spending habits and a healthier relationship with money. When we're breaking down a behavioural pattern like clothing consumption, working on understanding what we truly value can be extremely helpful.

You might have told yourself in the past that clothing is something you value. You might have told yourself you just love fashion or you love buying new clothes to wear—and, hey, that might be true. But if you've got this far into this book, I'll guess that your love of clothes isn't serving you all that well. There's a difference between a love of clothes and a love of consuming. And even when we do love clothes, we can still get stuck in the trap of buying the wrong things. Sigh. Why is nothing ever easy?

I'm willing to bet that there are far better uses for your money than the current way you're buying clothes. That's where values-based spending comes in. It's all about redirecting the money that's being gobbled up by spending traps, dopamine-hunting and that pesky fantasy self, and redistributing it into things that actually add to your life. Don't worry, there's still room for clothing purchases in values-based spending. The difference is you're in control, not the other way around.

Task: Understanding your spending values

When we understand what we value spending our money on, we can better align our decisions to those things and have more of what we truly want, and less of what we're told to want. I sometimes refer to this work as raising your 'money standards'. A bit like in dating when you decide to stop ignoring red flags and tolerating patchy communication—you're raising your standards. It's the same with money. You're ditching meaningless dopamine hits and sale bargains that don't quite fit properly, and raising your standards to allow for more of what matters.

Think of three of the best things you've ever spent money on. They can be experiences or material things—I'm not judging. Unsurprisingly, a lot of people bring to mind experiences here, which is telling. It's usually not their 16th pair of mid-wash denim jeans that comes to mind.

For each of the three things, write down words you associate with that spend. Be careful not to describe the thing or focus too much on the functions or logistics. I want to know how you feel about those things.

For example, let's say you're describing your sofa.

Instead of: It's a great colour and it's easy to clean and it looks good in my house.

Try: It makes me so happy because my family gather together there to get comfy for family movie night, and when I'm sitting on that sofa I feel so content and connected to my loved ones.

Or for a different perspective: Every time I walk into my home and see this sofa, I know I'm in my sanctuary of peace, calm and relaxation. I watch my favourite shows while snuggled up on it and it's my perfect 'me' space.

The first one shows values of family, togetherness and fun. The second one shows values of calm, peace, 'me time'. Same purchase, different values. Once you've done this for all three things, look for commonalities in your words. Themes that come up over and over again, or any similarities you notice, are all things to pay attention to. What you have in front of you is a range of things you value. That might be freedom,

(continued)

family, calmness, adventure, excitement, laughter, connection, self-care, luxury, ease, simplicity or friendship.

Understanding how money can be used to bring you more things aligned with your values can help you spend it more meaningfully. These values are strong enough and personalised enough to compete with that loud thrill we associate with clothing purchases.

Using your values to benchmark your clothing purchases can help you contextualise what you're giving up by buying more clothes. If $100 is half or a third of a night in a hotel, or the cost of a nice meal out with friends, or maybe a month's worth of having fresh flowers on your kitchen bench every Saturday, you're more likely to think before you add to cart.

Try condensing your values down into some smaller monetary chunks so you can train your brain to associate a clothing purchase at that price with what else it could be spent on. This creates a 'this or that' environment in your decision-making to highlight the ways your decisions to buy directly take away from things that matter to you.

Adding more variety to your spending

I speak to a lot of people who spend a high proportion of their disposable income on clothes. It's usually a combination of that pseudo joy we experience from buying new pieces, the novelty factor and the habitual pursuit of the perfect, complete wardrobe. As soon as there's money available, the first place they want it to go is on clothing.

On page 98, we talked about hedonic adaptation, and how adding more variety into your hedonic spending (as opposed to utilitarian spending) can help you outpace the natural adaptation and happiness flatline that we experience. This rings particularly true for those of you who relate to being stuck in the 'clothes-above-all-else' vortex.

It's worth noting here that you might not be in the vortex all the time. You might, at times, find some relief from the wardrobe treadmill, perhaps due to factors outside of your control such as higher expenses or a health challenge. But if you keep returning to this idea that more clothes will make you happy, you might benefit from finding value in spending on other things.

Take some time to zoom out and assess where your money goes, and what proportion of it goes on clothing compared to other categories. Using your values to direct your money to other things can help improve your overall happiness, allow you to feel like your money is being used as a resource to improve your life and, thus, reduce your reliance on always having more.

The 'yes, and?' method

I promised you there was still room for clothing spending even when spending in this values-aligned way, and there absolutely is. Primarily, we use these benchmarking methods to steer us away from those impulsive, mindless purchases by contextualising the consequences of those decisions.

But sometimes, there will be things you do want to buy. Those 'greatest hits' items we talked about on page 18 have to get into our possession somehow! So how does values-based spending fit into the equation?

I call this the 'yes, and?' method. When you've found something that's bulldozing through your benchmarking techniques and you're left thinking 'yeah, I really do want this', you can use your values as a sense check.

By saying 'yes' to the piece of clothing, you then ask 'and?' to consider your values. Yes, I love this piece of clothing, I don't think it's a mindless spend, and I want to hand over my money for it — and, how does it sit alongside my values?

If your values are ease and comfort, you might ask: Is it actually comfortable? Does it make getting dressed easy?

If your values are travel and adventure, you might ask: Would I pack this on my next trip? Does this match my ideal day exploring?

If your values are connection, fun, and joy, you might ask: Am I excited to wear this to my next social gathering? Does this colour or style make me feel joyful?

The 'yes, and?' method acknowledges and respects the desire you're feeling for the item, and then makes sure it fits with where your money is really best spent, rather than taking away from things that matter more to you.

Buying clothes is its own unique beast because we need to consider the financial implications and the wardrobe implications. Both of these things can carry an emotional load, making these assessments much more complicated.

These techniques we've just covered speak to the financial side. We're looking at where your money is going, where your money is best used and where we can redistribute your money better in your life.

The style side requires its own set of criteria, so we can assess not just what you're spending, but the item you're buying, too. Later, I'll teach you how to use everything you've learned in this book to consolidate a toolkit for mindfully adding to your wardrobe using three things:

∞ Your style code
∞ Your style concept
∞ Your style standard

Understanding your buying decisions

Ultimately, many of our wardrobe purchase mistakes come down to rushed decision-making. That doesn't necessarily always mean we bought the item impulsively, but we've rushed through the careful thought that should be going into the clothes we buy. Maybe we rushed ahead to the idea of looking like our fantasy self. Maybe we rushed ahead to the idea that it's the missing piece in our wardrobe. Maybe we rushed ahead to a place or a context in which we wanted to wear that item. Maybe we rushed ahead to get the thrill of spending.

Slowing down is one of the best things we can do to reclaim control of our purchase decisions, and allows room for both our financial assessment and our style assessments to happen. Slowing down allows the emotional part of our mind to quiet down after it's been activated, and leaves room for our rational, more conscious mind to come back online and take the wheel. We make emotionally charged decisions after a bad day, or when we're chasing our fantasy self. Our more conscious decisions are those that factor in who we really are, what we really want, and where our time, money and energy is best spent.

When learning how to slow down, it can be helpful to understand the process you go through when you're buying, and how the cycle repeats itself.

The image here demonstrates the trap a lot of people get stuck in when emotionally consuming, and how clothing consumption in particular can become a cycle of repeating behaviour.

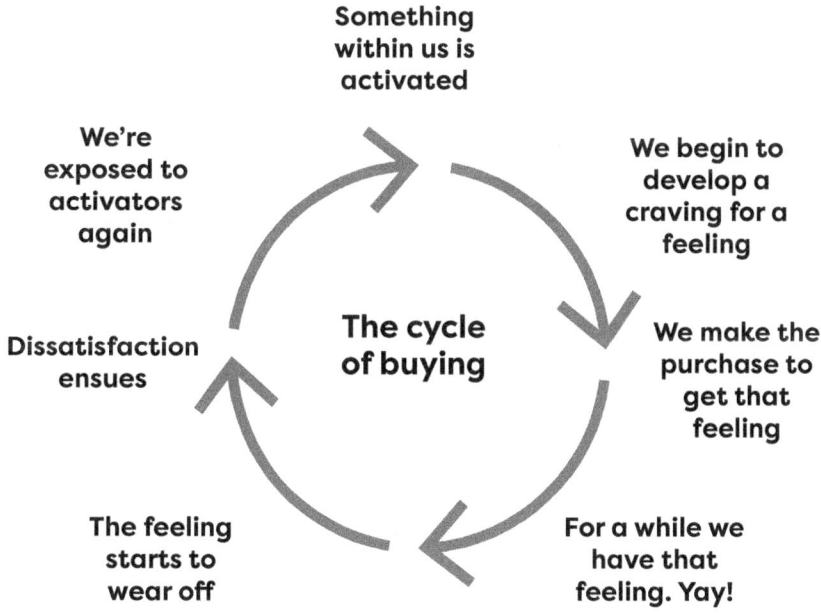

Something within us is activated

We're exposed to activators again

We begin to develop a craving for a feeling

The cycle of buying

Dissatisfaction ensues

We make the purchase to get that feeling

The feeling starts to wear off

For a while we have that feeling. Yay!

Something within us is activated. This is the trigger that moves us into purchase consideration mode. It can be anything from a bad day, to a negative thought about yourself or a social media comparison, to an exciting sale announcement or marketing email.

Then we begin to develop a craving for a feeling. This might be happening consciously or subconsciously, but the more you pay attention to what happens before you buy clothes, the more conscious this craving will become. This is the part where we want to feel that confidence, or that dopamine hit, or that illusion of self-care, or like we're treating ourselves.

Then we make the purchase. We add to cart or head to the till, and all of a sudden the item is ours. For a short period of time, we have the feeling we've craved. We might feel excited to wear something that we think will bring us confidence. We might be enjoying that bit of dopamine after a doom scroll. We might be feeling triumphant that we've got something on an amazing sale.

Then all of that starts to slide away. Dopamine begins to drop immediately after we've made the purchase. That heightened emotional state starts to quieten down, and the positive feelings we were experiencing start to taper off.

If the item we've purchased doesn't meet the expectations we had for it, *we start to feel dissatisfied* at the gap between what we wanted to feel and what we actually feel. This is extremely common when we're buying for our fantasy self or buying to fill an emotional void, because the problem we're trying to solve simply can't be solved with a purchase.

When we're in that state of dissatisfaction, *we're far more vulnerable to being activated again*, and going through the cycle again. The problem is, instead of remembering that the clothes-buying behaviour didn't bring any long-term relief, our mind focuses on the instant benefit, which is what drives more clothing purchases as we try to find the thing that makes it last.

Task: Contextualise the cycle

I want you to start thinking about what this buying cycle looks like for you. What are those activators that get you wanting to buy clothes? What are the feelings you're craving? How do you feel afterwards in the short term, and how do you feel as time goes on?

Draw out the below matrix and fill it in with as many observations as you can. Feel free to add to your lists each time you recognise a new feeling or experience. Then, next time you're buying or tempted to buy, ground yourself in this cycle and watch it play out. Observing your own behaviour without judgement is a great way to recognise the ways it's not serving you.

Activators	Feelings you crave from buying
Environmental/circumstantial activators (e.g., pre-holiday spending runway, bad day at work, lead-up to an event) Emotional activators (e.g. bad body image day, comparison, dopamine-seeking)	Excitement, confidence, satisfaction, relief, avoidance etc.
How you feel immediately after a purchase	**How you feel one week later**
Happy, giddy, anticipating wearing the item and experiencing confidence	I've forgotten about the purchase altogether, the excitement has worn off, regretful

So much of our clothing consumption happens on autopilot. We're scrolling and we tap a link. We're quickly adding to cart

(continued)

during a sale period and then getting back to work. We're grabbing something two days before an event.

When we can increase our consciousness around those purchases, we can better understand what's going on and slow down to consider whether we're behaving in a way that's helping us or harming us.

Slowing down your purchase decisions

Slowing down is all about creating speedbumps to halt your existing behavioural patterns.

Here is a flow you can use next time you find yourself hurtling towards a clothing purchase you may later regret.

∞ **Take a breath.** This is your moment to pause and begin the interception process. Ask questions. Do I really want this? Am I on a spending runway? What am I feeling here?

∞ **Stack it up.** How does this purchase compare to other things I could spend this money on? Use your benchmarking techniques from page 139 to quantify what you'd be giving up.

∞ **Create space.** Give yourself a time obstacle between you and the purchase. Some ideas include:

• Choose a set buying day. Schedule a day in the future to buy the item if it's still on your mind. There's a good chance it won't be.

• Save up double. Set yourself a challenge to save up double the cost of the item before you can buy it.

• Attach a reward. Use the item as an incentive to get yourself to do something you want to do; for example, buy the item when you've finished a big piece of work.

∞ **Rely on the 'default no'.** Earlier we discussed being in that default state of 'yes'. Activate your default state of 'no' by walking away knowing you can come back to the purchase again once you've had time to think about it.

Real people

Unpacking cycles of emotional behaviour can be vulnerable, especially when it comes to spending. Let's hear from some of our friends of the Project, who have so generously shared some of the emotions embedded in their relationship with clothes.

Rebecca

'Buying clothes was always an attempt to raise my self-worth.'

I love clothes and probably always will. In the past, even when buying the items that turned out to be mistakes, I felt euphoric at the time. Here was an item that I was going to feel so cool in! But, so often, that feeling soon crashed. Something happened between the changing room and the mirror in my own home. I'd think I looked great (or even simply acceptable) in the shop then later at home think 'WTF, you look ridiculous' or whatever negative thought came into my head. Then I would feel bitter disappointment, guilt and I despised myself that little bit more.

Olga

'Fashionable clothing was a manifestation of my lifestyle and status.'

A lot of my previous purchases were made out of an emotional desire to blend in or show off. For me, fashionable clothing was a manifestation of my lifestyle and status, even if it was more like a fantasy self version of both. And, to be completely honest, I still have a bit of that desire now, but at least it doesn't affect me that much in terms of money and emotion.

Previously (and especially during the COVID lockdowns), online shopping for clothes was my means of expecting at least something good from the future. Waiting for a parcel and then unboxing it felt like treating myself when the whole world was (and, to a degree, still is) a huge mess. 'I don't know what happens to the world tomorrow, but at least I have a delivery scheduled, and that's already a lot!' So I felt a little bit of relief when yet another parcel arrived. I needed more to keep feeling grounded (even if I didn't have a chance to actually wear these clothes out much).

Lizzie

'My number-one motivator for buying clothes was to re-gain control of a situation.'

Shopping has been a way for me to make sense of emotions, and help me regain control in a particular aspect of my life. While it is often a bandaid solution (funnily a new item of clothing doesn't fix your worries), it does provide enough to help me manage my own thoughts and emotions. A huge reason for a lot of my shopping is the dreaded fluctuation of weight, something I would say resonates with a lot of women who grew up in the 90s/00s. Plus, on top of that I have PCOS [polycystic ovarian syndrome], which makes it very easy to gain weight (in my instance).

There'd be times where you have to buy new clothes because clothes felt less comfortable or were no longer flattering — or in the opposite vein, if I lost weight, I'd like to celebrate that loss with a tangible outcome (e.g., celebratory shopping).

Before I started working on this, my number-one motivator for buying clothes was to regain control of a situation — positive or negative. It would be a bandaid to give me a hit of dopamine to feel good. Sometimes, there would be shopping expeditions where I legitimately didn't care what I bought, I just wanted to spend money (and often not money I had — enter credit card or buy now, pay later). Often these would result in purchases I regretted, or I had justified at the time for the dopamine, but in reality, did not need or work for my wardrobe.

Amy

'I often feel like I'm in a "before" state.'

My purchase behaviour was very much driven by fear of missing out. I didn't want to miss out on a viral, cult, must-have item. I'd get so invested in chasing the high of securing it and the emotional fuel that that gave me became quite addictive. I wanted to stay up-to-date and not stuck in what I worried was 'outdated fashion'. If there was a new trend and I liked it, I would jump on it, whether I really needed it or not. I was very much driven by not wanting to get left behind.

A whole spectrum of emotions are linked to the way I buy clothes. It makes me feel super buzzy and excited when I'm buying and then often disappointed when things arrive. I've gained weight since COVID that I've never lost, and I often feel like I'm in a 'before' state (before I get my old body back). I still shop for my size 8 body and then I feel deflated when the clothes arrive and don't make me look several dress sizes smaller. I also feel a lot of shame about the money I have wasted in the past, but I remind myself that I've come a very long way in a year and I still have growth ahead of me.

Jo

'I bought what looked good on others and hoped I would look as nice as them.'

Buying clothes would make me feel better in the short term. But I had no clear idea what would look good on me. I bought what looked good on others and hoped I would look as nice as them—fantasy self! I wasn't aware of my body shape, my colours, how clothes could be styled to suit my body...Also, being part of Facebook groups and online communities focused on buying and fashion meant I bought more as I was getting my validation from those groups. While they were supportive and kind, no-one ever tells you when something really doesn't suit you! And these people made money from selling clothes for brands. So, I did amass quite the wardrobe of clothes, but I still wasn't feeling entirely how I wanted to feel: confident, stylish, unique, good enough...

I learned about body types, colours, styles, patterns etc. that I could apply to myself through trial and error. Eventually, I developed my style to where I wanted it to be, but I was still buying a tremendous amount of clothes, spending approximately NZD$1000 per month.

I came to realise that, although I had satisfied myself, I was still trying to satisfy someone else who I knew would never be satisfied, and who I didn't need to try and please anymore. It helped me let go of focusing on my ex-partner, and shift to really acknowledging and appreciating myself, and my growth.

Chapter summary

- ∞ Spending runways represent the momentum of buying one thing and that leading to another and another. These can be based on a certain environment, circumstance or emotion.
- ∞ There's so much more to life than clothes.
- ∞ Benchmarking other things to spend our money on can help activate our more rational decision-making and help us walk away from purchases.
- ∞ Values-based spending can remind us of where our money is best spent.
- ∞ The 'yes, and?' method can help us understand when a purchase is worth our money by referencing our values.
- ∞ Buying clothes becomes a cycle when there are unmet emotional needs. When clothes fail to meet our expectations, we're left vulnerable to more temptations in the future.
- ∞ Slowing down your purchase decisions involves taking a pause, recognising the behaviour, asking key questions, using benchmarking techniques and installing time delays.

SEPTEMBER
The rebellion

It really can't have been a coincidence that breaking the cycle of looking outside of myself for confidence happened to be what made me accept myself truly and completely.

September was an interesting month for the Project, as I was once again met with the beginning of a change of season as spring started to take hold. As anyone who lives in Melbourne will know, spring can be any manner of hot or cold. It's not uncommon to wake up to temperatures close to zero, and sit shuddering in your poorly insulated house, only to be tearing off layers by lunchtime because the temperature has climbed up above 20 degrees.

Nonetheless, I got to experience the benefit of referring back to my outfit album from earlier in the year. As I was faced with the prospect of warmer weather, my usual confusion was remedied by the fact I had a bank of outfits I knew I could reach for. Revolutionary! This made it so much easier to not take a shortcut by buying new stuff I'd see in stores. It was a timely reminder once again of how much of our desire for clothes can be remedied by simply knowing what we own. I can't remember what I ate for dinner last night most of the time, so it's no wonder I don't remember what I wore last summer. Taking steps to catalogue what you wear so you have outfits to refer back to is a really simple way to quell that inner fashion goblin that whispers to you to browse the new arrivals the second you can't find the top you were looking for.

However, September also brought me my greatest obstacle of the challenge so far: an event with a dress code. My mother-in-law was turning 60 and had decided to throw a 'sparkling 60' party that called for a sparkly outfit. Well, colour me stumped. I had nothing. Shit.

Not only did I have nothing appropriate, for the first time, I actually felt like I was missing out during the discussions of what everyone was wearing. There were quite a few sparkly pieces in stores at that time, and a quick Google search set off the flashing hearts in my eyeballs. It was really hard not to just buy something, especially given I had the perfect excuse.

I considered renting something as a workaround, so I didn't actually purchase but could still meet the dress code and get sparkly, especially since I'd been exploring adding in a little more sparkle to my style as I leaned into what I really wanted to express and embrace about myself. Unfortunately, rental options for plus-size gals aren't particularly extensive, so that was a dead end.

Instead, I decided to roll my sleeves up and make something! I secured some champagne-coloured sparkly fabric, stretchy to minimise fitting errors, and cut a pattern from a midi-dress I already owned. A lot of swearing, a lot of sweating, two visits to the osteopath from hunching over my machine and some very bungled stitching on the shoulder later, I had a dress!

While it was far from well-constructed, and I definitely heard some kind of tearing of the stitching when I sat down on the night, I was chuffed with myself. I'd met the dress code without breaking my Project, and I'd got creative along the way. Just call me Lorelai Gilmore. I've got to say, it felt pretty good to be engaging with a creative dress code outside of consuming, and it really opened my eyes to the ways in which we've been conditioned into the default setting of buying something whenever we don't have exactly what we need.

The default option: Buy something new

Whether it's an event with a challenging dress code, or a celebratory event where we want to look special, our default setting has gradually shifted into the 'buy' setting. Online shopping, endless new retailers popping up and fast-fashion giants dropping thousands of styles left, right and centre means it has become easier than ever to just buy something.

When we're already juggling the demands of modern life, living further away from work, working longer hours for less pay and, as women, usually doing substantially more than our fair share of the caring load for children and perhaps even parents, too, no wonder we reach for the easiest option.

When you think about it, the gradual worsening of our quality of life as the years go by actually lends itself to overconsumption. Sixty-five per cent of women I surveyed agreed that they browse clothes online when they're bored, procrastinating or doom scrolling. When we're tired, burned out, anxious about the state of the world, and trying to put in more hours than ever just to afford a basic standard of living, it's no wonder it feels more appealing to place an order of three different dresses than it is to dig out one we already have, get it dry cleaned and style it up with accessories. And because exploitative capitalism really likes to fuck with us, it's actually oftentimes *cheaper* to buy something new than to care for what you already have.

All this to say: it's not necessarily our fault that we're in this default state of buying, but it is our responsibility to get out of it.

To break down the habitual patterns we've been conditioned to fall into, and to decide that, while it might be cheaper to order that new dress with free shipping than to get one we already have dry cleaned, that doesn't mean it's the right thing to do — for us, for your wallet, for the people exploited by the fashion supply chain or for the environment.

Body acceptance, is that you?!

Towards the last few months of the Project, I coincidentally joined a gym again for the first time in probably five years. I'd been pretty terrible at moving my body ever since I fell and broke my foot in 2022, so I signed up to my local council gym.

I was a little reluctant to join, if I'm honest, because I've had a bit of a rocky history with diet and exercise. I've never been a sporty person, and in my early 20s, I had a few years where I had a really unhealthy relationship with eating and fitness. I became addicted to shrinking myself and would do back-to-back gym classes all while only eating 1200 calories a day.

Over time, I gradually regained all the weight I'd lost, and had to grapple with what it meant to not be praised for my weight loss anymore. I was extremely lucky that I managed to get out of that phase of my life and start enjoying food again, and slowly accept my body as it was. But, as for many people, the pandemic threw my body image into question again, and I gained a lot of weight very quickly thanks to my weekends spent devouring a cheeseboard and a bottle of red wine in my one-bedroom flat, and amassing a grand total of about 17 steps a day.

Despite my reluctance, I realised within a couple of visits that my intentions around exercise felt completely different to so many of my other experiences with fitness. For the first time in my life, I could genuinely say I wasn't going to the gym to lose weight. It felt so unbelievably freeing to be moving my body without checking how many calories I'd burned, or without any association with burning off my food.

Now, don't worry, this isn't one of those stories where I tell you that because I'd stopped trying to lose weight, the weight 'fell off' naturally. It didn't! I actually think I gained a kilo or two, based on what I weighed at the doctor's for an unrelated reason. I'm a chunky gal and I simply always will be.

But, for the first time, I really experienced true body acceptance — and I don't think it was a coincidence. I had started to notice that I had been feeling somewhat happier in myself throughout the Project, and the shift in how I felt about exercise made me really stop and notice the difference that not buying clothes had made.

Given my history of wishing clothes would make me look thinner, trying to look like other people and, ultimately, rejecting my body and all of its worth simply because it didn't look like the body I wanted — it really can't have been a coincidence that breaking the cycle of looking outside of myself for confidence happened to be what made me accept myself truly and completely.

As I started to tune in more to how I felt about my body, it felt like a weight had been lifted — ironically I *had* lost some 'weight', it just wasn't from my body.

I started to question the beliefs I'd been holding about clothes, particularly as they related to my body, and started a sort of sub-experiment to see if I could change those deeply held rules I'd been following.

If you grew up watching shows like *Next Top Model* and *What Not to Wear*, style rules and body types and 'fashion faux pas' have been baked into us for years. We've internalised everything from hiding your tummy to never wearing horizontal stripes, to identifying with our bodies as fruits like apple and pear.

But the biggest one of all was this: clothes must be *flattering*.

The 'flattering' lie

I hadn't realised how much I was holding on to the belief that my clothes must be flattering until it slapped me in the face during the Project. The slow and gradual acceptance I gained for my body, coupled with the lessons I was learning about why I'd buy certain things and why I was stuck in a cycle of buying things I didn't feel good in finally made it clear to me how much I had pedestalled the idea of looking slim. Most of the clothes I was drawn to I was either trying to:

∞ dress like a slim person

∞ accentuate my waist or my smallest areas

∞ conceal the 'worst' parts of myself, most notably my cellulite-ridden thighs, wobbly bum and lower stomach

Don't even get me started on how I'd hold out hope that one day I'd find jeans that would magically give me the illusion of a thigh gap.

Really, when we say something is *flattering*, we mean it's *slimming*. Of course, there are many ways something can flatter you, from being a great colour on you to being a really nice fit to having characteristics that reflect your personality or demeanour. But, really, if we're honest with ourselves, the word *flattering* has become synonymous with *slimming*.

In fact, digital magazine *Bustle* announced in 2018 that it would no longer use the world 'flattering'. The inclusive side of the fashion world has also stopped to take a cold, hard look at the dangerous narrative hiding behind the word—clearly, I'm late to the party on this discovery.

A piece by Fordham University Center for Ethics Education also covered the topic of flattering clothing, referencing the importance of body inclusivity in the movement towards ethical and sustainable practice in the apparel industry.

Ethical fashion is about more than sustainable materials and fair wages; it's about creating a culture of respect and inclusivity that empowers all bodies, regardless of their shape, size or appearance. This means moving beyond traditional concepts of 'flattering' clothing, which is rooted in a system that values some bodies over others. Instead, we should embrace the idea that clothing is a form of self-expression and personal choice—a celebration of our unique, beautiful and diverse bodies.

Back in the Project, fresh from a stair-climbing session at the gym, during which I listened to Taylor Swift's *1989* vault tracks on repeat, I was eager to try my new resistance to looking as thin as possible on for size.

I'd always had this belief that I had to cinch my waist in as much as I could if I wanted to look good. It's the smallest part of my body and I suppose it's the part of me that gives me proximity to thinness. That meant there were certain things in my wardrobe that I didn't wear often, or that I only wore one way, because I'd been struggling to wear them according to the 'flattering' rulebook.

If I ever wore jeans and an oversized shirt, I felt like I had to tuck the shirt in to accentuate my waist. That's the *rules*, right? As a person whose weight goes up and down by a few kilos, and can pack a belly if I'm nearing my period or if I've had my wicked way with a large roast dinner and a family box of Maltesers, sometimes wearing a jeans with a shirt tucked in is just simply uncomfortable. Yes, even if the jeans have stretch in them—trust me, I ditched 100 per cent cotton jeans many years ago along with MyFitnessPal.

After this specific gym session where I was feeling particularly fired up about the fact I'd been buying into the flattering lie for too long, I marched home, washed my hair, hoped my tomato-red face would neutralise, and put on a pair of cream jeans and a baggy striped shirt ... and left it untucked.

Gasp! A woman with thick thighs, hips that do not lie and no thigh gap hiding her one redeeming feature beneath an oversized shirt? Breaking news: a woman is comfortable. Alert the authorities.

It was a revelation. I went outside. I looked at myself in my window as I walked to my car. I turned to the side. The shirt fell down my back, skimming the tops of my thighs. My small waist was taking a day off from being the one thing aligning me to conventional body standards. I'll admit, for a second I thought 'oh god, I should at least tuck in the front'.

But I didn't. I went out with a baggy shirt over wide-leg jeans, and you know what? I felt great. It felt freeing. It felt like an extension of that mental peace I experienced at the beginning of the challenge, when the weight of 'wanting' was lifted and I just knew I wasn't buying. This felt like the next phase of that lightness, and I'm certain my withdrawal from my consumption habits were what got me to start letting go of the clutches of 'flattering'.

Dressing for comfort is powerful. Dressing in what *you* think looks good is even more powerful. Thin women can wear baggy shirts and not accentuate their waist, so why can't I? After that, I found the confidence to wear a baggy dress that I'd never wanted to wear because it didn't give me any 'shape', and I started wearing more of my shirts with flowy wide-leg trousers and embracing a whole new way to wear them. It gave me more mileage in my wardrobe that way, too. I could wear them tucked and formal or untucked and casual, and in both, look absolutely fine.

What a revelation.

Ten ways to dress for resistance

Dressing in a way that bucks the rules we've been bound by is a profound act of resistance, and I want to see us doing more of it! Here are ten ideas to weave into your wardrobe

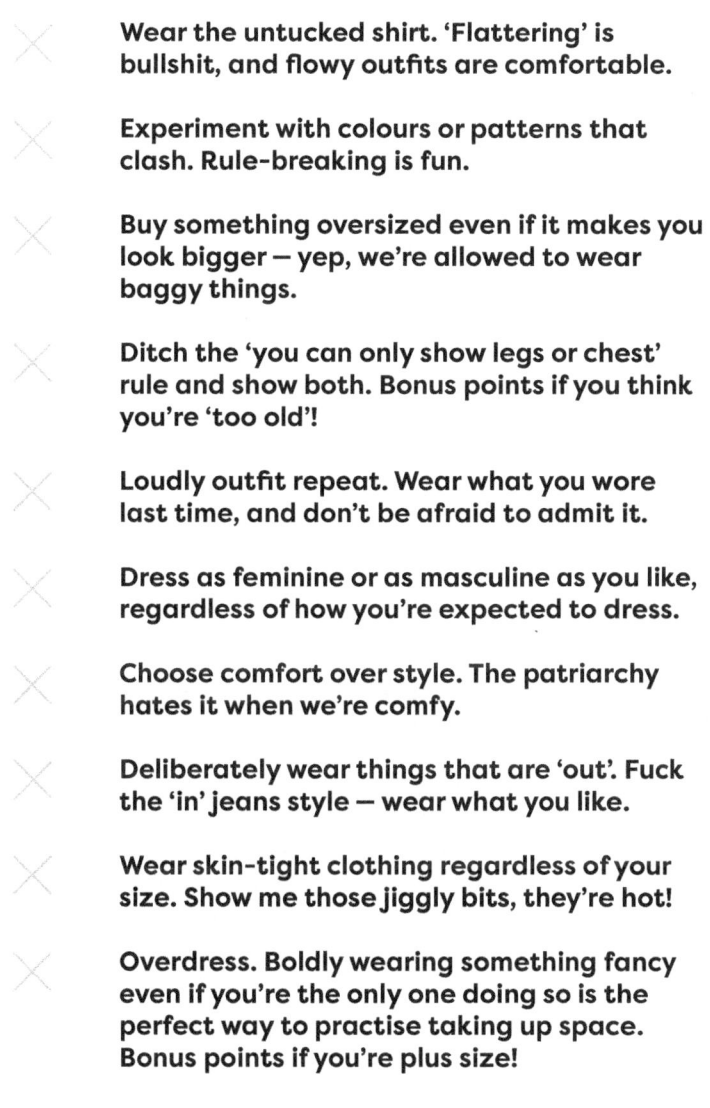

Wear the untucked shirt. 'Flattering' is bullshit, and flowy outfits are comfortable.

Experiment with colours or patterns that clash. Rule-breaking is fun.

Buy something oversized even if it makes you look bigger — yep, we're allowed to wear baggy things.

Ditch the 'you can only show legs or chest' rule and show both. Bonus points if you think you're 'too old'!

Loudly outfit repeat. Wear what you wore last time, and don't be afraid to admit it.

Dress as feminine or as masculine as you like, regardless of how you're expected to dress.

Choose comfort over style. The patriarchy hates it when we're comfy.

Deliberately wear things that are 'out'. Fuck the 'in' jeans style — wear what you like.

Wear skin-tight clothing regardless of your size. Show me those jiggly bits, they're hot!

Overdress. Boldly wearing something fancy even if you're the only one doing so is the perfect way to practise taking up space. Bonus points if you're plus size!

The weight of weight

Something that came up regularly when I talked about my Project on social media in real time was a question around weight fluctuations. A lot of people expressed to me that they couldn't do a period without buying clothes because they often change shape or size for various reasons. Weight (or perhaps, more accurately, size) plays an interesting role in the way we interact with clothes and, of course, the way we consume them. If our size goes up or down more than a couple of kilos or inches, there's a good chance the clothes we have won't fit anymore. Thus, there's a genuine need for new clothes.

I want to look a bit closer at the link between our weight and our wardrobes, particularly the way we behave differently around weight gain and weight loss. I speak from experience here when I say that, in the past, buying clothes after *losing* weight has been a significantly different experience to buying clothes after *gaining* weight.

When I've lost weight in the past, I've galloped out to the shops to buy things to fit me better, perhaps been excited about being able to fit into a smaller size, or finding that things sit differently on my smaller body.

When I've gained weight, though, and had to go and buy clothes to fit my bigger body, I've often given that process a lot less respect. We're conditioned by body standards and diet culture to view weight gain as a bad, bad thing. It's easy to internalise the idea that if you've gained weight, it has to be temporary and you must lose it again. I've had conversations with women about this in my social media community who have felt like they've been waiting to lose weight to be able to look good. In my 20s, I even bought into the 'I'll buy this and slim into it' vortex, where I'd buy an item that was too small with the belief that it would hold me accountable to lose weight until it fit. Please, if you're ever considering doing this, don't. Take it from me. It's not worth it.

Looking back, I bought much nicer clothes when I had lost weight compared to when I had gained weight, and was happier to be seen and take up space when I was smaller, but less so when I was bigger. It's almost as though I saw my slimmer body as something that should be held onto, and my fatter body as something that should be pushed away and rejected. Can we only 'take up space' if that space is smaller than an airplane seat?

Withdrawing from buying highlighted just how much I was using clothes to make peace with my body. When I was smaller, I celebrated that fact with clothes. When I was bigger, I tried to fix myself with clothes. Regardless of my size, the subtext was always the same: I'll like how I look if I have the right outfit. Removing the option to buy stripped back that deeply embedded belief. By no longer having the means to 'fix' my reflection in the mirror with clothes, my belief that I needed to be fixed started to fade away too. What I looked like hadn't changed at all—the way I saw myself was what changed.

I first learned that this was possible when I saw a video on social media that said something along the lines of:

If you look back at old photos of yourself at a time when you thought you were too big, but now realise you weren't at all, that's just proof that it was never about your size, it was about conditioning.

The photo hasn't changed. You just changed the way you saw yourself.

It's the same thing that happens when we're reminded of the vitriol celebrities used to get in magazines in the 90s and 00s. We'd thumb through pages and pages of photographs of women's bodies splashed across spreads like 'cellulite watch' or 'which popstars are piling on the pounds?'

Looking back now, there was nothing wrong with their bodies. Many of them are barely bigger than a size 10. The photos haven't changed; the way we see them has.

While realising just how warped our views on the way we look can be quite frightening, we can use this to our advantage. Just because we think something when we look in the mirror, doesn't make that thought true. The more we recognise that the way we see ourselves is completely fluid, the more we can flirt with the idea that, maybe, *we* get to decide how good we look.

Task: The Great Unfix

On page 117, I talked about neutralising negative thoughts that present when looking at a photo of yourself. That was your gateway. Now we're getting onto the hard stuff—mirror work. I call this 'The Great Unfix'. It's designed to get you to stop looking for things you want to fix about your body (and, by extension, your style) and allow yourself to just be.

If you haven't personally struggled with your weight or size when it comes to your style, you can still benefit from this exercise. It's not just about body hang-ups, it's about our whole self-image and style.

Step 1: Look in the mirror for one whole minute

Yep, set a timer and stare at your hot little reflection for 60 seconds. It will feel like an eternity, but it'll also remind you how infrequently you spend time looking at yourself.

Step 2: Write down or say out loud answers to the following prompts

- What thoughts came up about how I look?
- What feelings am I experiencing about the way I look?
- What things have I tried to change in the past?
- What parts of me have I considered not good enough in the past?

Step 3: Consolidate those thoughts into narratives you've been living by

Spending time looking in the mirror and reflecting on what we think and feel can present recurring narratives like:

- I'd look better if I was thinner.
- I'm too short to look stylish.

- This [item] doesn't look as good on me as it does on others.
- I shouldn't wear something this tight, it shows my stomach.

Then, rewrite or reframe each one into a series of more positive narratives. Some will be a gentle flip of language or intention. Others may require a completely new statement. For example:

- My body looks great in this.
- This fits me really beautifully.
- This colour really suits me.
- I'm really making this style my own.
- I love that I can see my powerful body in these clothes.
- I'm comfortable in this outfit so I will wear it with pride.

Try doing this once a week and observe how your thoughts start to change.

Weight-fluctuation-proofing your wardrobe

While a lot of the issue around sizing in our wardrobes is a mental game, as we've discussed already, there does remain a logistical challenge for those of us with fluctuating weight. If you are a multi-size baddie—that is, your size fluctuates up and down for whatever reason—that doesn't have to make it impossible to get dressed or feel comfortable in your wardrobe. There's plenty you can do to make your wardrobe work for you, without putting your body on trial all the time.

I'm right there with you. My weight tends to fluctuate, and the impact on my size and shape can make some of my tighter items of clothing more uncomfortable to wear if I'm a little bit bigger. Something I recognised during the Project was that some of my best-worn pieces in my wardrobe are those that are somewhat weight-fluctuation-proof. It wasn't something I'd consciously cultivated, but there were several things I noticed that made certain parts of my wardrobe instantly have more longevity because they could fit me across a couple of sizes. Plus, they were better for my mindset and self-image, too, because they fitted me well regardless of what my weight was doing.

I've collated some of my top tips for weight-fluctuation-proofing your wardrobe

Stretch is key, especially if you're plus size

Yes, there are valid concerns around microplastics in synthetic stretch fabrics, due to most stretch in fabrics coming from elastane, spandex or Lycra. Natural alternatives are being explored, but they're not widely available. However, ribbed and knitted fabrics can deliver more of a stretch without having to have a synthetic stretch component. Some of my most worn pieces are made of a compact knit or ribbed cotton.

Elastic waistbands

Where possible, look for elastic to give you that bit of extra room. I know people have hang ups about them, but honestly, if comfort is wrong and rigidity is right, I'm happy being wrong.

Bias cut skirts and dresses

Items cut on the bias have natural fluidity in size and fit due to the angled fabric forming a skimming quality akin to a slight stretch. I found huge versatility in these pieces, even pulling out a dress I'd worn when I was more than 10 kg lighter still fit me, albeit slightly differently, due to the expansion the bias creates.

Don't be afraid to wear something loose

This was a big one, as I'd realised that I had always tried to get the smallest size I could, or bought things tighter on the assumption that it would make me look smaller (or that I'd slim down eventually and it would fit better ... sigh). Being unafraid to wear something a little loose, or even opt for looser styles overall, gave me a bit more room for movement if I gained or lost a couple of kilos. Plus, my newfound ability to not have to cinch my waist meant I could always leave a button undone on my jeans and throw a baggy shirt over the top, and rebrand it as cool, laid-back and carefree.

Item report
Pink/red long-sleeve floral dress

Purchased from

Marks and Spencer

How I came to own it

I bought this while I was in the UK on one of my end-of-trip buying frenzies. I love nothing more than visiting my home country. There's a sense of home that's palpable to me the second I step off the flight. Unlike a lot of people who have migrated to another country, I didn't leave behind a big close family who eagerly anticipate my return and lay on dinners and reunions when I eventually do so. What I did leave behind was Marks and Spencer, and let me tell you, it yearns for me and I yearn for it in place of the extended family I don't have.

Over the years as I'd got better and better with money (ahem, nod to my first book, *Good With Money*) and relied less and less on buying material things to feel a shred of joy, I was better able to tame the monster inside me that growled to spend a month's pay in M&S on day one of the trip. However, where I struggled was in the last days of each visit. I'd be bouncing from supermarket to supermarket, filling my suitcase with Rolos and custard creams, Robinson's squash and Colman's Tuna Pasta Bake mix, grabbing one last coffee with people to bolster the big goodbye-till-next-visit.

Something about that discomfort, the countdown of a visit coming to an end, always made me vulnerable. I'd usually end up deciding to just buy the pieces that were living rent free in my head as some sort of completion mission. If I can fill my suitcase

(continued)

with enough treats, do my final round of goodbyes and buy these few items that I won't have a chance to get again, that'll make me feel better about leaving. At least, that was my thinking. So that's how this long-sleeved monstrosity (as I now call it) ended up in my wardrobe. It was a pinky-red, floral, long-sleeved midi-dress in a soft jersey fabric that was admittedly so comfortable I could've slept in it. Unfortunately, I knew pretty quickly after buying it that it wasn't right for me, but I really wanted to make it work. I really wanted to like it.

The verdict

It took me a few goes to actually wear this dress for the day because I really, really didn't feel good in it. This strategy of forcing myself to wear something, though, was really starting to work, because it gave me the clarity to understand why I didn't like it so I could use that data to better inform my approach to clothes going forward.

The problems with this dress were endless. The cut of the bottom of the dress was frankly hideous on me. It wasn't a tight midi, it was sort of wider at the bottom than the waist, which meant it hit my hips and just continued down to my mid-calf at a similar width. My dump truck ass was merely a speed-bump on its journey to the ground, which, tragically, made it fall slightly shorter at the back than the front.

On top of that, the floral pattern was so not me. On some level I always knew florals weren't for me, but they'd always manage to sneak in from time to time. This dress really taught me that I don't feel good in a wider skirt, and I don't like florals. I was right to think a long-sleeved stretchy dress would be great for low-effort cooler-weather dressing, I just forgot that the dress had to actually suit me for that to work.

Lessons learned

- I feel best in midi-dresses that come in at my lower leg to accentuate my curves.
- The cutesy, girly, dainty dress style really doesn't feel like it reflects my personality.
- I don't feel good in florals!

Chapter summary

- ∞ Body acceptance can often come from unexpected places—sometimes all we need is space to be with ourselves without trying to change anything.
- ∞ 'Flattering' is a lie designed to keep women pursuing thinness.
- ∞ Dressing in a way that serves you, not the rules, can be a form of resistance against patriarchal standards.
- ∞ Weight-fluctuation-proofing your wardrobe is possible with the right combination of stretch, fabric and cut. You don't have to put your body on trial by trying to fit into rigidity.
- ∞ Gaining weight is not a moral failing and shouldn't mean you enjoy clothes less.
- ∞ You can change the way you see yourself without fundamentally changing anything. You just need to believe it's possible.

OCTOBER
The outfit repeater

We tell ourselves we'll wear the dress again, but when that next event rolls around, there's an emotional disconnect between the person we were when we bought the item and the person we are now.

Following my sewing escapades of September, humbling me with the realisation that I wouldn't be the next Vivienne Westwood, October rolled around quickly and brought with it a wedding invitation. I hadn't attended a wedding for quite some time, and an outfit wasn't immediately coming to mind. Before you ask, the sparkly dress I'd made for the 60th was probably a touch too bridal to have been appropriate.

In the back of my wardrobe I fished out a cerulean blue dress that still had the tags on. Shameful, I know. It actually hit the trifecta of my past buying mistakes in that:

∞ I bought it because I saw it on an influencer I always wished I could look like.

∞ She had it in black, but black was sold out in my size so I bought it in blue (???). Like, okay … ?

∞ I bought it in a hurry without thinking it through because it was on sale and it was a really good price for the brand. I also bought three other things in that same sale that I definitely didn't need.

So, dear readers, I give you: the triple threat. Oh, and to add insult to injury, the dress was a size 14, and at the time of this wedding I was a 16 with benefits (basically a 16 but kinda a 17 after a salty meal). Give me strength.

Anyway, lucky for me, the dress was bias cut so it still fit me, albeit not at all like the picture of the slim model, but, thankfully, we'd unlearned a lot by this point in the Project.

Wearing this dress put me through one of the learnings I experienced over and over again during the challenge. I didn't exactly *want* to wear it (there was resistance galore when I first put it on), but it was my only wedding-appropriate dress, so I had no choice. So, I stopped being a whiny little bitch and got on with getting my rambunctious ass to the wedding. To my surprise, several people complimented me on the dress, and after moving around in it a little bit, I realised how much I actually liked it. Once again I'd like to thank my own brain for gaslighting me.

It was one of those moments that highlighted to me the power of novelty. There were so many things in my wardrobe that I'd written off, decided I didn't like, or could have quite easily gotten rid of had I allowed myself a clear out. Because at first glance, no, I didn't like them, but I'm now a big believer that your perception of your clothes can change if you just give them a chance. Being forced to wear that dress gave it a whole new life, and I wouldn't have given it that chance if I hadn't been committed to the Project.

You don't need a new outfit for every single event

One of the most common triggers for wanting to buy new clothes, and that you'll probably encounter if you're going to do The Wardrobe Project, is wanting an outfit for a specific event or occasion. It might be a wedding you've been invited to, a milestone birthday or some kind of work event that you want to look sharp for. That belief that all the clothes you have are somehow worse than the clothes you could buy will kick into overdrive when you find yourself in this position, and the excuse to buy something new will be strong.

I know you know you don't *need* a new outfit for every occasion. We all know we don't, but the pull is still there because the craving for novelty or to buy the specific version of ourselves that we want to present at this event is powerful. In the previous chapter, we talked about how often we're in that default state of 'buy'. Never has that state been stronger than when we have an event to go to and a sudden hatred for everything we own.

But here's the thing: buying for one specific event or one specific occasion is actually what creates the feeling of having nothing to wear. When we buy in this way, all of our decisions are based on how the outfit will work for that one use. We buy based on the practical stuff: the weather, the venue, the type of event, what everyone else is wearing, etc. But we buy based on all the emotional stuff too. How we feel in our body at that time, what trends we're drawn to, how our day has gone, how we feel about money right now, how we feel about the other people that are going, and most critically, how we feel about the version of ourselves that we want to put out there at that one occasion.

The problem comes when that very specific set of circumstances ends up hanging in our wardrobe long after the event is over. You probably told yourself you'd wear the dress again at another event, but when that next event rolls around, there's an emotional disconnect between the person we were when we bought the item and the person we are now. We don't want to wear that same dress because all of the decision-making was based around how you felt last time, not how you feel today.

While it feels like buying something new for a specific event will mean you have more to wear, it actually often means you have less to wear because you end up with a collection of outfits that don't really represent your whole self, just the version of you on that one given day, under one specific set of circumstances.

I believe it's actually better to buy your clothes independently of a specific occasion, so that you buy something that contributes wholly and completely to your wardrobe and your life than something that's stuck in a silo that you don't actually want to reach for.

Now, I'll admit that isn't all that helpful when you have an event to go to and you don't have anything you want to wear! I get it, you can't go back in time and buy a really versatile dress that you can have ready for this specific occasion.

But going forward, if you can reduce the amount of buying you do with a specific scenario in mind, I promise you'll thank yourself later. In the short term, can you borrow something from a friend, rent something or do what I did and force yourself to wear something you don't really want to wear? You might end up liking it more than you thought, or you might just survive the night without anyone even noticing that you're wearing something you didn't want to wear.

Long term, I actually recommend shifting the way you buy, so that you're buying things, particularly occasion wear, independently from the occasion. On the surface, it feels smarter to not buy a cocktail dress until you're actually going to a cocktail event, or a job interview outfit until you have a job interview lined up. However, you're more likely to buy a cocktail dress that you're willing to wear over and over again when you buy it for what it is, not what you need it for. Consider this your permission to buy clothes even if you have nowhere to wear them. Because when you really, really love something, you'll be excited to wear it when an event does roll around.

Of course, there's a line. If you rarely ever go to weddings, events or celebrations, it's smart to limit how many pieces of occasion wear you're buying. But if you do have a moderate rotation of events that call for something a little fancy—think back to your lifestyle pie chart from page 36 here—there's a lot of wardrobe value to be found in buying things before you need to wear them. When you have pieces you love, events aren't a burden, they're an opportunity.

Instead of 'what am I going to wear?!' you get to say 'YES! I get to wear that dress!'

The orange suit example

Since completing my Project, I've added an orange suit to my wardrobe that I purchased without a specific purpose in mind. I'll admit, it felt a bit wrong to buy in that way. I was being so mindful with my post-Project purchases (more on that later) that I wondered if this was my first mistake.

It absolutely wasn't. That orange suit is now my go-to outfit for work events, speaking gigs, important meetings, or even just a day when I want to show up like a boss. I dress it up, I dress it down, and every occasion that lands in my calendar is an opportunity to get more wear out of it. I'd never experienced that kind of excitement over something I already own before. That feeling was only reserved for novelty, when I had something new I couldn't wait to wear. To be able to experience it with things I've worn more times than I can count feels like such progress.

Task: The optimal wardrobe

Curating a wardrobe that works for your lifestyle outside of specific silos requires an understanding of how you spend your time. Earlier on at page 36, you completed the lifestyle pie chart task. Now, we're going to build on that.

For each slice of your pie chart, I want you to consider what the optimal outfit for that scenario would be based on how you want to look and feel when in that slice. For example, let's say you spend 40 per cent of your time in work clothes, 40 per cent of your time in activewear, 15 per cent of your time in casual leisure outfits and 5 per cent of the time in smarter leisure outfits. Your optimal wardrobe breakdown might look like this:

(continued)

Slice	When I am in this slice I want to look and feel...	Optimal outfit(s) for this slice
Work	Comfortable, smart, easy, simple, approachable, mature	Knitted midi-skirt, sneakers, blazer
Chilling/WFH/ activewear	Comfortable, organised, easeful	Leggings with pockets, zip-up jacket
Leisure casual	Feminine, cute, fun, relaxed, laid-back	Light denim jeans with a cardigan and ankle boots
Leisure smart	Bright, joyful, flowy, feminine, elegant	A pastel midi-dress with a bow detail and pink shoes

By thinking about how you want to look and feel when in each slice, and what an idea of that outfit might be, you gradually become more informed about the function of your clothes. This helps you make better buying decisions, as you can see how pieces might fit into one or more slices meaningfully, rather than just buying for one single leisure event or one single work presentation.

Outfit repeating is cool

Social media has created this perception that people have an endless trove of new clothes to wear. That desire to wear something new for every occasion is partly down to the fact that it feels like that's what everyone else is doing. Some creators or celebrities genuinely do avoid being seen in the same outfit twice, but for us regular folks, it's simply not necessary to always wear something different.

Outfit repeating has been considered a fashion faux pas in popular culture for decades. If you were born in the 90s, you probably associate the term with that iconic scene in *The Lizzie McGuire Movie*, where she's mocked at a school event for wearing an outfit she's worn before.

I think outfit repeating needs a rebrand. In the previous chapter, I talked about dressing for resistance. I suggested we should outfit repeat in order to buck the pressure to always have something new, and do so loudly. By that, I mean owning our outfit repetition.

Loud outfit repeating can look like:

∞ not being afraid to say 'I'm wearing my [insert item here] again because I love it so much'

∞ allowing others to recognise that you're outfit repeating by boldly being known for a certain outfit

∞ outfit repeating so frequently that people come to remember you in certain outfits.

That orange suit that I love so much? It's bold. It's bright. It's not quiet in any way. People know I've worn it before. People remember it (because it's a damn fine suit), so when I wear it again, they recognise I'm outfit repeating.

What a privilege it is to feel so good in an outfit that you can't wait to wear it again. What a privilege it is to be remembered for an outfit that suited you so perfectly. What a privilege it is to have something in your calendar that invites you to reach for that special piece.

Next time you go to outfit repeat, I want you to do so loudly, and think to yourself as you look in the mirror, what a privilege it is to wear this again.

Embracing style formulas

Something that I found helpful in breaking my ties with buying new things every time I didn't have something to wear was creating *style formulas* for specific purposes. This is not so much for everyday dressing, but for things that would trigger my desire to buy something new.

For example, what are the kinds of circumstances that would make you want to buy something new? Some of these circumstances might be events such as a:

- ∞ wedding
- ∞ work event
- ∞ formal gala dinner
- ∞ friend's birthday
- ∞ cocktail party
- ∞ dinner
- ∞ work presentation or meeting
- ∞ job interview.

A style formula is really just a cheat sheet of styles or combinations I could wear to one of these types of events, sort of like a pre-assigned go-to that I know I can rely on. When I brought the blue cerulean dress out of still-got-the-tags-on retirement, that became my go-to wedding guest outfit. After the Project finished, I bought the orange suit in my brand colour, and that's now my go-to outfit for business events or presentations. My blue knitted top-and-skirt set became my formula for when I wanted to look a little nicer but without fully dressing up, like someone's birthday or a dinner. My cream jeans, cream boots and my long brown coat became my go-to elevated winter outfit.

Having these formulas in my mind, and creating them as I discovered them during or after the Project, allowed me to see my clothes as components of an outfit that I had the agency to put together. It made me infinitely more creative with my clothes, and more connected to the things I owned, rather than flippantly adding more as though they meant nothing to me.

Chapter summary

∞ You don't need a new outfit for every occasion or purpose. When we buy with only one purpose in mind, we end up with a collection of clothes that feels disjointed.

∞ You may find it more helpful to buy clothes without a specific place to wear them, so that you're not siloing the item into one specific context.

∞ The optimal wardrobe task can help you tease out how you want to look and feel for different parts of your life, to help you curate a wardrobe that makes sense across those areas instead of a collection of one-hit wonders.

∞ Outfit repeating is cool, and we can embrace the privilege that it is to be recognised for wearing something that reflects who we are.

∞ Style formulas are outfit bases or structures for specific outfit purposes that you can refer back to over and over again to make getting dressed easier and ditch the pull to just go out and buy something in a pinch.

NOVEMBER
The clear out

Resistance to wearing items in our wardrobe isn't necessarily because the clothes are wrong.

The penultimate month of the Project was here, and I was experiencing a strange sense of duality. On the one hand, I knew I'd learned so much and was ready to replace some items in my wardrobe and implement my plans to buy better. On the other hand, I was starting to worry about spring back, and what it would be like in the big wide world of clothes again. Would I go gangbusters and undo all my progress? Would I buy the right things? Should I even buy anything? Should I never buy anything again? It was busy in my head. And, so, I thought it was as good a time as any to do a clear out and give me something to focus on.

You might remember that I didn't allow myself to clear out before the Project began. That's because I wanted to really try to wear everything I had so I'd know for sure what I liked and what I didn't so I could maximise my learnings. Now that I was nearing the end of the year and I was starting to look beyond the Project, I felt it was a good time to sell and donate some of the things I knew I was definitely done with.

The key things I got rid of were things that well and truly didn't fit, to the point they weren't wearable, and some of the things I'd identified really weren't me—the stunning Lee Mathews jacket I told you about on page 106 being one of them. Thankfully, I found a loving home for her on Facebook Marketplace, and she went to someone who would appreciate her in a way I couldn't.

The Project changed the way I bought and wore my clothes, but it also changed the way I let go of clothes too. You might have heard of the hanger flipping method for deciding what to keep in your wardrobe. If you haven't, the crux of it is that you turn all the hangers in your wardrobe one way, and then each time you wear something, turn the hanger the other way when you hang it back up so you know exactly which items you're reaching for. Any hangers that aren't flipped when you go to clear out are things you clearly don't wear.

In theory, I love this idea, but in reality, the Project had taught me that just because I *wasn't* wearing something, didn't mean I *couldn't* wear it. Let's not forget the 80/20 rule—we wear 20 per cent of our wardrobe 80 per cent of the time. That doesn't automatically mean we won't ever wear the other 80 per cent. It just means we need to get more creative and spend more time with our clothes and putting our outfits together. Resistance to wearing items in our wardrobe isn't necessarily because the clothes are wrong. Ditching anything you're not wearing may mean you miss out on something magical!

Instead, I only let myself discard things that I had really given a chance. Anything that was a maybe got put in the 'to-be-worn' pile so I could properly road test it before deciding. This clear out felt completely different to any other clear out I had ever done, most notably because there were really only a few things I was getting rid of—things that were totally unwearable due to fit or size issues, or things that really went against my view of my style I'd developed throughout the year. I discarded about 15 things, half of them sold on Marketplace, half of them donated to my local thrift shop, and had five 'maybe' items that I was still diagnosing.

To be honest, it was the first time I'd done a clear out and hadn't immediately felt a compulsion to buy something new, which was evidence to me of how differently I was viewing my wardrobe. I'd really started to see it as a collection of things I *wanted* to get dressed in. My plans to work with a stylist to replace a few key things were now based around adding life to what I already had, rather than getting swept up in the novelty of new items and ignoring my old ones.

Five tips for a mindful and successful clear out

One of the best things the Project taught me was to slow down my decision-making with both buying and getting rid of things. Here are my top five tips for a mindful clear out that you'll actually learn from, and that won't leave you dashing out to buy stuff that you'll be donating again in six months.

1. Be careful with things that don't fit

Clothes that don't fit are tough. On the one hand, it's unhelpful to get dressed from a wardrobe filled with things that don't fit you—especially if they're too small, as that can feel really deflating and could damage your body image. However, discarding things as soon as they don't fit can leave you high and dry if your weight then changes again. Be gentle with yourself, and be careful with your intentions. It can help to store some clothes in a separate box or room if you have one, so you still have them but without having to look at them every day.

2. Don't hang onto anything that you tell yourself you'll slim into

This is the one exception to the above—if you're telling yourself you're going to go on a diet to fit back into something, or if you're taunting yourself with an ideal version of yourself, get rid of it and move on. You don't need that kind of pressure—life is hard enough and you are fantastic as you are.

3. Don't get rid of anything without giving it a second chance

If you're ditching something that fits, don't do it without giving it a second chance. Wear it to pop to the supermarket, or, if you dare, for a full day out somewhere. We're very quick to discard clothes that aren't as exciting anymore, but I've salvaged so many items from people's donate pile just by getting them to give them another chance.

(continued)

4. Try things on while you're clearing out

Yep, no discarding until you've actually tried it on. Often we get an idea in our head about how something looks, or we assume it looks bad because we're not excited by it. If you're not trying things on, you're not learning and you'll just keep making the same mistakes again. Always try on!

5. If you plan on replacing something, be clear on what exactly you're looking for

Clearing out is prime time for consumption cravings. We empty our wardrobes and vow to start fresh and never make the same buying mistakes again, only to rush out too quickly, high on the permission to build a fresh new wardrobe, and do it all again. If you're replacing something in your wardrobe or filling a gap you've identified, get really, really specific about what you're looking for, right down to the granular details that you've learned about what you like and why.

Task: Yesses and nos

This task is about compiling learnings from the things you're keeping and the things you're throwing out. Every clear out is an opportunity to learn something to inform any future purchases you make.

Grab a piece of paper and draw a line down the middle so you have two columns. Label one 'yes' and one 'no'. Your challenge is to write down as many likes and dislikes in each column as you can.

I'm talking necklines, sleeve types, colours, specific shades, trouser lengths, fastenings, hardware, trouser rise, feel of fabric, weight of fabric, pattern, size of florals, colours within patterns or florals, smaller features like bows, silhouettes, skirt shapes, dress lengths…literally anything you can note down that is a strong 'yes' or a strong 'no' for you.

Get as granular as you can. The more specific the better, because this is going to help you niche down what you like and what makes you feel good, and get clear on the things that you don't love so you don't buy them again.

This is not to say you have to only ever buy things that meet these yesses and nos. It's more of a handy cheat sheet so that when you see something you like, you try something on or you go looking for something, you're led by your own decisions and what you know about yourself and your style, rather than the emotions that are present on that day.

For example, I'm always drawn to puff sleeves in stores. But I have puff sleeves and frills firmly on my 'no' list, because I don't feel good in them. I've made the mistake too many times, and they're just not for me.

Fill out your yesses and nos list, making sure to take note of anything you're discarding during a clear out (as this is where we learn most of our nos) and add to both lists over time as you discover more from wearing your wardrobe.

Here's a snapshot of what was on my list at the end of the Project:

YES	NO
High neck, racer back	Puff sleeves
One shoulder	Mini skirt/dress
Orange, dark orange, rust	Calf/knee length
Compact knit	Any pulling across the hips
Longline midi finishing around ankle/mid-calf (not above)	Light, floaty fabrics
Red	Dainty florals (e.g., light pink, green, pastels)

(continued)

Remembering these tiny details makes such a huge difference when I'm adding things to my wardrobe—especially if I'm shopping second-hand, as I tend to be slightly less fussy due to having less to choose from, but that can mean I allow things in that aren't right for me.

My top five most worn items and what they taught me

At this point in the Project I was reflecting on my most worn items (some of which because they surprised me and some because they were starting to need replacing). Here are the five things I wore the most and what they taught me about style and consumption.

1. Black wide-leg trousers

This item in my wardrobe is the one that was doing the absolute most. These taught me how much a looser leg trouser is better for my style and shape than the tapered trousers I've been chasing my whole life. My ultra-polished fantasy self would always be wearing sleek, slim-leg trousers and pointy heels, when actually a looser fitting, comfier version of that look gives me the style I like in a way that's more me-shaped.

2. Cream jeans

My cream wide-leg jeans were a big surprise to me. I'd bought them as an impulse purchase when I couldn't find exactly what I wanted, so I settled for something that would 'do for now'. This is usually a rookie error, but I won this one! By doing the Project and embracing them as they were, I fell in love with them and wore them at least once a week throughout most of the Project. They also helped me move away from my obsession with slim-leg styles (which was what I originally wanted) and start dressing for my curvy shape.

3. Statement belt

I'd bought this belt for a friend's hens party when I was back in the UK the year prior, and didn't have anything appropriate to wear, but it turned out to be a winner. I hadn't worn it since the hens as it was such an impulse purchase in a panic the day before, and I felt like it was somehow 'too much' to wear regularly. That belief came down to the fact I was constantly trying to shrink myself down into a minimalist, beige, plain style when actually the belt was perfect for my bolder, punchier approach to neutrals. This piece formed part of my espresso con panna and basics-with-benefits style anchor.

4. Black-and-gold accordion pants

Ahhh ... one of my lockdown purchases that stood the test of time. These were a pair of wide-leg trousers that had a subtle gold/bronze print and an accordion pleat. These formed part of my shift into my own take on the minimal, neutral style, as they felt simple and classic while still having a little something extra about them.

5. Blue knitted top-and-skirt set

And lastly ... my Kmart wonder. Every time I wear this I stand a little taller and feel so pumped up. It's ultra-soft and stretchy, but makes me feel a bit special without compromising on comfort. I love that it matches as a set, and it taught me how much knitted fabrications really give me the me-shaped version of styles I love.

Lessons learned, clear out complete. One month to go, and I'd officially done it.

 Item report
Taupe wide-leg trousers

Purchased from

Country Road

How I came to own it

I owned this exact same pair of trousers in black, and absolutely loved them. They were—chef's kiss—perfection, and they actually taught me a lot about the fabrics I liked most. They're made of a

(continued)

heavier viscose-type material, which I found hung really nicely on my curvy, jiggly body, and made me feel really confident in myself in a way that lighter fabrics didn't. However, this specific pair ended up in my wardrobe because I did what I now know is one of my cardinal wardrobe sins: I bought them because I loved the black and wanted another colour *shakes head*.

The verdict

Ever since I bought these trousers, I knew something wasn't right. I really wanted to like them, and I couldn't work out why I didn't, since I loved the black ones so much. Well, giving myself the time to actually interrogate why I wasn't reaching for them and why I felt blah every time I put them on helped me uncover the problem. Turns out taupe is actually really hard to style. It's one of those cooler neutrals, not quite grey, but not as warm as a beige or camel. I could only ever pair it with black or white, and they just felt really limiting. The coolness of the colour meant they didn't go with any of my warmer neutrals, like creams or browns, which I've since learned are my preference over cooler tones.

Lessons learned

Not all neutrals are made equal. This was when I started to realise why I often felt like none of my clothes went together—because there are so many different types of 'neutral'. Not all creams go together. Not all whites go together. Not all beiges go together. And without having several items in similar hues of taupe, nothing went with these goddamn trousers!

Just because you like something in black, doesn't mean you'll like it in another colour. I had to learn this lesson over and over throughout the project. I'm thankful for this pair of trousers and this year-long challenge for teaching me that running out to giddily repurchase something in every colour it comes in is a huge mistake (and terrible for your bank account!).

Chapter summary

∞ Clearing out your wardrobe can leave you vulnerable to feeling like you have permission to buy a bunch more stuff or 'start fresh' in your wardrobe.

∞ When doing a clear out, sort items into 'yes', 'no' and 'maybe' piles. Your 'maybe' items then form a 'to-be-worn' pile, so you give them a chance before immediately ditching them.

∞ Be careful with items that don't fit you. It's tempting to ditch them, but you might be setting yourself up for failure if your weight fluctuates again. Consider storing them in a box instead of hanging in your wardrobe.

∞ You can learn a lot from your most worn items. Reflect on what they are while doing a clear out, particularly if you're doing your own version of the Project.

DECEMBER

The end

I still wanted to be able to engage with style and with clothes, but I wanted to see myself and the role of clothes in my life in a new way.

…and just like that, it was the final month of the Project! Getting to December was a weird feeling because, in my mind, I felt like I'd finished as soon as it got to December. In reality, I still had 31 days to go. I think, by that point, I was so certain that it would get done that I started to calibrate my brain towards life after the Project.

After a fair bit of research, I'd found a stylist I wanted to work with. I explored a few options, including some people I had followed on social media for years. Ultimately, I was restricted by how much I could spend on the styling package itself, as this is generally in the thousands, and, of course, you still need to set aside some money for the clothes you purchase during the personal shopping portion. Nonetheless, I found a stylist that fit my price range, and booked a discovery call and initial consult. Her name was Maddy Forster from Mad About Fashion, and we connected instantly.

I went into our initial conversation thinking I was only looking to pay for a few hours of personal shopping because I wanted the support when buying again, but, ultimately, I ended up booking the full package, which included:

∞ a wardrobe revamp, where the stylist comes to your house and goes through your wardrobe with you to analyse everything you own

∞ personal shopping

∞ wardrobe integration, where the stylist returns to your home and helps you integrate the pieces you've purchased.

I'll tell you more about what that experience looked like on page 219, but it was the integration that really hooked me in. I'd done so much work with what I had that I knew my wardrobe inside and out. Seriously, I knew every damn item in my wardrobe in detail, and if it fit me, I'd almost definitely worn it at some point during the year, too. That, in itself, was an unfamiliar feeling. I'd been so used to only wearing a few items and ignoring most of my wardrobe purely because the novelty had worn off or I was looking for the next dopamine hit. But, good as this knowledge of my wardrobe was, I wondered if I'd struggle to integrate new pieces, and whether I might fall into the trap of seeing new clothes as separate or better than everything I already had. So I dove in head first and decided to go whole hog.

I think it's worth mentioning here that I did grapple a little with whether spending money on a stylist negated the money I'd saved during the Project. Having previously been an overspender and struggled to be good with money in the past—read my first book *Good With Money* for all the tea on that!—I guess I felt a little bit guilty at the idea of spending a big chunk of money on a stylist and new clothes. There was a small part of me that wondered if it meant I'd failed or cheated somehow by buying things at the end, especially as I was sharing my journey on social media and, now, in this book. I questioned whether what I'd done was still 'worthy', or if I'd done it 'right'.

This is common when a change of behaviour has involved abstinence or modification, especially where spending is concerned.

A lot of women in my Wardrobe Project program community have expressed confusion at what it means for their progress if they've shopped after their cohort has ended. In my money programs, it's common for people who have previously struggled to hold on to money to then learn to spend it healthily again once they've mastered the behaviour of saving. Learning to spend is a skill in itself. Even if you feel like you could compete in the emotional spending world championships (not a thing, but should be) it's a whole other thing entirely to trust yourself enough to spend wisely.

I was experiencing this in real time, and it felt familiar. It reminded me of my previous efforts to change my financial behaviour several years ago. Being a hot mess with money was something I identified with for so many years. Trying to save and not following through, existing in a state of chaos with my finances, and spending based on how I felt in the moment were all mainstays in my financial routine. When I went through the process of paying off debt and, at the same time, teaching myself to save money and take back control of my money habits and financial decisions, I had to learn what it meant to spend money outside of that state of chaos.

Here I was five years later re-learning the exact same thing, but in the context of clothes! I had to learn to buy again in a way that incorporated what I'd learned, and almost with a new identity. Just like I'd identified with being bad with money for so long, I identified as having a weakness for clothes. I needed to remould that identity, allow myself to leave that behind and evolve into someone who interacts with clothes, and themselves, in a completely different way.

Now, purists would argue that I could just not buy again. Or I could just live with what I have and only buy from a utilitarian perspective and become a proper OG minimalist, but that wasn't what I wanted. Firstly, we've already addressed in this book how the way we look as women does have implications for how much you can earn and how you're perceived. I'm a plus-size woman with a career that places me somewhat in the public eye. There's a degree of showing up that needs to happen. But, more than that, clothes can bring so much joy and a means of self-expression when used correctly. I actively wanted to buy again, so that I could buy differently and experience my style, and to a degree, myself, differently.

I still wanted to be able to engage with style and with clothes, but I wanted to see myself and the role of clothes in my life in a new way. I wanted to buy differently and curate a wardrobe of clothes that I can enjoy over and over again for years. I wanted to replicate more of the best things in my wardrobe and feel excitement to wear my favourite pieces, and experience the joy of getting dressed without relying on newness. I definitely saw myself buying less and less over time, but for now, I wanted to use my learnings to buy the *right* things, rather than buying nothing.

So while the Project as I first created it was almost over, the real work was still ahead of me.

My mindful buying toolkit

When it comes to buying clothes mindfully or minimising overconsumption, the internet is flooded with advice like 'buy staples that go with everything' or 'wait 24 hours before you buy' or 'only buy in three colours'.

While the intent of this advice is solid, and I'm not here to prove anyone wrong, personally, a lot of those rules didn't completely connect with me.

In fact, trying to buy classic, timeless staples that 'go with everything' was one of my biggest downfalls. As I learned the hard way, not all neutrals match, and finding 'basics' isn't as simple as it sounds. Plus, what's considered a 'classic' changes with time, and we change, too. Trying to dress as though no time has passed can be difficult, and to be honest, I've grown to feel like it erases the human experience. Time passes, we change and the version of ourselves we're expressing changes, too. We need to be able to dress in a way that doesn't tie us to one specific time.

Some swear by only buying things in specific colours, which I do partially subscribe to as my love of orange and red does help me to not get tempted by other colours, and it does drastically simplify the process. However, we need more context than this. We can be guided by key colours, while being careful not to buy things solely because they're in that colour.

To develop my mindful buying toolkit, I considered everything I'd learned throughout the year, and asked myself what I'd need to do to ensure that things I was bringing into my wardrobe were things I would genuinely love and reach for over and over again. I distilled it down into three things:

∞ My style concept
∞ My style code
∞ My style standard

My style *concept* was a big part of this: my 'espresso con panna' and basics with benefits. Having this anchor to guide the vibe and the feeling I wanted to experience in my outfits was going to be an important part of my mindful buying toolkit as it personalises the piece to me and I'm able to benchmark whether it's fitting the vibe that I'm looking for and, most importantly, that I want to *feel*.

My style *code* was the second thing in my toolkit. This was based around my yesses and nos list (page 186) and my lifestyle pie chart (page 35). Being crystal clear on the specifics I wanted in my clothes helped me cut the crap, and see through the dopamine haze we often feel when we see pretty things in stores.

Thirdly, I decided I would implement a 'return until proven worthy' rule that I'd call my style *standard*. As I've told you several times throughout this book, I had extremely low standards for what I'd allow into my wardrobe. I'd buy things that didn't fit quite right. I'd say I was going to get things tailored but I'd end up not bothering. I'd buy things because I was in such a rush to wear the style even though it wasn't quite what I was looking for. I'd buy things I liked for no reason other than I liked them and they were on sale. The 'return until proven worthy' rule was designed to hold me accountable to make better decisions. Effectively, it meant that I had to assume I was either not buying the item or returning the item until I could prove it was worthy of a spot in my wardrobe. This looks like:

- ∞ If the fit isn't right, no excuses.
- ∞ If it's not an immediate 'yes', it's an immediate 'no'.
- ∞ Not just saying it'll go with loads of other things; actually trying it on with those things.
- ∞ Planning complete outfits with the piece, not just theoretical combinations in my head.
- ∞ Trying it on properly in the context I plan to wear it to avoid convincing myself it'll look better when I'm wearing the right underwear/my hair is done.
- ∞ No open loops—never keep anything that requires more purchases to be able to wear it.
- ∞ Reference check against my spending values—is this really adding to my life?

Yes, this is comprehensive and, yes, this takes time. But style should be slow. That urgency we talked about on page 99 speeds up our decision-making and leaves us wondering how we ended up with so much stuff. Slow fashion means slowing down the pace at which we consume and raising the standards of what we consume.

I also made a Notion template for logging any purchases I made post-Project to help me ensure I was assessing the things I was adding, and to get a view of the types of things I was buying. You can access this template via the website thewardrobeprojectbook.com.

Task: Developing your mindful buying toolkit

As you take everything you've learned in this book back to your own wardrobe, I want you to start consolidating the things you observe in your wardrobe into your own style concept, style code and style standard.

Your style *concept* is that visual anchor that represents your personal interpretation of how you express yourself visually. It may take some time for you to come up with yours, but start paying attention to the overall vibe of objects, places, experiences and sensations and see if you connect with any on a visual level.

Your style *code* is made up of all the juicy data we can learn from our existing wardrobes. Your wardrobe categories from page 18 and your 'yesses and nos' list from page 186 are really helpful here.

Your style *standard* is your commitment to learn from your mistakes and break the buying patterns that are keeping you stuck. Our benchmarking techniques from page 139 will help you embed this, along with the lessons learned from your lesser-loved items in your wardrobe.

The Rule of Three

Having spent the year analysing my buying mistakes and unravelling why my wardrobe has been such a sinkhole for my money over the years, I spent a long time working out how I could condense those learnings down into something that could signpost better buying decisions in the future. I deeply understood them while I was in the safe cocoon of the Project, but would I still listen when I was able to buy again? I knew I needed something to anchor everything

I'd learned into my buying decisions if I had any hope of putting my learnings into practice.

That's what led me to come up with the Rule of Three: three questions I could ask myself when deciding whether or not to buy something.

Q1: Would I have liked this three years ago?

This question began as 'will I still like this in three years', but I found my answer was invariably 'yes'. That's partly because I'd tell myself I'd like something in three years if it meant I could justify buying it, and partly because it's hard for us to view our future self as a real person. Psychologically, that person is a stranger, and the life they'll be living isn't something we can fully conceptualise. By flipping it to ask if it's something I'd have liked three years ago, it grounds us in the passage of time, and shows us just how much we can change in three years. What were you doing three years ago? Who were you three years ago?

Now it's not to say that if your answer is 'no', you can't buy it. You might not have liked it three years ago because you weren't a parent then or you lived in a different place then or you've evolved and grown since then. This time anchor is an important pause point to remind you that you change, and life changes. Trends or styles or even things we identify with can feel timeless in the moment, but actually may not reflect who we are when we zoom out.

Q2: What are three contexts or environments where I would wear this?

This question has evolved from my attempts to make myself come up with three different outfits to wear an item with before I'd purchase it. As with my first question, I found it was easy for me to barrel on through and scrounge up three outfits in my mind just to justify the purchase. By changing the question to refer to contexts, I'm forced to not only consider outfits I'd build with the item, but where I'd actually wear them. This prompts a sort of mental visualisation of how you will actually wear the clothes in your real life. If your mind goes to fancy dinners or parties or glossy work meetings, you can check yourself and think, hey, when was the last time I dressed like Miranda Priestly's first assistant trying to get to fashion week?! Oh, wait, never! Boom. Purchase mistake swerved.

Q3: Would I be willing to wear this every day for the next three weeks?

This one is an interesting one, and I need you to not take it too literally. Of course, it's unlikely that you'll wear an item every day for the next three weeks. I'm not expecting you to rock into your all-staff Teams meeting wearing a cocktail dress. But the thread I'm pulling at here is steamrolling those impulse purchases of things that aren't quite right. I've told you endless examples throughout this book of purchases I've made of things that didn't fit quite right, or that I liked in theory but wasn't 100 per cent sure on. If I'd asked myself if I'd have been happy to wear that item every day for the next three weeks, I could've caught those excuses I was making before I purchased. The key here is giving yourself a pause point to assess the concessions you're making for an item that's less than perfect.

∞ ∞ ∞

You can mould the Rule of Three to suit what works for you, and I trust that you'll trust yourself(!) enough to discern when your answers are signalling towards a 'yes' or a 'no'. The beauty of these questions is that they're complex. They're not simple answers that you can easily override with an impulse and a hunger for a dopamine hit. They're things you really need to think about, and they'll get you thinking about how the item actually fits into your life.

My beliefs about clothes pre- and post-Project

Coming to the end of the Project, I was in major reflection mode over just how much had changed for me. It had gone so quickly and so slowly all at the same time, and I was really quite in awe of the fact it had been one whole year. I got to thinking about some of the beliefs I'd untangled throughout my time doing the Project, and explored what

I believed about clothes now. The year gave me the space to build a much more meaningful relationship with my clothes, and with myself.

I really started to recognise how much that transience had lifted, how I didn't see my clothes as temporary in the same way anymore. Don't get me wrong, there were a couple of heavily worn items I couldn't wait to replace or upgrade using the knowledge I'd gained, but for the first time in as long as I could remember, I wasn't craving a new version of myself. I didn't have this image in my head of how different I'd look after my styling session. It was about honing what I already knew to be true, not trying on a different life.

Beliefs before the Project	Beliefs after the Project
Buying clothes makes me happy.	I can be happy and feel good without buying clothes.
I look best when I'm in a new outfit.	I look best when I'm in an outfit I love and that really feels like me.
Feeling good comes down to what I am wearing.	Feeling good starts with a mindset, and an outfit is curated to compliment that.
I need to look more polished and put together in order to feel good.	I don't need to look perfect all the time to be able to feel like I look good.
I am less worthy because I don't look nice every single day.	It's fine to look fine!
If I buy more clothes, eventually I will have the perfect wardrobe and not want anything anymore.	Buying creates more buying. Satisfaction and contentment comes from working with what I have.
Nothing will fit me well because I am plus size.	I deserve to wear clothes that fit and feel good on my body.
If I find something I like, I have to buy it or I will be missing out.	There will always be more clothes, I won't be thinking about this in 20 years.

Task: Belief audit

Teasing out the things I believed about clothes, style and myself happened gradually throughout the Project, and were a result of me focusing in on my relationship with clothes throughout the year, but I'd like you to start investigating what beliefs you might be holding of your own. Luckily, I've come up with some prompts to help you untangle what yours might be without having to go through the whole year process (though I totally invite you to do the year as well if you want to!).

Finish these sentences with the first thing that comes to mind. Go gently with this as it can be confronting, deflating or overwhelming, but just allow yourself to observe what answers you find.

Prompt	Complete the sentence
I'd look better in my clothes if I...	....
I wish I could wear...	....
If I had the right clothes I could...	....
When I feel like I have nothing to wear it's because...	....
I wish I felt more...in my clothes	....
I wish I looked more like...	....
The thought of giving up buying clothes feels...because...	....
I always end up buying more clothes because...	....
Getting dressed feels...	....
When I buy clothes I feel...	....

(continued)

Not every prompt will resonate with you, and that's okay. Just follow the threads that tell you something. Once you've done this exercise, let these responses settle in your mind, and see how they start to come up when you're engaging with your wardrobe. Whenever you find one of your unhelpful beliefs making you think, feel or behave a certain way, stop and take a pause. A big deep breath goes a long way here! Then, recognise the behaviour or response that this belief is prompting. Is it making you want to buy? Is it making you reject your wardrobe? Then ask yourself, is this belief really true, or is this a story I've got comfortable telling myself? See if you can challenge the belief.

As you spend more time with your clothes and you implement some of the exercises we've gone through in this book, try building out some counter-beliefs. The goal isn't to change the way you think overnight, but gradually, you build up the muscle that intercepts these unhelpful beliefs, shifting your relationship with clothes over the long term.

Real people

Withdrawing from consumption had such a profound impact on my life and my confidence, which highlights just how harmful emotional consumption cycles can be. I don't just want you to take it from me, though. Let's hear from some of our friends we've met throughout this book about how their habits changed after spending time inside my Wardrobe Project program and hitting pause on their clothing consumption.

Rebecca

'I've become so much more intentional.'

I have become so much more intentional. I have been so much more honest about what suits me at this stage of my life. I have looked for gaps in my wardrobe. If I like something, I think about where and when I will actually wear it and do I have anything it will go with already? It's a waste of money to buy it just to own it because it's pretty or cool.

Having more clothes that work well together (no more buying random individual pieces) and buying a dress that works well for me (i.e., trying to practise 'The Ultimate Rule'— we'll learn more about this on page 218) makes me feel much more confident when I look in the mirror. I am more accepting of myself. I'm not 100 per cent there yet but I am so much further along.

The clothes I am choosing and wearing now are actually sitting on my body in a way that I like. Also, working with what I have and making myself *actually wear* the things I have is really satisfying. Things I may have thought were 'special' have become everyday apparel and I get compliments about the items I have. Friends tell me 'you always look nice'. I feel more confident in my ability to choose correctly. I'm also trying really hard to buy things that will last, made from materials that I like.

When I started looking at the money I was wasting on clothes, it had a knock-on effect on other areas of my life. I now question everything I am getting my debit or credit card out for. Is this really worthy of my cash? I love this side effect! I'm spending money on things I enjoy and that feels great.

Jo

'I channel my money into meaningful connection, rather than five minutes of dopamine.'

I implemented much of the information Emma gave us in The Wardrobe Project, embarking on a wardrobe pause, tracking spending, setting some savings and spending goals, and really assessing and utilising (and culling!) what I already had.

Things remain in my cart for 24 hours, unless it is something I have been coveting for a long time and, even then, 24 hours is useful. Ninety-five per cent of the time, the tabs are closed after a few days, because I forgot to go back, and I don't remember what it was anyway.

Every now and then I fall back into mindless spending. I know this because packages turn up and I can't recall what I bought. If this happens two to three times in a short period, I take the time to think about what is happening for me right now. What am I stressed or upset about? Then I tend to put the call out to friends to do an activity or workshop together, and channel my money into genuine connections and hours spent meaningfully, rather than five minutes of dopamine-hitting buy now.

Olga

'Having the opportunity to enjoy events is worth way more than a new dress.'

I noticed a significant shift in my spending from shopping for clothes to paying for experiences so that waiting for parcels wouldn't be the only pleasant thing in my life. As Emma wisely said on Instagram once, no-one will remember if you wear the same dress to two events in a row, but having the opportunity to enjoy these events is worth way more than a new dress.

Honestly, I don't always take selfies at these events and, a month or two later, I can't remember what I was wearing at a show where I didn't take one. I do take pictures of my surroundings, the musicians on stage or the type of show I'm in and this is what I end up remembering through the years. If I'm at a restaurant with my family, I enjoy talking and eating more than being obsessed with details on my blouse. Sure, I still aim to look good and fit the environment I am in (because I already have an outfit for pretty much any occasion), but when there are many events and experiences, it makes one care less about all the stuff in the closet. And this is a very liberating feeling!

Lizzie

'I now have a few different options I circulate for the events, depending on their dress code and love how I feel in all of them.'

I got heavily inspired by my own wardrobe—taking photos of the styled outfits every day made me realise how underutilised my wardrobe was. And while I was constantly looking for something new, instead of buying something, I just created a 'new' outfit from my existing wardrobe—realising it gave me the same hit of dopamine.

There have been a number of things that have helped me change the way I consume clothing:

- Being open and transparent with my husband and my friends (who form my jury) about what I want and why. It's not that I need their permission to spend my own money, but sometimes they ask the questions I need to really get to the 'do I really need to make this purchase?'

- Getting to know your wardrobe. After doing The Wardrobe Calculation (page 68), I think I calculated I could make upwards of 200 different clothing combos ... when I thought I had a pretty small wardrobe. That was very eye-opening. It has made me create new and different options, some that work, and some that absolutely don't, but it is a good first choice to shop what I have before purchasing other things.

- Spending money on other things that may give dopamine, but won't make me sacrifice decision-making at the time (e.g., my go-to is now a foot massage, or buying a face mask).

- Being comfortable with outfit repeating in life (e.g., at work, on weekends, at events). It is such a 'pick me' moment, where no-one really cares, but we all get in our heads about it. I now have a few different options I circulate for the events, depending on their dress code and love how I feel in all of them.

- I am far more picky about the fabric or fit of an item of clothing (e.g., I will not actively purchase anything I need to iron, or dryclean).

- I am less concerned about flattery and more so classic comfort.

- I am far pickier on what shops I support and generally will only support shops that stock a wide range of sizes (shops that have supported me when I'm 'bigger' as well as when I am smaller).

I definitely still fall for my own emotions, and love to spend (or the idea of spending) when feeling any loss of control, but this is something I will have to work on to re-train my mind as it is second nature. However, while it is still a thought, it is generally quite fleeting. I am no longer really worried about what size clothing is (because clothing sizes are beyond confusing and straight out stupid), but how I feel in them. And, for once, I am not just saying this. I have done a lot of work to remove emotion from weight, and that has trickled into my clothing habits also.

Amy

'I no longer use buy now, pay later or my credit card for clothing purchases.'

Honestly, after cutting myself off from buying for six months, I realised I still had something to wear to everything and that the world did not end when I missed out on an item or a trend. What actually made me feel confident and happy with how I looked was doing simple hair and make-up, applying fake tan and wearing my jewellery. None of that has anything to do with spending on clothes, and that realisation has really helped me to reduce what I buy.

- I have learned to pause and give my logical brain time to get back online before I go into chaotic, frenzied shopping.

- I am able to consider if the item actually fits my lifestyle and if I'll realistically wear it.

- I order one or two things at a time now and keep only what I love.

- I no longer use by now, pay later or my credit card for clothing purchases.

- I'm in the habit of always looking in my wardrobe first before I buy for an event or for a holiday.

- I carry a lot less stress (admin of payments and returns) and shame (from wasting money).

Chapter summary

∞ There is an incredible sense of accomplishment on the other side of committing to yourself for a whole year.

∞ Building out your mindful buying toolkit is all about developing criteria and standards to help you buy in a more considered way.

∞ Your mindful buying toolkit takes into account your style *concept,* your style *code* and your style *standard.* This helps you buy in accordance with what feels truly 'you', factoring in what you know about the things that make you feel good and that add to your life, rather than take away from it.

∞ The Rule of Three gives you an easy-to-remember set of questions to help you make better buying decisions in the moment.

∞ Your beliefs about clothes drive your behaviour towards them. Breaking down the ways your beliefs are keeping you stuck in a spending cycle can give you the awareness to intercept repeating patterns.

The emergence

As the shops closed on 31 December 2023, I sat with an immense feeling of accomplishment. I'd bloody done it. I'd gone one whole year without buying clothes, and not only that, I'd enjoyed it! The satisfaction I felt was really quite remarkable, and I'm genuinely not overselling that. Not only did I have the pride of completing something I'd set out to do for one whole year, but I was certain I wasn't the same person I was a year ago. I saw someone else in the mirror looking back at me.

If you'd have told me before the Project that I'd be forever changed afterwards, my mind would be leaping and bounding through every iteration of my fantasy self, giddy at the thought of undergoing some kind of transformation. But real change isn't like that. Real change isn't the flip of a switch or a complete 180 on your identity. Real change occurs gradually, and actually becomes part of who you are and who you've always been.

I knew I'd changed because I felt different. But I knew I'd undergone *deep* change when I realised that the person I saw in the mirror hadn't fundamentally changed from the outside. We're conditioned to believe we'll feel differently after big external changes, such as weight loss or a new style or a new haircut or a new outfit — as though we're candy in a wrapper. For years I'd been trying to change the wrapper, but never what was underneath. Now, though, I knew for certain the change was real because, to an outsider, the wrapper looked the same.

The key shifts I never expected

There were three key parts of the major shifts to how I felt at the end of the Project, and I want to break down each one individually, because they all represent a different aspect of the change I underwent.

1. I felt happier

It's sometimes hard to pinpoint exactly why I felt happier, but I think it came down to the fact I'd stopped relying on those external things to feel good. I hadn't realised how much the seemingly enjoyable process of buying clothes was keeping me stuck until I cut it off completely and learned to create my own joy without it.

In the time since completing the Project, I've paid extra attention to online content about people's decisions to do low-buy or no-buy periods, whether for clothes or just stuff in general. Not once have I heard anyone say they weren't happier afterwards, or that they were happier when on the consumption hamster wheel. And bear in mind, it doesn't really serve algorithmic advertising for that message to be pushed. If there were an alternative perspective (i.e., that withdrawing from consumption was a miserable feat), I'm almost certain we'd be hearing it.

While my no-buy was only for clothes, the knock-on effect meant I consumed less overall, and felt broadly less reliant on 'stuff'.

2. I felt more confident

If there's one message you take from this book, let it be this: I found more confidence from not buying clothes than I did from buying them. Yikes. What does that say about my previous pursuits? Confidence is something I'd chased for years, and I conflated so much of my idea of confidence with the way I felt about my body. It was always a case of 'when' something had changed, I'd be free to be confident. As if the confidence was in there, just shackled by a few extra kilos or a few flyaway hairs or the absence of the perfect white T-shirt.

It was always *when* I lose weight, *when* I look polished, *when* I get that job, *when* I have a thigh gap, *when* this, *when* that. Experiencing confidence without any of those changes I thought I needed was eye-opening, and it taught me that I could change the way I saw myself whenever I wanted, without the need to consume.

This realisation got me thinking more about our culture of clothing consumption and its effect on us. We buy all of these things to look a certain way—but is that actually what's stopping us from seeing our real selves, the ones that don't need shiny things to be worthy, but who just are worthy for the very reason that we exist?

We're conditioned to have these insecurities, and then offered up psychological relief in the form of avoidance by hiding in the clothes we see on racks, chasing the images we consume online, and never really, truly seeing our reflection in the mirror. When I took away the option to hide my body or contort it into clothes to fit a mould, so many of my flaws went away too. So it begs the question: do our insecurities exist without the solutions we're sold to fix them? I'm starting to think they don't.

3. I felt free

The mental peace of withdrawing from clothing consumption is one of the most important things I took from this experiment. I'd had absolutely no idea how much my mind was cluttered with things I could want, with decisions to buy or not to buy, with fantasy stories of what an item would do for me, with battling priorities—save or buy this thing? Should I, shouldn't I? I'll just check cashback sites. I wonder if it's on sale. I wonder if my size is back in stock.

Taking all of that away felt like a weight had been lifted. We often think of saying 'no' as something restrictive. Like we regress back to our childlike selves being denied an ice cream. In this context, the 'no' was liberating. I wasn't saying 'no' to things I needed, or things I even wanted. By saying 'no' to clothes, I was saying 'yes' to so much more.

∞ Yes to having enough—and therefore to being enough.

∞ Yes to more choices, more agency over my decisions.

- ∞ Yes to more money in my bank account, and less pull to impulsively buy something that I think will make me happy.
- ∞ Yes to more space in my wardrobe.
- ∞ Yes to less packaging.
- ∞ Yes to more mental space and less decision-making.
- ∞ Yes to creativity with what I had, and with a hobby I'd always wanted to reignite (sewing).
- ∞ Yes to a more sustainable way of participating in clothes.
- ∞ Yes to myself as I am, without the need for a shiny new 'wrapper'.

Not buying clothes freed me up to do so much more

Don't worry, this isn't the part of the book where I reveal I took up 16 new hobbies and was amazing at all of them. I'm still forever envious of those with a natural talent for dance or sport. I have the athleticism of a slug and I cry a lot—trust me, if there's one place you won't find me it's at Wednesday night mixed netball.

Withdrawing from buying clothes did free me up to do more with my money, my time and my interest in clothes. Throughout the year I was able to:

- ∞ *Book two trips: one to Queensland and one to Bali*
  While this money wasn't directly and completely saved from not buying clothes, the total for both trips came in well under the $6000 I'd spent on clothes the year prior to my Project.

- ∞ *Pay off my postgraduate study*
  During the Project, I was finishing up my year-long postgraduate study in financial psychology, and because I studied via a college in the US, I had to pay for it as I went rather than adding it to my student loan balance. A blessing for future me, for sure,

despite being a challenge in real time. Time and money I gained back from my overall shift in consumption behaviour definitely contributed to making this achievable.

∞ *Increase my savings and investments*

I experienced an increase in my income of around $10 000 during the year of the Project, and despite high costs in my personal life thanks to a hefty year of health expenses, I was still able to increase my personal investments and savings using that extra money. Being self-employed often means you don't know what you'll earn in a year before it happens, so I couldn't set out to contribute this additional amount upfront. When it happened, the clarity and focus the Project had given me, along with having no option to treat myself to clothes with my extra money, allowed me to put the funds aside for future me. The knock-on effect of my consumption behaviour meant I simply spent less overall on discretionary expenses, from make-up and skincare to food delivery, freeing up money for more important things in my life.

∞ *Take up sewing again*

Sewing is one of those things that so many of us say we want to learn. I'm lucky that my gran and mum were big sewers — my mum made all my clothes as a child, and I'd sew with my gran when I went to stay during school holidays. She died when I was 15, and I hadn't sewn since. As with so many things we say we want to do in life, I could've done it at any time. The fact I finally got around to it during the Project wasn't a coincidence. Slowing down the way I interacted with clothes, finding creativity again and disconnecting from the instant gratification of buying all led me to finally thread my sewing machine and get stitching. There's something so therapeutic about making and crafting and spending time on something in a way we just don't anymore, and the Project gave me the space to do that. I started setting myself sewing goals, first to make an item of clothing, then to learn to insert a zip. I devoured YouTube tutorials and booked myself into a sewing class to learn how to do a zip and facing on a skirt. I've dipped in and out of sewing since then, but I keep coming back to it. The Project gave me the space to start it again, and I'm so glad I did.

Buying again

While I basked in the satisfaction of completing the year, I did begin to feel somewhat unsettled at the idea of being out the other side of the Project. I knew I had a challenge ahead of me, and I can't lie, I was nervous to buy again!

Luckily for me though, on 1 January 2024, I was in Bali. I was sitting poolside, reading my Kindle, guzzling a coconut, and hoping I knew where my Imodium tablets were for the flight home (if you know, you know). Most critically, I was outside of my real life. Not only did I have distance from the new year sales that would be plaguing social feeds and email inboxes, I also wasn't having to get dressed for my real life. The humidity in Indonesia meant that for a sweaty gal like me, outfits rarely went beyond a swimsuit and a throw-on midi-dress. Anything more and I'd look like I'd taken a swim fully clothed thanks to my apparently being born with five times the sweat glands of an average human being.

Getting to spend a bit of time in a temptation-less state was helpful in many ways, as it gave me a chance to exist outside of the Project, but in somewhat of a holding pattern before being flung back into my normal life. Within 24 hours of returning home to Melbourne, I came down with a horrendous bout of what turned out to be COVID, which rendered me bedbound for three further weeks. A vile way to start the year but, hey, at least I wasn't being tempted by clothes!

Nonetheless, I did eventually make my first purchase. I'd found something that ticked all of my criteria and so I added to cart. Pulse racing, I entered my card details and said goodbye to the part of myself that was hinged on being the girl that hadn't bought clothes all year. The bandaid was ripped off. I'd done it!

I'll admit I had to do a bit of mental work around that purchase. Around letting go of the satisfaction that was bolstering my progress. Around being willing to make a mistake, or be bad at the next part of what I was trying to do. I think on some level, I surprised myself at how well I took to the year, and how much I'd learned and gained in the absence of buying, so much so that I was reluctant to let that feeling go and move on to the next part. But I knew I had to move on and learn to buy differently in order to make it all worth it.

That purchase was my first experience of truly mindful clothes buying, which is quite scary to admit. Because of the year I'd just completed, I had a unique opportunity to make what would probably be the most considered clothing purchase of my life, because it would always be the first thing I bought after a whole year in the Project. I wasn't going to waste that one purchase on something I thought might be a dud, or on repeating old patterns I'd uncovered and dissected with tweezers during the year prior!

The item was a beige, knitted, longline midi-dress, which nailed so much of what I'd learned during the Project:

- ∞ It was a thick-knitted fabric that hung nicely on my body.
- ∞ It was a longer-line midi-length, closer to my ankle than my knee.
- ∞ It was easy to wash and low maintenance to keep fresh.
- ∞ It had the neckline I liked.
- ∞ It could stretch or shrink as I needed it to.
- ∞ Coincidentally, it was from a store that made their clothes breastfeeding friendly, so hey, I'll be able to wear it if I ever breastfeed too! (Bet you didn't see that benefit coming.)

The process I went through to select this item involved a lot of consideration. I looked at everything from the fabric to the length to the care instructions. I thought through how I'd style it, I considered whether the shade of beige tied in with my beige sandals and bag. I looked at others that were similar to make sure I wasn't just impulse buying an idea that I'd later wish I could refine. And, most critically, I visualised it on my body. That visibility I had over my reflection in the mirror meant I was no longer imagining myself looking totally different in clothes. When I pictured how it would look on me, I finally saw … well … me! My fantasy self was nowhere to be seen, and god, it felt so freeing. It felt so distinctly different from how I'd bought before, and I knew this was how I wanted to consume going forward.

Hot tip: *When buying something online, utilise the 'you may also like' feature that many sites offer. It shows you items that are similar to the one you're looking at, especially on larger sites that sell multiple brands. Something about seeing how many other similar items there are to the one you're looking at can help you take the idea of the piece you're looking at down off the pedestal you've put it on, and show you just how many other options there are available. We have a tendency to feel as though we only have one chance to have the thing we're looking at, but once we make it less special, that urge to buy neutralises.*

Buying technique: The Ultimate Rule

I want to share with you a mindful buying technique from my first book, *Good With Money*, that you'll find helpful in making better clothing consumption decisions.

The Ultimate Rule is all about buying with the same consideration you would if it was the last item of that kind you ever bought. How discerning would you be over a black dress if it were the only black dress you could buy for the rest of your life? (Of course, it most likely won't be, but you never know!)

The Ultimate Rule prompts you to:

- seek out multiple options before making a decision to buy

- never settle for something that isn't quite right just to get the dopamine hit sooner

- walk away from sale bargains that you feel compelled to buy just because it's a good deal

- buy things to be worn again and again rather than for one specific context

- approach trends with caution and say 'no' to those that don't align with your style concept, style code and style standard

- adopt a 'curate, not consume' mindset with your wardrobe where you select each item carefully rather than rushing through your decision-making

- buy based on what your wardrobe will benefit from, rather than just what catches your eye in the moment

- plan what you want to add to your wardrobe independently of what you see in stores or online. Instead of 'that's a nice coat, I'll buy it', it becomes, 'I want to add a black coat to my wardrobe, I'm going to look for one'.

Next time you're buying something, consider The Ultimate Rule. Is this item good enough to be the last of this thing I ever buy? If not, it's a 'no'.

...And then I hired a stylist

By February, I'd recovered from my lurgy and was finally ready to have my styling session, which involved my stylist, Maddy, coming to my house, doing a three-hour deep dive and sort out in my wardrobe, before setting off on our personal shopping adventure a couple of days later.

Hiring a stylist is one of those things so many people want to do at some point in their life. It's up there with having a private chef as one of those top luxuries that we crave. Someone to tell us how to look well-dressed, what to buy and how to put it together. There was definitely a degree of that when I giddily booked my session, but what became apparent to me was how much the learnings from my Project were going to help me get the most out of the styling process.

When we were working through my wardrobe, noting down the things we wanted to replace or ditch altogether, I could almost see a previous version of me next to me, acting completely differently in that session. Had I had a styling session before I'd committed to the Project, I know exactly what I'd have done—tried to use a stylist to dress me as my fantasy self and emerge a different person. I'd have been conjuring up visions of how glossy and put together I'd look after the session, how I'd somehow look totally different and have a different body shape, and how I'd be this immaculately groomed person all of a sudden. I could almost see that version of reality playing on a screen in my head as I went through the session, hyper aware of just how different I was approaching this based on everything I'd gained from the year. I had no wild ideas of reinvention, and that felt unfamiliar. I hadn't engaged with clothing consumption in this way before, and it was a noticeably different emotional experience—in a good way.

The outcome of that wardrobe revamp was a list of things we were looking for during personal shopping, almost all of which were replacing items in my wardrobe that either didn't fit well, or were more appropriate versions of the *almosts* that I'd settled for despite them not being perfect.

List complete, we headed to the shops where I experienced conscious consumption in a new way once again. The first things I tried on and purchased were basic T-shirts, replacing the crusty old ones I had. But where I'd usually run in and grab a T-shirt I thought would fit, I took the time to try them on, try different sizes and a couple of different cuts or fabrics to be sure. It was revolutionary. The urgency was gone. The rushed decision-making was gone. The settling was gone.

As we moved through our shopping list and my arms started to ache from trying on clothes, what struck me was just how many things

I tried that weren't right, but that I'd previously have settled for. Being able to identify when things aren't right and why, and being able to walk away from the imminent dopamine hit of a purchase until I found what I actually wanted was empowering in a way I never even expected.

This is really where buying again was its own part of the journey. Continuing my learnings into the shopping process meant I could meet my mistakes in the real world, not just in hindsight from my wardrobe, and see where I'd previously have let my emotional ideas of how I *wanted* to look dictate my buying decisions. Being meticulous in what I accepted into my wardrobe was key, and felt like a form of resistance against the instantaneous culture we live in. I must have tried on about 20 tank tops looking for the perfect neckline based on what I knew I liked, and it made me realise how different clothes can be when you respect yourself enough to find what actually works.

During that three-hour shop, we purchased two pairs of jeans, a blazer, some basic tank tops and T-shirts, a nice top to go with jeans, and a couple of tops that could be dressed up or down. Almost everything was replacing existing themes in my wardrobe, but in a much more me-shaped format.

We then integrated those things into my existing wardrobe and made outfits with the things I already had. Not only was this a great way to make sure I didn't get stuck in that 'new things good, old things bad' mindset, but it was a really good way to verify the things I'd bought before keeping them. I ended up returning two of the tops as I didn't feel confident in styling them independently, which is previously something I'd have glossed over and ignored.

How to be your own personal shopper

Now, of course, the glaring problem with my rave review of having a professional stylist help me with my wardrobe is that it's not something that's available to everyone, and it's not something I can afford to keep doing regularly. However, I did learn a lot of things between my session and my Project on how to be my own personal stylist and shopper that I'm going to share with you here. These are things I come back to again and again, and that have changed the way I shop forever.

Audit your wardrobe

Personal shoppers don't just help you buy shiny new things. They're buying from a place of being informed about what you wear, what you like and what your wardrobe will benefit from—so make it a habit to audit your wardrobe before going shopping (or do your own Wardrobe Project to get to know what you have!).

When auditing your wardrobe, it's important to look beyond just things you don't wear. There's temptation to simply get rid of the things you don't like and then go and buy things you do like. This leaves little room for the nuances in your wardrobe.

You might find it helpful to revisit our wardrobe categories from page 18 to identify things like your *greatest hits*, your *almosts* and your *ghosts*. In addition to that, the following questions can help you extract important data to inform your buying decisions:

∞ For things you love and wear often, ask yourself 'what makes me reach for this again and again?'

∞ For things you don't love but wear often, ask yourself 'what makes me reach for this even though I don't love it?'

∞ For things you don't know how to wear, ask yourself 'what makes this hard to wear?'

∞ For things you love but don't wear, ask yourself 'what stops me from wearing this?'

∞ For things you don't like, ask yourself 'what don't I like about this, and why do I have it?'

Give yourself time

How often do we grab things we've seen on impulse? Or quickly check out after seeing something on social media? Or pop in and grab the first thing we see and say 'that'll do'? You can become your own personal shopper by carving out a chunk of time to go and properly browse.

Even if you shop online for size needs or brand preferences, it's still worth going to a couple of shops if you are able, feeling fabrics and textures and experiencing clothes on a more meaningful level than just clicking and adding to cart. Not only can seeing clothes physically help you better understand how items will feel and fit, you're engaging all of your senses and being present in the process of buying.

In such a fast-paced world, we skim over so many experiences as we rush to the next thing. Slowing down and buying clothes more visually can help you connect to your style concept and develop your knowledge of how fabrics and colours fit and feel.

Try things on properly

If you're shopping in store, give yourself plenty of room in your shopping time to try things on. Go dressed to try on—something comfortable that you can easily get in and out of. Trying things on properly helps you make better decisions and not have to settle for things that aren't right. Plus, make use of other items in the store to try items in the context you'll wear them. For example, if you'll wear trousers with a black T-shirt, grab a black T-shirt to try on with them to get a better idea of how they'll look in the context you plan to wear them.

If you're an online shopper, make it your mission to try things on once they arrive—and try them on properly! I've been guilty in the past of trying something glam on while I'm wearing pyjamas with my greasy hair pulled back in a bun. I'd then make concessions for anything that was wrong with the item, thinking that it would all be solved once my hair and make-up was done. Trying things on in the right context helps you make better and more considered decisions about whether they're keepers.

Wear good underwear

When you're shopping or trying on, make sure you're wearing suitable underwear for what you'll be trying on. Again, you don't want to be making excuses for something not fitting right on the basis that it'll fit with the right bra or lighter underwear. Wear your best underwear for trying things on, and if it's been years since your last bra fitting, go and get fitted!

Shop with a list and stay in your lane

You know when you go into a supermarket hungry and end up buying a tub of potato salad, a bag of mini cucumbers, a family-sized pizza and everything from the specials aisle? Yeah, clothes shopping is the same. Having a list and staying in your lane can stop you from straying from your intentional purchases.

When I was shopping with Maddy, my stylist, I found myself stopping to look at other things we weren't trying on while I was walking through a store or queueing to pay. We have a tendency to feel like we have to see every single thing in store to be sure we have the right item, but when you shop with intention and have a clear idea of what you're looking for, you can stay in your lane and not get distracted by pretty things you're not looking for.

My styling session gave me the perfect foundation from which to take the next step post-Project. I had replaced the staple items in my wardrobe and knew I had everything I needed to integrate new with old, as well as to really continue honing my style and my new perspective on my wardrobe.

I adopted somewhat of a mindset shift as I got used to life after the Project, in that I viewed my wardrobe as more of an asset that I wanted to curate over time. Rather than that transient, temporary view of my style that had held me back for so many years, I now saw my clothes as things to keep and care for, and my style as something to be playful with and to actually enjoy outside of the familiar pseudo joy of shopping. Embedding my learnings into my day-to-day style meant shifting from the experimental phase of my no-buy period into a phase of cultivation. And that all began with dressing myself differently.

Dressing differently

When I wasn't buying during the Project, I dressed with experimentation. I was trying new combinations and wearing the things I already had in the absence of being able to rely on novelty and newness. Afterwards, I found myself being far more methodical, and actually locking down some of the things I'd learned from experimentation into systems and methods that would make getting dressed easier in the future. Here are some of the techniques I found the most valuable.

Style formulas

On page 180, I talked about the idea of style formulas, which helped me lock down combinations, shapes and silhouettes I felt good in. I continued to use these methods when I was integrating new items again, and found that it was a great way to get solid wear out of things I was buying. Seeing how an item (such as my cerulean dress that became my go-to wedding outfit) could fit into a new style formula was helpful in resisting that temptation to carbon copy the things we see on other people.

Anchor styling

Anchor styling involves using one anchor piece as the main focal point of your outfit, and keeping everything else around it really simple. I'd started to do this in my shift from iced latte to espresso con panna that I talked about on page 104. That basics-with-benefits approach represented a slightly bolder take on basics and neutrals. For example, a black blazer with a Dolman sleeve, or a black midi-dress with fringing on the hem.

When I discovered anchor styling being talked about on social media, I was keen to explore it as a way to incorporate some bolder pieces in my wardrobe. Since then I have added a pair of very excellent orange velvet platforms that I wear to pretty much *any* event now, and often put together entire simple outfits around the idea of my bold shoe doing the talking. It's really helped me make the simpler styles I used to copy from others feel much more *me*.

The signature system

As I continued to feel more and more confident in myself and my style, I started to recognise the value of having 'signature' things. A signature colour, a signature outfit, a signature lip colour, a signature hair style, a signature accessory you wear often.

Something we often forget is that style and fashion are *hard*! There's a reason people are professional stylists, and celebrities pay experts to dress them—us normal people shouldn't actually be expected to know what to do!

Having 'signature' things simplifies just about every aspect of your life, and especially your wardrobe and self-image. Not only does it make it easier to get dressed and express yourself, it actually helps you resist all of the ways you're sold to on a daily basis. There are endless things to buy and want, but when you have your signature system, you automatically become immune to 90 per cent of that noise. You buy within your signatures, and you use your signatures to tie together just about anything. Wearing a simple jeans and a T-shirt and feeling a bit blah? Draw it together with a signature bag or belt. Feel like everyone else looks amazing in a black dress and you don't? Finish it off with your signature lip and nail colour. So much of the way we look is *perception*, and your signature system helps you perceive yourself in the right context.

In the year after my Project, I really leaned into having a signature brand colour, which was easy to choose as it's my business brand colour. I have a visceral connection to that orange colour, and it brings me back to myself in so many ways. When I incorporate it into my outfits in subtle ways, whether that's with my orange velvet shoes or painting my nails or wearing a top in that colour, it's like it adds that little sprinkle of me to whatever I'm wearing, which keeps my style feeling cohesive and considered. Perhaps most meaningfully of all, though, is the very act of selecting and working with a personal brand colour serves as a way to remind you of yourself, your values, your identity and your personality, and keep you aligned to what you're expressing in your outfits.

Themed days of the week

On page 35, we talked about the lifestyle pie chart, which helps you understand how you're spending your time—and what you actually need in your wardrobe for your day to day. The battle many of us have is actually finding the motivation to dress in the things we like when we *could* get away with wearing leggings and a jumper. I hear this from a lot of people who work from home, don't have to wear a specific standard of attire for work, are in caring roles or on parental leave.

Being self-employed, I relate to the same struggle. I am my own boss (read: chaotic maniac with not a leadership bone in my body) and, let me tell you, we have no dress code in my office (read: my living room) and zero image guidelines in the employee handbook (read: my notes app). I'll be honest and say that some weeks I do 90 per cent of my workload unsure if I've brushed my teeth and certain I should've worn a bra.

And, look, working this way is a privilege and I cannot understate that. It's also true that living the slob outfit life impacts the way I see myself—not so much that it makes me feel bad about myself, but I do notice that I miss out on the enjoyment that comes from serving a certified *look*.

The solution? Theme days! Assign certain themes to certain days to hold yourself accountable to actually wearing the clothes you love and expressing yourself the way you want to. These give you specific days of the week where you put extra effort into your outfit, and the rest of the time you're allowed to just exist. Remember, as we discussed on page 63—it's okay to look 'fine'! For example:

∞ Fancy Fridays: Wear something fancier than usual.
∞ Main character Monday: Dress like the main character of your life and command attention.

∞ Maximalist Mondays: Push the envelope and wear something bolder than usual.

∞ Wildcard Wednesdays: Wear that thing you never quite dare to wear.

∞ Icon days: Dress like the icon you truly are.

Picking just one themed day and scaffolding out opportunities to wear more of your wardrobe helps you integrate the clothes you love into your real life. It also gives you space to just exist in whatever's comfortable the rest of the time, knowing you'll get your chance to put the effort in on your next theme day.

Far too often we try to change everything about how we get dressed at once. We say we'll start getting dressed to work from home or putting more effort in for our office days, but that overcommitment to do everything all at once is just too much. Choosing just one day a week to be stylish is so much more achievable and, more importantly, realistic. Most of us aren't living a glossy life trotting up and down the halls of *Vogue*, so why pressure ourselves to dress like we are? If it still feels overwhelming, start small with one day a month and build up from there.

Wardrobe optimisation

Getting dressed starts with your wardrobe—but we're all guilty of neglecting the space where we keep our clothes. Every few weeks I find myself sliding into 'floordrobe' territory, and I need a couple of hours and a good podcast to sort through the chaos. Rather than just tidying up to a good enough level, I've begun treating my wardrobe more like a boutique that's nice to shop at.

Now I could sit here and lie to you and say that since my Wardrobe Project I now keep my wardrobe in pristine shape, always organised and never, ever allowing piles to form under a plume of cat fur. But I shan't.

I'll be dead honest with you—I have a messy house. Yep, I'm a messy person. I'm not neat or organised, my house never looks like a show home and I have a strict 'no turning up at my door without a warning' rule with everyone who knows me because I will have to gallop around the house picking up random things from the floor and giving the bathroom sink a quick once over to rid it of toothpaste grime.

But periodically, I get myself to restore my wardrobe to some semblance of order, and take a few small steps towards making it somewhere I want to get creative. Even just setting a timer for ten minutes and putting away that pile of laundry you've been ignoring can make a huge difference.

Here are some other handy ways to make your wardrobe more enjoyable to dress from:

∞ Put away seasonal pieces: Saves clutter and ensures you're pulling things you can actually wear.
∞ Box up things that don't fit: Dressing from a wardrobe that doesn't fit can make getting dressed a negative experience.
∞ Get some nice hangers: This makes your wardrobe feel luxe and plentiful!
∞ Use a wardrobe freshener: Give your wardrobe that boutique store smell.
∞ Explore organising solutions: Being unable to find what you're looking for can create overwhelm and leave you wanting to buy as an easy way out.
∞ Organise by colour: Merchandising your clothes in a way that's pleasing to the eye can make getting dressed a more exciting experience.

Moving forward

As I moved through the year after finishing the Project, I started to realise that the Project hadn't ended on 31 December, it had just evolved into its next stage. When I embarked on this journey, I thought it would be a case of not buying for a year and the rest taking care of itself, but for me, life post-Project has been an extension of the Project itself.

Throughout the rest of the year that followed, I made some more purchases, all of them considered, and about 90 per cent of them were absolute hits. There were a couple of misses, largely due to the item itself being sub-par rather than mistakes I was making. For example, a really great pair of trousers I bought ended up washing terribly and losing their colour.

I'll admit, I did grapple, at times, with how easy it would be to go back to the dopamine cycle of buying. Being able to buy better brought me a whole new type of joy from clothes, and while it was more meaningful than a quick-hit impulse purchase of the past, it's still something that you can be left craving.

While I had broken the cycle of buying when I was sad or insecure (or buying for the person I wished I was), there's still no arguing with the *allure* of buying. It's almost muscle memory. We remember how good it feels to buy clothes (even if it's, ultimately, short-lived). Calibrating everything I'd learned against that muscle memory definitely felt challenging. There was some grief there: in a way, that that old coping mechanism wasn't there anymore, even though I knew it didn't serve me. It felt vulnerable to admit that, even after my year without clothes, I could still see a path where I tumbled back into temptation. So much of this comes from the fact we can't change the world we live in. There are marketing messages everywhere, everything is shoppable. Every conversation is an opportunity to say 'where did you get that?'

Ultimately, though, in a testament to what I learned in the Project, I really didn't slip back into my old ways. Did I get tempted by shiny things and my newfound ability to buy for my real self? Yes. Did I slide back into old purchasing patterns based on outsourcing my identity to pretty things on a rack? No.

But I did really miss the mental lightness of the freeze period. I liked who I was when I wasn't buying, and I liked my style and my clothes more without the noise of being able to consume. In August I decided to do another freeze period for three months, just to halt any temptation I felt and remind me of how fine I was with what I had, particularly given the things I'd added to my wardrobe that year. The familiar sense of peace that came from not buying returned instantly, and I knew that periods of not buying would likely become part of the way I consume going forward.

I am forever changed

Regardless of the ups and downs, I know one thing for certain: The Wardrobe Project changed me forever.

Wow, could I be more dramatic?! It's not lost on me that it's kinda wild to sit here and say that I didn't buy clothes for a year and it changed me forever, but I'm being 100 per cent genuine when I say this. It truly speaks to the power of clothes, and the impacts of mass production, overconsumption culture and ever-evolving image standards for women.

For so many years I struggled with my self-image, with my body and with the way I looked. I grew up dieting, struggled with disordered eating, often felt like an outsider in social settings and, honestly, never really felt attractive. I'd struggled with my finances, identified with being 'bad with money' and been stuck on the hamster wheel of spending and credit card debt before I knew better. Clothes were present in both of these challenges, acting as an emotional crutch, an outlet when I needed to feel something or absolve myself of emotional discomfort. Spending brought relief, and clothes did, too. I was able to overcome a lot of the financial challenges through working on my money beliefs and habits—you can read about that in my first book, *Good With Money*. But the clothes stuff required its own inner work to break. I might not have been in financial debt anymore, but I remained in debt to myself. I owed myself respect and love and care and acceptance, and the Project taught me that.

Withdrawing from the wardrobe treadmill meant actually meeting myself and confronting who I'd been trying to be, and why I'd been trying to dress up as a different person. Having no choice but to see myself, and to get comfortable with who I was outside of newness, allowed me to gradually neutralise the way I felt about myself, and start to find the joy in being creative with myself and my style, without relying on bolstering my confidence with the dopamine of buying.

I could see so clearly how much the dopamine hit of a new outfit had had a hold over me, and just how damaging the behavioural aspect of fast fashion and social media trends have become on our buying habits. The ever-moving goal posts for women keep us in a trap of buying to be somebody, without ever stopping to look in the mirror at who we already are. And that's opened me up to a whole new approach to clothing, style and consumption on every level.

Beyond changes to my identity and self-image, though, the Project shifted so much more in terms of the kind of consumer I want to be. Here are three profound mindset shifts I've experienced since completing the Project.

1. I'm ready to embrace sustainability

Sustainability in the fashion industry has been on my mind for years. The human exploitation in the supply chain that brings endless outfits for our comfortable consumption. The use of plastic in fabrics and the emissions created by the volume of clothes we have in the world, almost entirely for the benefit of the Global North, and to the cost of the Global South. The sickening amount of landfill that's caused not just by the overproduction of clothes, but because of the throwaway mindset we've normalised. It's something I think about often. Every time I do a clear out, I have a visceral reaction to the amount of *stuff*, clothes and otherwise, that I've somehow accumulated. I'm struck by the stat that 70 per cent of clothes donated to thrift stores goes to landfill—and often that means our unwanted garments are exported for offshore disposal in what's known as *colonial waste*.

Up until the Project, my approach to sustainability was a bit all over the place, if I'm honest. I didn't ever fall into the trap of shopping at ultra-fast fashion brands that are some of the worst offenders and, thankfully, my rambunctious booty excluded me from the likes of Zara and H&M years ago. But I felt somewhat lost in how to approach sustainable fashion outside of abstaining from the 'bad' brands. I wasn't shopping with the top-tier bad guys, but I wasn't really seeking out brands doing things differently, either.

I'd sort of dance this tango of becoming overwhelmingly disgusted by fashion waste and the journey our clothes take to get to us, deep diving into sustainable brands and fabrics and production methods only to get even more overwhelmed and end up in avoidance mode. Additionally, trying to reconcile how I *wanted* to behave in terms of the brands I was choosing and the ways I felt *compelled* to behave based on my fraught relationship with myself and clothes made matters worse. It's like there wasn't room for me to focus on finding sustainable brands when I was still using clothes as a means to emotionally soothe.

What the Project gave me was room to address the stuff about myself outside of a focus on sustainability. The fact I didn't buy for a year in itself had a positive impact on my consumption footprint, but that wasn't the focus. The focus was on healing the parts of me that had those beliefs about clothes that drove me to keep wanting to buy. It's as though I feel *ready* now; like I'm giving *myself* enough respect when it comes to clothes to finally be able to take that next step with sustainability.

Giving myself the room to do that fundamentally changed my relationship with clothes, which made the space for a more conscious and meaningful approach to sustainability—because it was underpinned by a shift in behaviour. Regardless of how sustainable or ethical a brand is, the most sustainable outfit you can wear is one you already own. When we charge into sustainability pursuits without addressing *why* we're buying things in the first place, we often run into friction. The beliefs I held about clothes weren't conducive to exploring slow, sustainable fashion because I was still ultimately conflating style with shopping. This mindset is deeply embedded in overconsumption.

Now that I know why I over-consumed and have been able to change the way I see myself, my style and the role of clothes, I can approach sustainability with the slowness it needs to actually mean anything.

Here are some ways I've begun exploring sustainability in the time since the Project:

Exploring sustainable brands

The world of sustainable/ethical fashion can feel overwhelming, especially with the rise of greenwashing. If you're not familiar, *greenwashing* refers to brands that make claims of sustainability or ethics for marketing and PR benefits, without actually following through on many of their claims. When you do land on a sustainable brand doing good things, prices are generally much higher — wild what not exploiting people does to the cost of clothes, right? On top of that, finding ethical brands that cater to plus-size women, I'll admit, is hard, but they do exist. For a long time, I probably used this as an excuse. On my deep dives during a particularly strong bout of climate anxiety, I'd vow to make changes to where I shopped and how much I shopped, only to find stores that stop at a size 14. But now that I rely less on newness in my wardrobe, I have the space to take a curious approach to finding inclusive and ethical brands.

A great tool to use is the Good On You website (goodonyou.eco) that ranks brands based on evidence of their ethics and sustainability. It's global, so you'll find stores from all over the world listed on there, but do your own research too. There are a lot of smaller brands doing great things too. Again, slowness in our approach to buying gives us room to find them. We must break the pattern of Googling whatever we want and being able to check out within seconds if we want to shop more sustainably.

A return to thrifting

Earlier in this book I told you about my challenges with thrifting. How the thrill of the hunt and the affordable dopamine hit made it easy to just buy anything and everything I saw, and that while I wasn't upholding a supply chain fraught with human rights violations, I was still participating in a 'fast' mindset around fashion.

Thoughts I had when I was a 'fast thrifter':

- ∞ If it doesn't fit I'll just re-donate! [Pats self on back for being so generous.]
- ∞ I don't actually like this but it's a good brand and it's a good price so I'll buy it.
- ∞ I already have six tops like this but I'll get this one because it's a good find.
- ∞ I'll get this and sew with it! *proceeds to never sew*

Since completing the year-long no-buy, I've been gradually dipping my toe back into the world of shopping second hand, because let's face it, there truly is no joy greater than a crisp weekend morning mooching around a thrift store and getting a coffee and a croissant. But now that my mindset is different, I feel differently when I'm thrifting. I used to thrift with energy pulsing through my veins as I hunted for treasure, that familiar urgency to find something good making the entire experience about the sole purpose of *buying*. Now, though, I'm much more considered. I thrift with the expectation that I won't find anything, but being open to goodies if I do find them. I tend to stick to certain categories based on things I know will make my wardrobe better, or things I'm actively looking for, so as not to get tempted to buy stuff just because it's there.

More than anything else, I think the biggest shift is that move away from transience in my wardrobe. I no longer find myself thinking 'this'll do until I find something better' or 'this'll do because it's a great price'. If I'm not willing to keep something, wear it regularly and love it for more than a day, it's not coming home with me. The Rule of Three from page 199 is super helpful when thrifting, because the dopamine of a good deal is an easy way to get led astray.

Online preloved marketplaces

While Australia's online preloved shopping game could use some work—it's no patch on the UK's Vinted offering, which appears packed with gems every time I'm there—my newfound slowness in my clothes shopping habits have given me much more room to hunt for things I'm looking for via preloved marketplaces rather than rushing out to buy new.

Just like thrifting, we have to be careful not to get swept up in the hype—the number of women who tell me they're addicted to Vinted is unreal. A friend of mine swears by buying her favourite brands preloved. Every time I see her she's decked out in brands like Alpha 60 and Ksubi, all in immaculate condition and all sourced from Depop. Knowing your brands and sizing is key to minimise purchase regret.

Clothes swapping

I've never been much of a clothes swapper, bar two years at uni where my friend and I had an 'open wardrobe' policy where we shared everything and even split the cost of new clothes when we bought them. Honestly, we were onto something. Sadly, as I've got older, I've found fewer opportunities to share clothes with friends, in part due to not living close enough, but mostly due to my sizing incompatibilities.

Swapping is something I've become increasingly curious about. I didn't allow any swapping during my Project because I didn't want to accidentally find a cheat code to living without novelty in my wardrobe and find myself relying on clothes swaps to keep up my 'fast' mindset with clothes. Now I'm out the other side, I've booked my first clothes-swapping event, where I plan to take two pieces I'm not getting much wear out of in the hopes of finding them a new home and exchanging them for something I can love.

2. My body image is the best it's ever been

I know, I know, I've waxed lyrical about this for so much of this book, so I'll keep this brief. The change in my body image is the single best thing to come out of The Wardrobe Project. I feel the best in my body I've ever felt, despite the fact I've spanned a 10 kg variance in weight since beginning the Project. Seeing myself differently, dressing for me, wearing clothes that already fit me without putting my body on trial with new things all the time, and not trying to be someone I'm not has been the most empowering shift of my life.

Thinking back even just a few years, where I had rampant body dysmorphia and every day I'd look in the mirror and felt like I was a failure because I wasn't thin—not hating my reflection and obsessively trying to change it is honestly one of the greatest feelings of relief.

The better I feel in my body, the less I feel compelled to buy. Don't get me wrong, there's an element of loving the way I look that can make me want to buy nice things that I know I'll look great in as a plus-size jiggly puff, but that emotional pull of performing as someone else is gone, which makes it so much easier for my rational brain to step in, remember I have plenty, and remind me that I have other financial goals that clothes aren't going to derail.

3. I now love everything I own

I've never loved my clothes like I do now. Don't get me wrong, I don't feel amazing every single day, I simply don't have the energy or lifestyle to get fully dressed in an amazing outfit every day—and I'm so okay with that. But when I do put an outfit together, it's *so much fun*.

What I found interesting after the Project was how much I loved reaching for clothes again and again and again. It wasn't something I'd ever really experienced before. Every season brought with it a craving for newness, and an inherent lack of connection to my existing clothes, that view that everything I don't have is nicer than everything I do have. But in that year post-Project, I found myself giddily reaching for things I'd worn the summer prior, referring back to my outfit album on my phone, knowing I had things I loved and felt good in already and, therefore, didn't need to look for newness to feel good.

That was a real turning point for my wardrobe, and a marker that I knew something had drastically shifted. I no longer felt the need to pull money out of my savings to have something I'd clapped eyes on just minutes ago. I no longer pedestalled new things over what I already had. I no longer felt the same pull towards what influencers were wearing, nor the sense of urgency I felt to try and look like them.

Recognising these shifts as the year following the Project went on made me so grateful to my past self for deciding to commit to going one whole year without any new clothes. As I stood almost a full year on, reflecting on how completely different I felt having integrated both a year of not buying at all and a year of buying better, I felt a whisper of curiosity. What would it feel like if I did the no-buy year again, this time with clothes I love? The original Project was an experiment, the year that followed was a recalibration. I felt ready to challenge myself again.

And so on 1 January 2025, I commenced a year of not buying clothes all over again …

Epilogue: The integration

Yes, you read that last page correctly. I decided to go a whole year without buying clothes—again. Why? Well contrary to what some might say, I haven't completely lost the plot. I just found so much value in taking a break from consuming clothes that I wanted to see what would be different if I did it again from a new vantage point. Where my first year was a complete experiment, this second time felt like an integration of all my learnings, of the things I'd bought, of the person I'd uncovered by stepping back from the hamster wheel of buying.

By the time this book is in your hot little hands, reader, I'll be nearing the end of that second year. At the time of writing this, I'm almost halfway (yes, this book's turnaround from manuscript to print was quick!), and I can honestly say, so far, I'm loving it—and it's totally different from the first time!

A lot of people ask me, 'Is it easier or harder the second time?' To be honest, at first it felt harder. The first month was challenging, because there was part of me (my ego, mostly) that felt like I didn't need to do it again. Like I'd already learned all there was to learn, because I'd already made such progress. That overconfidence was part of why I wanted to do it again. I learned the first time that by doing something radical like not buying for a whole year, I could push my buying habits to the edges.

Once I settled into it, it was easier in so many ways. After about five weeks, the mental lightness set in again, that feeling I missed so much from the experiment year. It was freeing to not have to make decisions over whether something was worth buying, whether it was mindful enough or considered enough. The decision was made for me.

Second, it's easier because I genuinely love my wardrobe. I still wear, still reach for and still stand by everything I bought during the recalibration year. In the experiment year, I had to push myself to wear things I didn't often reach for, or get myself to wear things that I'd discovered were past purchase mistakes, but now I get to wear the things I love all the time. Seasons roll around again and I'm reaching for things I loved last summer. I sent a dress to the dry cleaners and it got snagged (yes, I'm still seething), and I was gutted because I loved it so much. Previously, that would have been an excuse to buy something new. Now, I'm finding a way to repair or reimagine it.

I've done a few exposure therapy trips, trying clothes on to meet my desire to buy. But honestly, I've got to a point where I love the clothes I have more than what I see in stores. I attribute that to the fact my clothes are more *me* now. I don't feel as compelled to buy new things because I'm not outsourcing my confidence to newness.

Sure, I still have my weaknesses. I love coats (and I actually do want to buy a new one at some stage), but I don't have that urgency anymore. I know I'll be fine without it.

I'm beginning to explore clothes swapping as a way to integrate new ways of acquiring clothes when I do want or need them, and while I'm not currently buying from thrift stores or online marketplaces, I'm browsing second hand options again, for fun. I'm bringing in a five-item limit for preloved pieces for the latter half of the year to integrate second-hand shopping into my lifestyle again to gently try to shift any clothing consumption I do engage with to be more sustainable and circular.

I really can't understate the value of taking a step back from consumption, addressing why you're buying, who you're buying for, what emotional needs your clothes are filling, and what beliefs you have about clothes that aren't helping you feel good about yourself.

My goal for this book was to inspire you to uncover the secrets lurking in your wardrobe, unlearn the patterns you've been conditioned to repeat, and unlock the money and confidence that awaits when you free yourself from the hold of clothing.

I hope you've learned something about yourself, your style and your identity in this book, and if I've inspired you to do your own Wardrobe Project—whether for a full year or even just a month—you'll find my best advice on how to get the most out of it on the next page.

I'm proud of you for reading this book—and for choosing yourself over a polyester dopamine hit. If you can do one thing for me (besides rating this book five stars and recommending it to a friend), please wake up tomorrow morning, take one look in the mirror and say to yourself: I look fabulous today.

Go get 'em, hot stuff.

Emma x

Advice for your own Wardrobe Project

If I've inspired you to take on your own Wardrobe Project and get to grips with how and why you buy clothes—firstly, yay, that means you liked the book. Thank god.

But, more importantly, I'm so proud of you for feeling ready to make a change. There are all kinds of ways you can make The Wardrobe Project into something that works for you, from duration and rules to exceptions and goals—you call the shots on this, so let's get you set up.

Here's my best advice on setting up your Project based on what I know now from the other side of the fence.

Consider setting a good/better/best goal

If you feel overwhelmed at the idea of trying to go cold turkey on clothes for a whole year, set yourself stepped goals so you can succeed no matter what. This means setting a goal that's considered 'good', one that's considered 'better' and one that's considered 'best'—your ideal outcome. You might choose to step your goals based on duration or number of items purchased throughout the year.

For example, you might choose to do a Project that looks like:

	Good	Better	Best
Option 1 (duration)	No clothes buying for three months	No clothes buying for six months	No clothes buying for 12 months
Option 2 (purchases)	Maximum five purchases all year	Maximum three purchases all year	0 clothing items purchased all year

Set your own rules

When it comes to doing any kind of challenge, whether it's a no-buy or a daily step goal, it's tempting to copy and paste someone else's goals and guidelines and run with it. This is your mind getting ahead of itself, wanting to race ahead to the good bit where we've done the big thing and are out the other side. Instead, set your own Project rules based on what you know about yourself.

Wear your clothes

So many of the valuable learnings that await you during your Project will come from the clothes you own, so do your best to wear what's in your wardrobe in as many ways as you can. Try things on like your wardrobe is your own personal store, wear something you're unsure of for a day and see if you feel differently afterwards, and do Wardrobe Workouts (page 65) periodically to build versatility in your wardrobe.

Be open to the process

It's important not to go into your Project with rigid expectations. You might find you settle into it quickly, or you might meet resistance early on. You'll probably alternate between feeling really motivated and wanting to quit multiple times throughout your Project, and that's okay. There's no right way to grow.

Listen to the stories your mind is telling you

Taking on The Wardrobe Project will challenge a lot of beliefs you have about clothes, about spending and about yourself. Our brains love stories, and we use them to understand the things we experience. Listen to the stories you notice coming up again and again as you work through your Project, as these give you clues as to the beliefs driving your behaviour.

Be prepared to see yourself differently

Yep, you're gonna start to see yourself in a whole new way and, I'll be honest, that can be scary. It's a vulnerable thing to let go of the boxes you've kept yourself in for so long, so being open to a shift in perspective will help you embrace them when they come.

Pay attention to the money stuff

Cast your mind back to when we talked about the ways spending can be coming from something deeper within us. It's important to pay attention to what comes up for you about money during your Project, as this will tell you a lot about where your spending behaviour is coming from.

Four mindset anchors to take into your Project

Before I leave you to go and discover all the juiciness to be found in your wardrobe (and in the mirror) let me give you four mindset anchors to carry into whatever comes next for you after finishing this book. Keep these in the back of your mind and recall them whenever you find yourself tumbling into the familiar territory of wanting to buy to feel good or fix yourself.

1. Outfit repeating is cool

Yep, let's bring it back people. Outfit repeating has been demonised by movies and media as some kind of sartorial failing. But y'know what? I reckon it's time we change that. Outfit repeating is not a result of lack or cluelessness. It's a signal that you buy well, dress well and care for your clothes well.

2. Urgency rarely creates good outcomes

Remember this next time your inner shopping goblin fixates on the thing that'll supposedly change your life or complete your wardrobe. Mindful purchases aren't urgent or hurried, they're considered and intentional.

3. You won't find your style just by buying

We've been sold the idea that style and shopping go hand in hand. Why? Because it's profitable. Remember that style, confidence and the life you want doesn't exist on a rack, it's created by you. Just like a basket full of groceries doesn't become a delicious meal without your input, you can have all the clothes in the world, but without a strong self-image, they won't give you the outcome you crave.

4. Change your mind, not yourself

For many of us, style has long-existed on the other side of transformation. I call bullshit. You don't need to change yourself in order to like yourself — in fact, it's safest not to. The best thing you can do for your style is not to lose weight or find the perfect pair of jeans, it's to change the way you see yourself.

And one final reminder … you can't 'complete' buying clothes

Throughout this book, I've taken you through the many layers of how we buy clothes and brought you along on my journey to finally taking new clothes down off the pedestal I'd put them on. What held me back for so long was this idea that there was some kind of end destination I could get to. If I just bought that one thing, if I could just find the perfect wardrobe, then I'd be done.

Honestly? It's all bullshit. You cannot complete your wardrobe. You can't complete buying. What you can do, though, is make the decision that you *have* enough and that you *are* enough. When you embrace this shift and take steps towards embedding it in your life using the tools from this book, you'll soon start to notice that whatever new shiny thing that catches your eye doesn't actually matter.

Because what if you're actually just really fucking *hot* as you are?

Imagine that.

Let's keep in touch

Here's where to get more from Emma Edwards and The Wardrobe Project:

- ∞ Website: www.thewardrobeprojectbook.com
- ∞ Instagram: @thewardrobeprojectbook
- ∞ Join The Wardrobe Project six-week behaviour change program: A community learning and accountability experience to help you discover the joy in your wardrobe and in the mirror, and leave you feeling hotter, happier and richer! Find out more on the website.

Emma Edwards is also the author of *Good With Money* and founder of The Broke Generation by Broke Media. Here's where you can find out more about changing your money habits, beliefs and behaviours for a better life:

- ∞ Website: www.thebrokegeneration.com
- ∞ Instagram: @the.brokegeneration
- ∞ Podcast: The Broke Generation Podcast

Acknowledgements

Bringing this book to life has been a whirlwind, so I must say the hugest thank you to my publishers at Wiley for all the graft that went into making this book a reality. To my commissioning editor Jordon, who not only commissioned this book, but completed the year-long challenge herself at the same time. You definitely win the award for most dedicated application to a book's production!

To the entire team who worked on this book—Chris, George, Renee, Leigh, Lucy and my fabulous copyeditor Melanie—thank you all for putting up with my chaos. And to George Saad, thank you for a stunning cover once again.

To the wonderful women who so generously shared their stories with me for this book, and to the many more who backed my vision for The Wardrobe Project in all its forms since day one—thank you. I adore you all, and meeting some of you at events across Australia and London has truly been a highlight of this work.

Behind every book, there are people who make it happen. Of course, there are the words and the production and the pages and the PR. But there are also the meals cooked. The hugs given. The 'you can do it!' messages when you've hit a wall with word count, or you've got to that god awful point where you think you've run out of things to say. Behind this book is my wonderful husband, who always manages to make me laugh, pull me out of the darkness, or suggest a 7-Eleven coffee break right when I need one.

To my stylist-turned-friend Maddy, thank you for all you have helped me discover in my style—who knew you'd find me jeans to fit. To Jenna—thank you for being one of the first people on board with The Wardrobe Project program and sharing your sustainability insights with us. To my chaos twin, podcast co-host and esteemed colleague Victoria, thank you for always backing and believing in me and The Wardrobe Project, and for enduring the insufferable part of my personality that comes out when I write books. I'd say this is the last time, but I can't promise anything...

And lastly, of course, thank *you*, reader, for coming on this journey with me. I hope you've found companionship and laughs in this book, and I hope you'll return to your wardrobe with a fresh perspective on just how freaking fabulous you are.